MENTAL HEALTH IN AGEING: CURRENT PERSPECTIVES

MENTAL HEALTH IN AGEING: CURRENT PERSPECTIVES

Edited by

SUSMITA HALDER
AKASH KUMAR MAHATO

Prints Publications Pvt Ltd

Published by

Prints Publications Pvt Ltd
Viraj Tower-2, 4259/3, Ansari Road,
Darya Ganj, New Delhi-110002
Tel. : +91-11-45355555
Fax: +91-11-23275542
E-mail : contact@printspublications.com
Website : www.printspublications.com

First Edition : 2022 (Hardbound)

ISBN: 978-93-93674-12-8

Price: Rs. 995/-

Published and Printed by Mr. Pranav Gupta (Director) on behalf of Prints Publications Pvt Ltd, New Delhi.

PREFACE

Being in clinical practice for last 15 years, we have had the opportunity to come across clients of different age groups from different socioeconomic and cultural backgrounds. Each of them has come with their own challenges, but elderly clients have always intrigued us with their complex presentations. Older adult clients are usually lesser in number compared to children, adolescents, and relatively younger adults to consult or to be brought for consultation in outpatient clinics. A common reporting by caregivers and family members of elderly clients we came across was, "they thought, its usual at this age". Some of our elderly clients have discontinued their sessions as family members find the whole therapy process for anxiety or depression or other mental health issues as eventually futile. But there were also a good number of elderly clients who benefitted from the sessions. The idea of writing this edited book on mental health issues of elderly came from feedback of elderly clients and their family members who benefitted from therapy sessions, and we thought of sharing the different perspectives in mental health of elderly, which could be useful for practitioners, researchers, and students.

The chapters included in the book throw light on different aspects of elderly people which not only influence mental health of elderly, but also impacts its symptomatology and its intervention. It starts from the most important extraneous variable in elderly mental health which is ageing and deploring physical health itself and focusses on role and relevance of physical health condition in elderly mental health. It further progresses to cover the implications of ageing brain functions in relation to mental health. Late life depression and suicide in elderly need to be looked from a different perspective compared to young or middle-aged adults and covered in next chapters. Loneliness though is not a diagnostic entity but an emerging area of importance, as elderly find themselves lonelier compared to yester years. The chapter on loneliness covers this aspect in background of increasing social media use across all age groups. There are two chapters on two very less discussed but equally important domain in elderly, i.e., substance abuse and sexual health and sexuality. There are separate chapters on perception of death and dying in elderly, spirituality, the transition process in ageing, the sociodemographic, cultural as well as environmental factors affecting ageing process and related mental health issues. Considering the timeline of this book, which was parallel to COVID-19 pandemic, we also have included one chapter on impact of COVID pandemic in elderly in light of research findings. The last chapter focuses on psychotherapeutic intervention, it's need and approaches in elderly population as well as the challenges in its delivery.

It was a challenging task to complete this project. At the time of conceptualization of this book, the COVID pandemic was already at peak, and the stress of lockdown and handling grief of relatives, neighbors, known as well as relatively lesser-known people had created a gloomy picture all around. We acknowledge all the authors who overcame their own struggles during the pandemic and contributed with their valuable contribution towards this book. A special mention for Ms. Shinjini Samajdar, who contributed in multiple ways in completion of this book.

We hope that this book will stand useful to mental health professionals, researchers as well as postgraduate students and add some insight into mental health of elderly.

SUSMITA HALDER
AKASH KUMAR MAHATO

EDITORS

Susmita Halder is Associate Professor and Head of the Department of Psychology at St. Xavier's University, Kolkata. She is a licensed Clinical Psychologist registered with the Rehabilitation Council of India. An alumnus of Ranchi Institute of Neuro-Psychiatry and Allied Sciences (RINPAS) Ranchi, Dr. Susmita has been into clinical teaching and consultancy for last 15 years and has worked in different leading institutes including Manipal College of Medical Sciences, Pokhara, Fortis Hospital, Medica Superspeciality Hospital and Crystal Minds Kolkata. She also headed the Dept. of Clinical Psychology at Institute of Psychiatry, SSKM Hospital Kolkata in the past. She had been a Research fellow at the prestigious Centre for the Study of Developing Societies, CSDS, New Delhi. She worked as Research Psychologist in 'The Cognition Group' assisting in development of the Cogtest Neuropsychological Battery and had also been associated with the Pearson Group for standardization of psychological scales in India. Her research interest lies in Neuropsychology, Cognitive Remediation and Cognitive Behaviour Therapy with children and adolescents. She gainfully uses her experiences to have a broader insight of customizing psychotherapy process particularly CBT with her clients. She has over 60 publications in peer reviewed and indexed journals and conducted workshops, delivered lectures and talks in national and international platforms.

Akash Kumar Mahato is Associate Professor in Clinical Psychology and Head of the Amity Institute of Psychology and Allied Sciences, Amity University Kolkata. An alumnus of the Ranchi Institute of Neuro-Psychiatry and Allied Sciences; Dr. Mahato has an experience of over 15 years in the industry and academia. Previously, he had been faculty and Principal at Sweekaar Academy of Rehabilitation Sciences, Secunderabad. He has also contributed as faculty and Clinical Psychologist in Postgraduate teaching departments in medical colleges and Universities the past including LGB Regional Institute of Mental Health, Assam and Amity University Jaipur. His interest areas lie in Evidence-based Psychotherapy, Therapeutic indication of Neuro-cognitive functions, and Community Mental Health. Dr. Mahato has over 45 peer reviewed, national and international publications to his credit.

CONTENTS

MENTAL HEALTH IN RELATION TO AGEING AND PHYSICAL HEALTH

Akash Kumar Mahato and Susmita Halder

Introduction

Ageing is a universal and unstoppable phenomenon, and is synonymous with growing old, maturing, and accomplishment. Ageing has been defined as a continuous process, beginning at birth, which ends with death, and is associated with physical, social and psychological changes throughout this whole journey (Bodnar et al., 1994). On other hand, the ageing body is also enroute depleting vigor, gradual slowing and weakening of bodily systems, and increased risk of medical ill health conditions. It would be wrong to conceptualize that elderly people essentially have illness condition. However, the common mass may perceive the contrary, though the illness conditions in old age may not be caused directly due to ageing, rather than other risk factors.

Prevalence of Elderly and Aging Population and its Health Consequence

Advancements in medicine and treatment facilities have marked a direct impact on the longevity of people globally and have reduced mortality rate across the world. The longevity of human population has increased globally at significant level. On an average, a person aged 65 years in 2015-2020 could expect to live, an additional 17 years globally. By the year 2045-2050, this figure will increase to 19 years (UN, 2019). In the twentieth century, especially after the 1950s, a change in world's age pyramid has occurred. The relatively healthy aging process which was previously restricted to developed countries is now taking place in developing countries and that too with a quick pace (Reher, 2004). This change in the age pyramid has made studies on aging and old age a focus of attention and has led to actions by social and governmental agents, in addition to actions by healthcare professionals (Benedetti et al., 2008). According to the United Nations (2019), by the year 2050, 1 in 6 people in the world will be over the age of 65; up from 1 in 11 people in 2019, or 37 million in 2019 to 120 million in 2050 (225%). While this growth is more in the Eastern and South-Eastern Asian, Latin American and the Caribbean countries, the fastest increase is projected to take place in the least developed countries, which will be home to more than two-thirds of the world's older population (1.1 billion) in 2050. This gradual increase in elderly population is going to impact support systems to the older people and require strategic planning to provide unabated financial opportunities and support, social inclusion and health care provisions.

Why Mental Health in Elderly is Important

Mental health is important not only for elderly but for any individual of any age. However, it is important to talk about mental health of elderly, as they are usually not in the same stature of physical as well as financial health compared to their yester years. Though not all, but a significant number of elderly people do not have a retirement plan and their resources are limited. With a gradual decline in joint and composite families and shift of younger population to nuclear setups, traditional care giving for the elderly is not the same as it used to be earlier, and elderly people are often on their own to take care of themselves. There is a rise in social isolation of elderly people post retirement, as elderly people find it difficult to engage in meaningful social and financial roles. However, this can be changed.

It is a matter of grave concern looking at the available data, which suggest that a sizeable proportion of elderly population suffers from mental illness in addition to their failing health and general medical conditions. Reports suggest that at least one in four older adults experiences some mental disorder, such as depression, anxiety, or dementia (PAHO, undated). Further, depression is the most common mental health problem in older people and the suicide rate is highest for elderly people above 85, compared to any age group. A majority of elderly people do not have access to health care or get the desired treatment, and by the year 2030 the number of elderly people with mental disorders is expected to double (PAHO, undated). These western numbers are no different than Indian context, where the reported prevalence of geriatric psychiatric morbidity in the community has been found varying from 8.9–61.2% (Shaji, Jithu & Jyothi, 2010). The mental disorders frequently encountered in the Indian elderly include dementia, and mood disorders, depression in particular. Other disorders include anxiety disorders, drug and alcohol abuse, delirium and psychosis (Prakash & Kukreti, 2013; Seby, Chaudhury & Chakraborty, 2011). There is great evidence of a rise in morbidity, mortality, hospitalization and loss of functional status related to common mental disorders in the elderly patients. Overlap of depression and anxiety is very common with up to almost half of the elderly patients reporting significant depressive and anxiety symptoms (Parkar, 2015).

Now the question is whether this presents a very pessimistic scenario. The answer would be a definite no. While this is true that the proportion of elderly people is increasing globally, it is equally true that despite a significant prevalence of psychiatric morbidity in elderly, the larger proportion of this population is age appropriately physically and mentally fit and capable of contributing to diverse and more important social responsibilities through their mature experiences.

What makes Elderly People more at Risk of Mental ill Health

While every individual strives for a healthy ageing, not all succeed in this. A general decline in different body systems is inevitable and many of them are linked with increased risk of depression and cognitive dysfunctions. While secondary psychological impact of ill health is possible, rather happens in all age group, they are mostly temporary and reversable in nature. However, compared to other age groups, elderly people experience physical illness and functional disability in late life more commonly leading to loss of autonomy, isolation, pain, increased burden on social networks, and the development of depression (Fassberg et al., 2016). It may not be possible to cover all the physical illnesses and age-related factors together; however, the relatively important conditions are being highlighted:

- Vision and hearing impairment:
- Pain
- Loss of grey matter
- Sleep disturbances
- Cardiovascular disease
- Immunological deficits
- Grief
- Loss/reduced autonomy

- Reduction in functional status
- Reduced/loss of psychosocial support

Vision and hearing impairment is common in elderly people, and its severity typically increases with increasing age. Correction glass as well as hearing aid, though are available, not all elderly people have easy access or comfortable using them. The lowering of these sensory capabilities is a big reason of impairment in functional abilities making them dependent on family members. In event, both vision and hearing are affected, the cumulative effect is much larger on daily functioning. Studies suggest that individuals with reported loss of visual function (e.g., difficulty reading newsprint, going down steps) endorsed higher levels of depressive symptoms, with around 21% experiencing moderate-to-severe depression, as compared to about 5% of people with no impairment in visual function (Demmin et al., 2020; Schuster et al., 2018; Zhang et al., 2013). While this study was on younger population, the phenomenon is more relevant for elderly, and studies from India suggest prevalence of depression upto 60.0% in the elderly with combined visual impairment and hearing impairment compared to 20.9% among those with visual impairment only and 37.8% among those with hearing impairment only. After multiple logistic regression analyses, depression was approximately 5 times higher among the participants with dual sensory impairment after adjusting for other covariates (Marmamula et al., 20210).

Pain

It is common that elderly people are facing major surgeries, hospitalization, injury and disease resulting in high risk of experiencing pain. Unrelenting pain is characteristically more universal in institutional surroundings such as in hospitals or nursing homes. Approximately 5% of the elder adult population will be inherent in nursing homes in the urbanized world and over half of these will experience cognitive impairment or dementia (Gibson, 2007). Also, the use of polypharmacy for medical conditions, and decreased physical activities also trigger the pain experiences. The occurrence of abdominal pain, headache, back pain, and chest pain all hit the highest point during later middle age from about 55 years of age and then turn down thereafter, whereas joint pain in particular areas and pain in the legs or foot have been accounted to augment with advancing age while becoming old well into the ninth decade of life phases (Tsang et al., 2008). Chronic pain represents a most important intimidation to quality of life of the older segments of our community (Blyth et al., 2001). Chronic pain has high potential to reduce mobility in elderly and inducing a sense of disability, a further risk of enhanced sense of depressive feelings. Speaking from an Indian perspective there is a lack of prevalence data on pain. The WHO Study on Global Ageing and Adult Health (SAGE) - a multi-country project included India and was implemented in six states of Assam, Karnataka, Maharashtra, Rajasthan, Uttar Pradesh and West Bengal (WHO, 2021). As per the preliminary data among the 6,557 adults aged over 50, the overall prevalence of arthritis was much higher than those below 50. There was much more arthritis among older women than older men and the women were less likely to get treated (Arokiasamy *et al.* 2013). Pain was reported as a silent pandemic, and considering its higher prevalence in elderly, its psychological consequences too are severe for elderly.

Sleep Disturbances

Sleep disturbances and insomnia in this age group is very common and should be measured as a multifactorial geriatric health state (Marengoni, 2011). As people grow older, they find it difficult to falling asleep on time, having disturbed sleep at night, or stay awake for long. Symptoms of insomnia amplify with advancing age, with increased frequency and intensity in adults aged 65 and above. Obstructive Sleep Apnea (OSA) increases with age and prevalence of OSA estimates in older adults may be as far above the ground as 70% in men and in case of women it is at 56%. Periodic Limb Movements of Sleep (PLMS) enhance in occurrence and intensity with proceeding of age and contain the potential to cause sleep complaints in older adults. PLMS is a disorder characterized by recurring episodes of stereotypic limb movements associated by muscle contractions during sleep (Bloom et al., 2009). Problems in sleep or insomnia cause anxiety, irritability, and depression among them. (Ji & Fu, 2021). Many healthy elderly people tend to adapt an altered sleep pattern, usually instigated by lack of structured engagement and sleeping in daytime, leading to reduced need of sleep or delay in sleep onset, which could be misconstrued as sleep problem.

Immunological Disorders/Diabetes

Slowing down of immune competence is a feature of getting old. It is accompanied by an increase in the frequency of autoimmune diseases in elderly. Aging of the immune system, or immunosenescence, is described by a decline of both T and B cell role, and in contradiction the incidence of low-grade chronic inflammation (Fulop et al., 2013). Thus, elderly peoples are not able to respond to immune challenge as vigorously and energetically as their younger counterpart. With ageing, the immune system gradually loses its capability to accumulate an effectual reaction against pathogens and cancer cells. Over 25% of the U.S. population who are in the age range of 65 years (Centers for Disease

Control and Prevention. National Diabetes Fact Sheet, 2004) or more are diagnosed with diabetes, and the growing age of the whole population is a noteworthy driver of the diabetes outbreak (Luhar et al., 2021). The burden of diabetes is repeatedly described in terms of its effect on middle aged adults, however; diabetes in older adults is associated to higher death rates and reduced overall functional capacity, and amplified risk of institutionalization and hospitalization. Elderly people with diabetes are at considerable risk for both acute and chronic microvascular and cardiovascular difficulty of the disease (Brown et al., 2003). Community based studies from India too report diabetes as a significant risk factor of depression in older adults (Bincy et al., 2021).

Cardiovascular disease: The risk of cardiovascular disease increases with age and increasing volume of literature suggest depression being particularly prevalent in cardiovascular disease. This aspect is elaborated further in the chapter, in context of depression. Depression is suggested to manifest rehospitalization, slower recovery, disability, mortality, and increased health care costs in cardiac patients (Krishnan et al., 2002).

While each of these conditions have their own longstanding impact on mental health status of elderly people, the impact is often cumulative due to several of these conditions usually happening in comorbid condition in different severity. Comorbidity typically is a rule rather than exception in mental illnesses. In elderly, the impact of comorbid conditions is more difficult to manage considering the limitations of drugs to be prescribed, as well as its additional side effects. As rightly pointed by Sartorious (2019), comorbidity does not mean the simple addition of two diseases that independently follow their usual trajectories; rather simultaneous presence of two or more diseases worsens the prognosis of all the diseases that are present, leading to increased complications and making the treatment of all of them more difficult and, possibly, less efficacious. Contrary to earlier notion where physical illnesses were perceived to have a psychological impact; psychological ill health conditions are gradually being established to have a two-way relationship with physical illness. This often is a major reason for misunderstanding the nature of illness, and misdiagnosis at primary level for the elderly, as well as a potential reason for families not turning up for early consultation of their elderly members.

Mental Health Issues in Relation to Ageing and Physical Health/Illness

As we discuss about mental health and illness issues in elderly, it is important to understand certain perspectives that affect mental health in elderly. The mind-body relationship is more established than ever before and has strong implications especially for the elderly. It is also important to understand the psychosocial perspectives, which has significant bearing on how health care is provided or sought for elderly. The multicultural, pluralistic society with enormous socioeconomic disparities in countries like India, make the task of providing care to the heterogeneous population with variable knowledge of attitude and practices a huge daunting task. Further, symptoms of illness are often disregarded both by patient and family as part of the "normal aging process" or something "not serious" (Prakash & Kukreti, 2013).

As human body ages, it gradually sees a loss in its vigor, slowing down of bodily functions, changes in sleep and appetite patterns, as well as an increased propensity of physical illness. The common conditions in older age include hearing loss, cataracts, and poor eyesight, back and neck pain and osteoarthritis, chronic obstructive pulmonary disease, diabetes, depression, and dementia. With growing age, they are more likely to experience several conditions at the same time. As per World health Organization, there is little evidence that older people today are in better health than their parents. It further stresses that the elderly in low- and middle-income countries carry a greater disease burden compared to rich countries, but irrespective of place of living, heart disease, stroke and chronic lung disease were the biggest killers of older people. In addition, sensory impairments, back and neck pain, chronic obstructive pulmonary disease (particularly in low- and lower-middle-income countries), depressive disorders, falls, diabetes, dementia, and osteoarthritis were the greatest causes of disability (WHO, 2017).

As morbidity risk of elderly people increases, so does the distress and care burden that comes with it. There is a growing body of literature that suggests link between physical and mental health in elderly. In a mediation analysis of 10,693 individuals aged 50 years and over, to study direct and indirect effects of past mental health on present physical health and past physical health on present mental health, researchers have found significant direct and indirect effects for both forms of health, with indirect effects explaining 10% of the effect of past mental health on physical health and 8% of the effect of past physical health on mental health (Ohrnberger, Fichera & Sutton, 2017).

We take a broader look over common mental ill health conditions in elderly in relation to growing age and physical health.

Depression: While epidemiological data on this population from Indian context is still scarce, researchers have termed the burden of geriatric mental health as a silent epidemic (Prakash & Kukreti, 2013). Depression is one of the most common mental ill health conditions in elderly. It is the most common psychiatric disorder in the geriatric population with prevalence ranging from 22.2% to 55.2% of elderly patients as reported in different studies from India (Tiple, Sharma & Shrivastava, 2006). In a review of fifty-one studies published (1997-2016) from 16 States in India, the prevalence of depression among elderly population was estimated as 34.4% (Pilania M et al., 2018). In further sub-group analysis, the pooled prevalence was higher among females, rural populations, and in the eastern part of the country. The WHO Study on Global Ageing and Adult Health (SAGE) conducted from 2007 to 2010 in six core countries found prevalence of depression among older adults to be highest in India, followed by Mexico and Russia (Anand, 2015).

While depression is common in elderly group, it is not normal. There are several risk factors in elderly, that make them more prone to develop depressive symptoms. Some of the frequently studied risk factors include educational background, gender, previous physical and mental health status, presence of physical illness, multiple medication, and poor psychosocial support (Varma, 2012; Heun & Hein, 2005). However, these risk factors may not have universal risk of alleviating risk of depression. Review study by Maier et al. (2021) found a heterogeneous results for education, female gender, self-rated health, cognitive impairment, and older age as risk factor of depression. Whereas chronic disease, difficulty initiating sleep, mobility impairment, impairment in activities of daily life and vision impairment were mostly identified as significant risk factors of depression. It clearly implicates that risk factors found most homogenously for developing depressing symptoms were related to ageing or disease conditions. Psychosocial factors as risk for depression yielded heterogenous results in the study.

It could be a consequential error to ignore depression in elderly as it is an important public health problem. It is important to note that compared to younger population, depression seen for the first time in elderly are different in terms of clinical presentation, etiology, response to treatment and prognosis. While minor depression and sub-syndromal depression could be common, major depression is not common. Further, elders as well as caregivers too are less likely to recognize or endorse depressed mood. Unlike younger adults, mild depression or even sub-syndromal depression has greater impact on overall health in elderly. Untreated depression can delay recovery or worsen the outcome of other medical illnesses via increased morbidity or mortality.

It could be tricky to diagnose depression in elderly especially when they have certain comorbid major physical illness; however, it is established that depression rates are increased in elderly who have other medical condition. The common medical conditions which are related to depression could be:

- Cardiovascular disease
- Thyroid disorders
- Parkinson disease
- Cancer
- Stroke
- Dementia (such as Alzheimer disease)
- In addition, overuse of alcohol or certain medications can make depression worse.

There is substantial literature on biological correlates of depression in elderly, however the exact causal factors are difficult to impress (Tiemeier, 2003). Talking of cardiovascular disease, depression is significantly prevalent in cardiovascular disease. As per an estimate, approximately up to 50% of heart disease patients experience depressive symptoms, out of which 20-25% patients experience major depression, and another 20-25% have subliminal or subsyndromal level of depression not meeting criteria for major depressive disorder (Carney & Freedland, 2003). With growing age, the risk of cardiovascular disease also increases. Age is a known independent risk factor for cardiovascular disease in adults, which is compounded by additional factors including frailty, obesity, and diabetes, which are again proportionate to age (Rodgers et al., 2019). Relationship of depression and cardiovascular disease is intricate and suggested to be a two relationship where depressive symptoms in long term enhance risk of cardiovascular disease, and individuals with cardiovascular disease have depressive symptoms. The prevalence of depression among cardiac patients ranges from 20 to 30%, which is much higher compared to 10% prevalence of this treatable condition in the general population (Stewart & Rollman, 2014). While the exact causality of one on the another in terms of pathways is not completely understood, the likely explanations suggested by researchers include dysfunction in the autonomic nervous system, elevated cortisol levels, and elevated markers of inflammation (Dhar & Barton, 2016).

Healthy Ageing

Good general health and social care is important for promoting good health, preventing disease and managing chronic illnesses. Educating and spreading awareness regarding age related issues in community is most important for prompt recognition and treatment of mental, neurological and substance use disorders in older adults is essential. Only medical treatment is not enough to cure physical illness, but much can be done to support and improve the health of elderly population by,

- Early diagnosis, in order to promote early and optimal management;
- Optimizing physical and mental health, functional ability and well-being;
- Identifying and treating accompanying physical illness;
- Detecting and managing challenging behaviour; and
- Providing information and long-term support to care givers.

Training all health providers in working with issues and disorders related to ageing is therefore important. Effective, community-level primary mental health care for older people is crucial. It is equally important to focus on the long-term care of older adults suffering from mental disorders, as well as to provide caregivers with education, training, and support. An appropriate and supportive legislative environment based on internationally accepted human rights standards is required to ensure the highest quality of services to people with mental illness and their caregivers. Mental health problems are common among seniors and may include isolation, affective and anxiety disorders, dementia, and psychosis, among others. Many seniors also suffer from sleep and behavioral disorders, cognitive deterioration, or confusion states because of physical disorders or surgical interventions. It is evident that seniors always get maximum benefit from supportive social connections and close personal relationships but suffer as a result of disrupted personal ties and loneliness.

Healthcare providers, especially those in primary care, can play a central role in promoting mental health for seniors by working with mental health professionals, local governments, different NGOs, families, and communities to provide comprehensive mental health care and support. In addition, older people should be encouraged to take care of their physical as well as mental health and actively participate in their communities and in society at large for overall wellbeing.

Summary: With an increase in elderly population the physical and mental health needs of older adults is of major concern. The general decline in physical health and presence of conditions like cardiovascular disease, diabetes, chronic pain and immunological decline make elderly at risk of developing mental ill health conditions. Some physical conditions particularly immunological deficiencies may mimic depression. Contrary to layman percept conditions like depression is not hallmark of elderly, but the physical health and other psychosocial circumstances may manifest the symptoms. General people need to come out of the perception that dysfunction is inherent of elderly and take measures for early screening and intervention to let elderly lead a healthy ageing.

References

- Anand, A. (2015). Understanding depression among older adults in six low-middle income countries using WHO-SAGE survey. Behav Health, 1(2), 1-11.
- Arokiasamy, P., Parasuraman, S., Sekher, T. V., Lhungdim, H. (2013). Study on global Ageing and adult health (SAGE) Wave 1, 2007. India National Report retrieved from https://www.iipsindia.ac.in/sites/default/files/SAGE_Wave1_India_Report.pdf
- Benedetti, T. R. B., Borges, L. J., Petroski, E. L., & Gonçalves, L. H. T. (2008). Physical activity and mental health status among elderly people. *Revista de SaúdePública*, 42, 302-307.

- Bincy, K., Logaraj, M., Ramraj, B. (2021). Depression and its associated factors among the older adults in rural, Tamilnadu, India,. *Clinical Epidemiology and Global Health*. 10 (100677).
- Bloom, H. G., Ahmed, I., Alessi, C. A., Ancoli-Israel, S., Buysse, D. J., Kryger, M. H., ... & Zee, P. C. (2009). Evidence-based recommendations for the assessment and management of sleep disorders in older persons. *Journal of the American Geriatrics Society, 57*(5), 761-789.
- Blyth, F. M., March, L. M., Brnabic, A. J., Jorm, L. R., Williamson, M., & Cousins, M. J. (2001). Chronic pain in Australia: a prevalence study. *Pain, 89*(2-3), 127-134.
- Bodnar, J. C., & Kiecolt-Glaser, J. K. (1994). Caregiver depression after bereavement: Chronic stress isn't over when it's over. *Psychology and aging, 9*(3), 372.
- California Healthcare Foundation/American Geriatrics Society Panel in Improving Care for Elders with Diabetes, C. (2003). Guidelines for improving the care of the older person with diabetes mellitus. *Journal of the American Geriatrics Society, 51*(5s), 265-280.
- Carney, R. M., & Freedland, K. E. (2003). Depression, mortality, and medical morbidity in patients with coronary heart disease. *Biological psychiatry, 54*(3), 241–247.
- Centers for Disease Control and Prevention. (2011). National diabetes fact sheet: national estimates and general information on diabetes and prediabetes in the United States, 2011. *Atlanta, GA: US department of health and human services, centers for disease control and prevention, 201*(1), 2568-2569.
- Demmin, D. L., & Silverstein, S. M. (2020). Visual Impairment and Mental Health: Unmet Needs and Treatment Options. Clinical ophthalmology (Auckland, N.Z.), 14, 4229–4251.
- Dhar, A. K., & Barton, D. A. (2016). Depression and the link with cardiovascular disease. *Frontiers in psychiatry, 7* (33).
- Fassberg, M. M., Cheung, G., Canetto, S. S., Erlangsen, A., Lapierre, S., Lindner, R., Draper, B., Gallo, J. J., Wong, C., Wu, J., Duberstein, P., &Wærn, M. (2016). A systematic review of physical illness, functional disability, and suicidal behaviour among older adults. *Aging & mental health, 20*(2), 166–194.

- Fulop, T., Larbi, A., & Pawelec, G. (2013). Human T cell aging and the impact of persistent viral infections. Frontiers in immunology, 4, 271.
- Gibson, S. J. (2007). IASP global year against pain in older persons: highlighting the current status and future perspectives in geriatric pain. *Expert Review of Neurotherapeutics*, *7*(6), 627-635.
- Heun, R., & Hein, S. (2005). Risk factors of major depression in the elderly. *European psychiatry : the journal of the Association of European Psychiatrists*, *20*(3), 199–204.
- Ji, X., & Fu, Y. (2021). The role of sleep disturbances in cognitive function and depressive symptoms among community-dwelling elderly with sleep complaints. *International Journal of Geriatric Psychiatry*, *36*(1), 96-105.
- Krishnan, K. R., Delong, M., Kraemer, H., Carney, R., Spiegel, D., Gordon, C., McDonald, W., Dew, M., Alexopoulos, G., Buckwalter, K., Cohen, P. D., Evans, D., Kaufmann, P. G., Olin, J., Otey, E., & Wainscott, C. (2002). Comorbidity of depression with other medical diseases in the elderly. *Biological psychiatry*, *52*(6), 559–588.
- Luhar, S., Kondal, D., Jones, R., Anjana, R. M., Patel, S. A., Kinra, S., ... & Narayan, K. V. (2021). Lifetime risk of diabetes in metropolitan cities in India. *Diabetologia*, *64*(3), 521-529.
- Maier, A., Riedel-Heller, S. G., Pabst, A., & Luppa, M. (2021). Risk factors and protective factors of depression in older people 65+. A systematic review. *PloS one*, *16*(5), e0251326.
- Marengoni, A., Angleman, S., Melis, R., Mangialasche, F., Karp, A., Garmen, A., ... & Fratiglioni, L. (2011). Aging with multimorbidity: a systematic review of the literature. *Ageing research reviews*, *10*(4), 430-439.
- Marmamula, S., Kumbham, T.R., Modepalli, S.B. *et al.* Depression, combined visual and hearing impairment (dual sensory impairment): a hidden multi-morbidity among the elderly in Residential Care in India. *Sci Rep* **11,** 16189 (2021).
- Ohrnberger, J., Fichera, E., & Sutton, M. (2017). The relationship between physical and mental health: A mediation analysis. *Social science & medicine (1982)*, *195*, 42–49.
- PAHO, undated. Seniors and Mental Health. Retrieved 14.11.2021 from https://www3.paho.org/hq/index.php?option=com_content

&view=article&id=9877: seniors-mental-health&Itemid=40721&lang =en

- Parkar, S. R. (2015). Elderly mental health: needs. *Menssana monographs*, *13*(1), 91.
- Pilania, M., Yadav, V., Bairwa, M., Behera, P., Gupta, S. D., Khurana, H., ... & Poongothai, S. (2019). Prevalence of depression among the elderly (60 years and above) population in India, 1997–2016: a systematic review and meta-analysis. *BMC Public Health*, 19(1), 832.
- Prakash, O., Kukreti, P. State of Geriatric Mental Health in India. *Curr Tran Geriatr Gerontol Rep* **2,** 1–6 (2013).
- Reher, D. S. (2004). The demographic transition revisited as a global process. *Population, space and place*, *10*(1), 19-41.
- Rodgers, J. L., Jones, J., Bolleddu, S. I., Vanthenapalli, S., Rodgers, L. E., Shah, K., Karia, K., & Panguluri, S. K. (2019). Cardiovascular Risks Associated with Gender and Aging. *Journal of cardiovascular development and disease*, *6*(2), 19.
- Sartorious N. (2013). Comorbidity of mental and physical diseases: a main challenge for medicine of the 21st century. *Shanghai archives of psychiatry*, *25*(2), 68–69.
- Schuster AK, Tesarz J, Rezapour J, Beutel ME, Bertram B, Pfeiffer N. Visual impairment is associated with depressive symptoms—results from the Nationwide German DEGS1 study. *Front Psychiatry*. 2018;9.
- Seby, K., Chaudhury, S., & Chakraborty, R. (2011). Prevalence of psychiatric and physical morbidity in an urban geriatric population. *Indian journal of psychiatry*, *53*(2), 121.
- Shaji, K. S., Jithu, V. P., & Jyothi, K. S. (2010). Indian research on aging and dementia. *Indian journal of psychiatry*, *52*(Suppl1), S148.
- Sözeri-Varma, G. (2012). Depression in the elderly: clinical features and risk factors. *Aging and disease*, *3*(6), 465.
- Stewart, J. C., & Rollman, B. L. (2014). Optimizing approaches to addressing depression in cardiac patients: a comment on O'Neil et al. *Annals of behavioral medicine: a publication of the Society of Behavioral Medicine*, *48*(2), 142–144.
- Tiemeier, H. (2003). Biological risk factors for late life depression. *European journal of epidemiology*, *18*(8), 745-750.

- Tiple, P., Sharma, S. N., & Srivastava, A. S. (2006). Psychiatric morbidity in geriatric people. *Indian journal of psychiatry, 48*(2), 88–94.
- Tsang, A., Von Korff, M., Lee, S., Alonso, J., Karam, E., Angermeyer, M. C., ... & Watanabe, M. (2008). Common chronic pain conditions in developed and developing countries: gender and age differences and comorbidity with depression-anxiety disorders. *The journal of pain, 9*(10), 883-891.
- United Nations, Department of Economic and Social Affairs, Population Division (2019). World Population Ageing 2019: Highlights (ST/ESA/SER.A/430). Retrieved 15.11.2021, https:// www.un.org/en/development/desa/population/publications / pdf / ageing / WorldPopulationAgeing2019-Highlights.pdf
- W.H.O (2017) 10 Facts on ageing and health. Retrieved 14.11.2021, https://www.who.int/news-room/fact-sheets/detail/10-facts-on-ageing-and-health
- Zhang, X., Bullard, K. M., Cotch, M. F., Wilson, M. R., Rovner, B. W., McGwin, G., Jr, Owsley, C., Barker, L., Crews, J. E., & Saaddine, J. B. (2013). Association between depression and functional vision loss in persons 20 years of age or older in the United States, NHANES 2005-2008. *JAMA ophthalmology, 131*(5), 573–581.

* * *

THE AGEING BRAIN: COGNITION AND IMPACT ON DAILY LIFE

Susmita Halder

People now are living longer owing to the improvements in health care facilities and technology (Craig, et al., 2015). It is not very unlikely to come across individuals who are in their 70's-80, and functioning adequately well. This increase in adult longevity is a kind of step forward in human adaptation. The geriatric population is increasing in an ever increasing manner throughout the world. While many older people remain in good mental as well as physical health, some tend to have aging associated problems as well. In the coming years the world's population aged sixty years and older is predicted to total 2 billion, up from 900 million in 2015 (Baltes & Carstensen, 1996; Hofer & Sliwinski, 2001). At present one hundred and 25 million people are aged eighty years or older as estimated by the World Health Organization (W.H.O). The population of the elderly population in the Indian subcontinent has been on the rise in recent years and this trend is likely to continue in the coming decades.

Aging is a process that begins at birth and ends with termination of one's life. Every individuals ages, and in the younger years its denoted by being called growth and maturation while with increasing age, its often referred to as senescence. One way to define aging is in terms of increasing age, while the other way is in terms of changing biological and physiological functioning of the body, both of which combined tend to impact one's overall functioning, which becomes evident in the older population (Hepworth, 2003).

It is essentially a biological process that has psychological consequences. With passing years it is natural to experience several changes including biological, psychological and social and these tend to be part of normal aging, however when these changes exceed the normal threshold they begin to cause problems. In case of the later scenario, the need to intervene becomes more pronounced and intervention may be required to facilitate the elderly's adaptation to the changes. Some changes are brought about in all individuals with aging. These progressions are persistent all through life, from losing infant teeth to the loss of taste buds. A few changes are evident inside the manner in which they modify physical appearance or in their noticeable impact upon body frameworks. Some changes are less evident, in that they influence the frameworks inside the body.

The progressions of changes differ in degree and rate from person to person. The aging of the brain is one such change and is expected due to pathophysiological changes that take place over the time of an individual's life expectancy. The aging of human brain is a gradual and complicated process beginning with inflammatory changes leading to abnormalities at the cellular level, proceeding onto a kind of neuronal adaptation and finally resulting in degeneration in some but not all individuals. There are several age related changes that occur at the structural and functional level of brain functioning, which further manifest in terms of cognitive changes. With the advent of latest neuroimaging techniques it has been possible to study in great detail the changes that happen in the brain with increasing age (Peters, 2006).

In terms of brain structure, the neurons in the brain tend to be have multiple connections, each receiving and sending signals. This exchange of signals tends to be majorly mediated by the white matter, which begin to deteriorate with increasing age, further also resulting in reduced brain size (Whalley, 2012). This also reduces the efficiency of communication between neurons thereby leading to several signs of cognitive impairments (Whalley, 2012). The common most critical changes related to the brain functioning associated with aging is a general reduction of brain weight and volume as found by Berg and others in between 1978-1998. Myelin loss as a result of increasing age is most prominent in areas where myelination takes place generally much later during the formative process (Kemper, 1984).

Articulated losses tend to be most significant in the human cortex especially in the frontal, the premotor cortical areas, and the association areas of the temporal lobe. The temporal limbic area (region 38) and association areas of the somesthetic and visual cortex (regions 40 and 18, separately) additionally show loss in cell count with increasing age, yet to a lesser degree (Kemper, 1984). Many regions of the hippocampal development show age-related neuronal losses, yet in the amygdala, subcortical forebrain, brain stem, and cerebellar formations, changes are progressively specific (Albert et al., 2011).

While existing literature has pointed towards several changes in the brain structure as a result of aging, the following tend to be common to almost all individuals and further deterioration of these may result in neurocognitive disorders in the elderly as well:

1. Enlargement of the ventricles
2. A decrement in volume of the brain

3. Reduced volumes specifically in the temporal, frontal regions
4. Atrophy of hippocampal and parahippocampal regions
5. Decreased neuronal communication
6. Loss of brain plasticity
7. Increased presence of neurofibrillary tangles.

Along with the structural changes several neurochemical changes are inevitable with aging, recent researchers have identified a number of neurotransmitters, as well as their receptors which exhibit alterations in various regions of the brain with the aging process. The most important function of these neurotransmitters is synaptic communication, which is important for neuronal transmissions to occur. Glutamate and Gamma-Aminobutyric Acid, or GABA, tend to be two of the most important ones, where in the former tends to have an excitatory function while the latter has an inhibitory role. Glutamate concentrations also reduce with age and this is especially seen in the motor cortex. With respect to aging dopamine and serotonin tend to play a major role, as they are deeply involved in synaptic plasticity and neurogenesis in the adult brain. Findings on Positron Emission Tomography (PET) studies showed a significant decline in domine synthesis which results in metabolic complications in normal human beings (Ota et al., 2006). Dopaminergic pathways tend to mediate several cognitive functions as well as behaviors such as arousal, cognitive control and working memory emotion and mood, motivation, motor function, positive reinforcement, sexual arousal, orgasm, and refractory period, all of which shows a decline with increasing age. The PET studies in human subjects show that with age the number of the serotonin receptors in the caudate nucleus, putamen and frontal cerebral cortex decrease. There is also a decreased binding capacity for serotonin transporter in the thalamus and midbrain (Marcusson et al., 1984). Serotonin in seems to have a role in depression and it has been seen that depression tends to be common in the geriatric population, further it modulates several functions like body temperature regulation, emotion and mood, aggression, and have a minor role in reward response, appetite, sleep, memory and learning, all of which begin to show a decline as a person ages (Chow & Herrup, 2015).

Further brain aging may be in terms of its functions, as structural changes are likely to result in functional manifestations. These can include changes in cognition and memory impairment as changes in brain structure and function are intrinsically intertwined to one's cognitive functioning. Cognition described very simply is the ability to think, reason, remember, solve problems, focus, be able to inhibit ones response and localize oneself in space. While not all of these functions are impaired or show a decline in every aged individual, a mix of some of this seems to be inevitable as one ages. There occurs cognitive slowing, which may be evident on attention tasks or when it is necessary to multitask or when switching from one task to another (IIHS, 2014). The most subtle signs of cognitive aging can be:

- Difficulty remembering facts
- Slowed reaction time
- Remembering names or locations
- Holding attention for long
- Paying attention to multiple stimulus at the same time
- Slower visuomotor coordination

In spite of these changes, not all of them show any deficits in terms of everyday activities. If given enough opportunity, they may be very functional. A slow decline in overall brain functioning starts from 60s which progress slowly; however, they maintain good cognitive health with appropriate life style, it deteriorates further with more age, which is common for all. The changes in old age are results of life events, habits, practices, heredity, history of medical illness as well as socialcultural impact which influence the cognitive functioning at later stage (Kapur et al., 1989).

Since the late 20th century interest has been increased to understand ageing and cognition connection and researches has been conducted largely in this area. The broad domain of cognition has been divided by neuropsychologists into subdomains that include attentional processes, language functions, learning and memory, processing speed, and the executive functions. While the overall trend seems more of cognitive decline, there tends to be tremendous variation across individuals. Even it is found, elderly perform better than their younger counterparts in certain cognitive tasks, or atleast almost at same level as the young population do (Melzer et al., 2001).

The cognitive changes often seen in the elderly can include but are not limited to:

1. **Attention:** Deficits in orientation tends to be an initial symptom of brain disease. There tend to be declines in orientation as a person ages, which is considered part of normal aging. However this tends to impact their attention capacity as well. Older adults tend to face prominent difficulties on tasks that assess attention and focus upon dividing as well as shifting of attention between several sources of information. There is relative conservation of implementation on tasks which them to select relevant stimuli; although they tend to be slower than younger adults, distractions don't weaken their performance on a comparable

level, rather they are able to hold attention for a considerable time for different tasks. The errands on which these adults demonstrate impedances will in general include adaptable management of attention, which tends to be related with the frontal lobes. Critically, these sorts of undertakings have the potential to improve if provided with appropriate training (Kretschme et al., 2011).

2. **Working memory:** Working memory which is a key element of executive and overall cognitive functioning also impacted with age. Deficits in working memory also disturbs other related psychological functioning, including long term memory, language, flexibility, problem solving capacities, and decisions making, because of its multi component constructs. The elderly often show critical deficits in tasks that include rearrangement, manipulation, or an integration of the elements of working memory. Although the mechanisms fundamental to these age-related shortfalls are up 'til now ineffectively comprehended, the impacts of such deficiencies are likely to be extensive. Numerous complex ordinary errands, for example, decision making, problem solving, and planning of goal directed activities require an amalgamation of information from an assortment of sources. It appears to be likely that attention, speed of information processing as well as response inhibition are terrifically important functions for powerful performance of superior cognitive tasks (Thapial et al., 2016).

3. **Long term memory:** Memory is one important cognitive function which affects most with ageing, but not all domains of memory slow down equally within same time. The ability to recall new information gradually declines long before ageing, its start almost in 40s. The older adults are less likely than young adults to freely recall most of the new

information, though they can recognize when the content is mentioned. Numerous elderly individuals mention about excessive slips in memory with increasing age, thus the significant focal point of studies has involved an attempt to recognize memory decreases owing to typical maturing in comparison to those characteristic of neurotic maturing. Similar to the concept of attention, memory tends to be a singular function; a few sorts which tend to remain moderately flawless with a gradual process of aging while on the other hand few manifest hugedecays. Long term memory, in contrast to short term and working memory, may require recovery of data which may never again be present or may be kept up in a functioning condition (Davis et al., 2003).

Aging mainly influences episodic memory, in particular traces for specific events and interactions that took place sometime earlier in the past. Albeit numerous older adults accept that their recollections for remote occasions are superior to their recollections for late occasions, all things considered, more established recollections have gotten increasingly semantic or gist like, holding the general core data however deficient with regards to subtleties, especially spatial and temporal setting. Elevated levels of stress and emotions, be that as it may, further for the most part has a detrimental impact on memory.

4. Speech and language: Learned early in life the language skills are retained during adulthood. However, trying to remember a familiar name or a particular word often becomes difficult for older adults. With maturing, there happens decrease in the errands identified with word recovery, perception of sentences, synthesis and production of sentences, influencing the totality of the verbal undertaking. Discourse and language processing are to a great extent unblemished in the elderly under ordinary conditions, in spite of the fact that handling time might be to some degree more slow than in young adults. Evidence in fact shows that verbal skills really improve with age. More seasoned individuals frequently tell well-organized expound narratives that are considered by others to be more fascinating than those told by young adults (Kemper, 2000). They typically have progressively broad vocabularies; and in spite of the fact that they display the intermittent word-discovering trouble, they are effectively ready to give circumlocutions to cover the issue. They are gifted conversationalists and seem to have hardly any challenges in preparing progressing discourse (Santiago et al., 2016).

5. Executive functioning: Executive control is a multipart construct that comprises of a variety of processes which may involve planning, organization, coordination, implementation, and evaluation of many non-routine activities. Executive control is especially significant for novel undertakings for which a lot of constant procedures is not promptly accessible. It relies basically upon prefrontal cortex, which applies its expansive controlling impact through broad reciprocal associations. Moderately scant studies have been undertaken to study the impacts of maturing on decision making. The vast majority of the literature has featured the effect of attentional and working memory impediments on the capacity to decide, yet in addition has incorporated ideas involving motivation, relevance, emotional investment, and prior knowledge as significant arbitrators of those impacts, especially, in actuality, settings. Decision making is by all accounts a domain that makes clear demands on processing resources, yet in regular daily existence those requests might be diminished by life-applicable information or expertise in the domain of problem solving (Lin et al., 2007; Allain et al., 2005).

However none of these cognitive functions can exist in isolation. Several cognitive abilities like attention, memory and reasoning, are involved in carrying out daily activities. It is often seen that there tends to be an inverse relation between cognitive abilities and dependence in terms of activities of daily living (ADL) in the elderly. In terms of the aging brain, the ADL most affected tend to be the instrumental activities such as handling money, housekeeping, and dressing, using telephone, transportation and meal preparation tend to get impacted much earlier than the basic life tasks. The elderly with significant brain changes, and subsequent cognitive manifestations may have difficulty in maintaining their independence in the community and daily life. Everyday life activities, including social interaction and behavior much dependent on cognitive functioning, and it becomes more difficult to keep control over these functions with conative decline in ageing. In unfamiliar situations brain aging interferes with performance when information has to be processed, while in familiar situations, older adults tend to make more accurate interpretations of the behaviors of others as their experience helps them focus attention.

Research in the field of neuroscience additionally underpins the idea that emotional regulation requires cognitive control. Ochsner and Gross (2005) have suggested that emotional regulation relies on prefrontal and cingulate control systems that feedback into, and change activation in, subcortical structures like the amygdala and insula related with emotional responding. Emotional regulation includes a goal coordinated procedure in which people change the dynamic highlights of feeling, including intensity and timing of behavioural, bodily and experiential reactions (Thompson et al., 2008). Connection between emotional regulation and cognitive capacities seems, by all accounts, to be equal. Executive functions assume a significant role in emotional regulation, and cognitive dysfunction may prompt enthusiastic regulations. There is an ascent in capacity of geriatric individuals to oversee emotional responses to push stressful circumstances contrasted with younger individuals, yet in addition having high paces of despondency and cognitive decays identified with neuroanatomical basic and practical changes is deserving of further examination.

Assessments to Measure Changes in Ageing Brain

Addressing patients' concerns and family members queries regarding changed activities of cognitive functioning are challenging for a clinician. Providing information in accordance to decreased functioning, i.e., memory loss or limited flexibility is required to increase the awareness and treatment adherence. Cognitive impairment in older adults may cause from different factors, including physical illness, side effects of medications; metabolic or endocrine difficulties; delirium due to medical conditions; infection as a urinary tract or COVID-19 infection; depression; and dementia. Comorbid physical and psychological conditions can be improved with pharmacotherapy or psychotherapy, but irreversible conditions like dementia cannot be improved only can be prevented from deterioration. For proper understanding of the problems and to take timely action families need to be educated and should be prepared for predictable changes. Management of these sort of problems can only be start with proper identification and screening. Information about daily life activities, emotional and social expressions should be taken from a person who has frequent contact with the person, such as a partner, close family member or other care provider, is the best way to more fully assess cognitive impairment (Willis, 2004). Interviews are conducted to assess memory, behavior, mood, and daily living functioning. It is recommended to do the interview and assessment with the patient alone, so that family members or companions cannot prompt the person and individual can feel free and comfortable (Bunn et al., 2012). For further management, if available, a local memory disorders clinic or center for treatment of Alzheimer 's disease may also accept referrals.

Ageing Brain and Emotional and Behavioral Changes

Emotional changes and impact of positive and negative emotion in elderly is not well studied domain. Emotional arousal as a controlling factor of behavior need to be understood (Streubel & Kunzmann, 2011). Changes in emotions with age are complex, as older adulthood is not simply a time of emotional well-being and tranquility. Strong emotions exist and reactions to important life events may increase with age, rather than diminish. Negative emotional experiences may impact the cognitive functioning and family members as well as the individuals involved with geriatric care should learn the connection to support them in a better way.

Regulation of emotion requires control over cognitive abilities such as focusing and maintaining attention, controlling and inhibiting the distractive elements in thoughts (Mather & Knight, 2005; Ochsner & Gross, 2005; Schmeichel, 2007).

Associated Activities

Although aging of the brain is an inevitable process, there still tend to be individual differences in aging related cognitive decline. In some individuals the decline tends to be minimal, often highlighting the role of an underlying cognitive reserve.

It is often seen that individuals who were more intellectually active at a young age, had better cognitive activity through continued education, occupation, or stimulating activities, having right genes and social network and friends, and enjoying activities with others retain cognitive skills with aging better than those who are less accomplished, they have been shown to be associated cognitive reserve. The level of education and intellectual effort, which improve cognitive skills, seem to protect brain against aging as well. Such intellectually stimulating activities cause the brain cells to grow and regenerate, replenish loss of neurotransmitters and retards the neuronal aging, and improves the cognitive reserve. As one ages the changes that occur side by side in neural activation, causes differential stimulation in different areas, with increased activation in some areas and decreased activation in others. Compared to younger adults, more brain activity is utilized when an elderly person performs a cognitive task. The physical frailty with age is accompanied with proportional cognitive decline, and can be leveled as normal aging process (Jasperson et al., 2014).

Brain Reserve

The concept of brain reserve tends to be highly evidence based, and along with it the high prevalence of brain changes and associated pathology at both clinical and subclinical levels are of major concern, thereby providing a useful theoretical framework for the development of programs aiming at the promotion of brain health in the elderly. In the old, issues with memory and other subjective capacities are so regular they're frequently viewed as "typical for age". Unfortunately, a significant number of those individuals develop dementia sometime later. Between benign memory issues and dementia there are "in the middle of" conditions that seem, by all accounts, to be the primary indications of what may become dementia. This implies numerous individuals with Mild Cognitive Impairment (MCI) are very progress to dementia. The limit setting a boundary between aging that is normal and early cognitive impairment is getting expanding consideration in many research settings (Petersen et al., 2001). Thus there tends to be a gradual progression from the normal changes associated with ageing towards these changes becoming pathological and ultimately resulting in disorders. The most common disorder in the elderly being dementia. While the effect of these programs may not be immediate or quite drastic, even the most modest impact would be a sign of successful intervention for the aging at the population, all across the world. Further concept of brain plasticity, which focuses on the ability of the brain to modify and replace neurons and neural connections throughout life tends to form the major principle guiding neurocognitive interventions. Although the plasticity tends to change as one ages, from childhood to old age, yet this capacity of the brain drives most researchers and clinicians to explore and develop intervention and neurorehabilitation programs for the elderly with both clinical and subclinical brain related problems.

Promoting Healthy Brain in Elderly Population

While it is inevitable that with age brain function will deteriorate, it also can be protected by following healthy behavior and positive engagements (Halder & Mahato, 2018). Involving into regular cognitive tasks strengthen the neural connections by using the alternative neural circuits and optimize the ability of individual's performance in his/her daily life functioning (Stern, 2012). Barulli and Stern (2013). An elderly person can engage himself into healthy life style, including proper diet, regular physical and brain exercise to keep them psychologically and cognitively active. Healthy and positive habits prevent deterioration, also promote, and support the brain's structural integrity and function, namely 'brain health' (Jackson et al., 2016).

Conclusion

The impact of ageing on the brain and cognition are widespread and multi-factorial. Understanding the cognitive, behavioural, and emotional changes would help in understanding the general continuum as well as help identify what changes occur prior to onset of dementia in the elderly that are most likely to have an impact on the individual. This may be an attempt to compensate and recruit additional networks or because specific areas are no longer easily accessed. Family history, presence of medical conditions, neurobiological and factors all play a major part to bring changes in ageing brain. But it is not all negative, higher levels of education or occupational attainment may act as a protective factor. Also protective are a healthy diet, low to moderate alcohol intake, and regular exercise. Biological ageing is not tied absolutely to chronological ageing, and it may be possible to slow biological ageing and even reduce the possibility of suffering from age related diseases such as dementia.

References

- Albert, M. S., DeKosky, S. T., Dickson, D., Dubois, B., Feldman, H. H., Fox, N. C., & Phelps, C. H. (2011). The diagnosis of mild cognitive impairment due to Alzheimer's disease: recommendations from the National Institute on Aging-Alzheimer's Association workgroups on diagnostic guidelines for Alzheimer's disease. *Alzheimer's & dementia, 7*(3), 270-279.
- Allain, P., Nicoleau, S., Pinon, K., Etcharry-Bouyx, F., Barré, J., Berrut, G., ... & Le Gall, D. (2005). Executive functioning in normal aging: A study of action planning using the Zoo Map Test. *Brain and cognition, 57*(1), 4-7.

- Baltes, M. M., & Carstensen, L. L. (1996). The process of successful ageing. *Ageing & Society, 16*(4), 397-422.
- Barulli D. & Stern Y. (2013). Efficiency, capacity, compensation, maintenance, plasticity: emerging concepts in cognitive reserve. *Trends Cogn. Sci,* 17, 502–509. 10.1016/j.tics.2013.08.012.
- Bunn, F., Goodman, C., Sworm, L. et al. (2012). Psychosocial factors that shape patient and carer experiences of dementia diagnosis and treatment: a systematic review of qualitative studies. *PLOS Med.* 9(10):e1001331.
- Chow, H. M., & Herrup, K. (2015). Genomic integrity and the ageing brain. *Nature Reviews Neuroscience, 16*(11), 672-684.
- Craig, T., Smelick, C., Tacutu, R., Wuttke, D., Wood, S. H., Stanley, H., ... & de Magalhaes, J. P. (2015). The Digital Ageing Atlas: integrating the diversity of age-related changes into a unified resource. *Nucleic acids research, 43*(D1), D873-D878.
- Davis, H. P., Small, S. A., Stern, Y., Mayeux, R., Feldstein, S. N., & Keller, F. R. (2003). Acquisition, recall, and forgetting of verbal information in long-term memory by young, middle-aged, and elderly individuals. *Cortex, 39*(4-5), 1063-1091.
- Halder, S., & Mahato, A. K. (2018). Cognition in ageing: implications for assessment and intervention. In *Handbook of Research on Geriatric Health, Treatment, and Care* (pp. 118-133). IGI Global.
- Hepworth, M. (2003). Ageing bodies: aged by culture. In *Discourse, the body, and identity* (pp. 89-106). Palgrave Macmillan, London.
- Hofer, S. M., & Sliwinski, M. J. (2001). Understanding ageing. *Gerontology, 47*(6), 341-352.
- Insurance Institute for Highway Safety (IIHS) Arlington (VA): IIHS; 2014. Fatality facts 2013, Older people. [cited 2015 Mar 26].
- Jackson, P. A., Pialoux, V., Corbett, D., Drogos, L., Erickson, K. I., Eskes, G. A., & Poulin, M. J. (2016). Promoting brain health through exercise and diet in older adults: a physiological perspective. *The Journal of physiology, 594*(16), 4485–4498. https://doi.org/10.1113/JP271270
- Jasperson, K. W., Kohlmann, W., Gammon, A., Slack, H., Buchmann, L., Hunt, J., ... & Schiffman, J. D. (2014). Role of rapid sequence whole-body MRI screening in SDH-associated hereditary paraganglioma families. *Familial cancer, 13*(2), 257-265.

- Kapur, N., Young, A., Bateman, D., & Kennedy, P. (1989). Focal retrograde amnesia: a long term clinical and neuropsychological follow-up. *Cortex, 25*(3), 387-402.
- Kemper, S. (1984). The development of narrative skills: Explanations and entertainments. In *Discourse development* (pp. 99-124). Springer, New York, NY.
- Kramer A. F., Bherer L., Colcombe S. J., Dong W., Greenough W. T. (2004). Environmental influences on cognitive and brain plasticity during aging. *J. Gerontol. A Biol. Sci. Med. Sci.* 59 M940–957. 10.1093/gerona/59.9.M940
- Kretschmer, V., Griefahn, B., & Schmidt, K. H. (2011). Bright light and night work: effects on selective and divided attention in elderly persons. *Lighting Research & Technology, 43*(4), 473-486.
- Lin, H., Chan, R. C., Zheng, L., Yang, T., & Wang, Y. (2007). Executive functioning in healthy elderly Chinese people. *Archives of Clinical Neuropsychology, 22*(4), 501-511.
- Lynn, R. (1963). Personality changes with ageing. *Behaviour Research and Therapy, 1*(2-4), 343-349.
- Melzer, I., Benjuya, N., & Kaplanski, J. (2001). Age-related changes of postural control: effect of cognitive tasks. *Gerontology, 47*(4), 189-194.
- Mondini S., Madella I., Zangrossi A., Bigolin A., Tomasi C., Michieletto M., et al. (2016). Cognitive reserve in dementia: implications for cognitive training. *Front. Aging Neurosci.* 8:84 10.3389/fnagi.2016.00084
- Ochsner, K. N., & Gross, J. J. (2005). The cognitive control of emotion. *Trends in cognitive sciences, 9*(5), 242-249.
- Peters, R. (2006). Ageing and the brain. *Postgraduate medical journal, 82*(964), 84-88.
- Petersen, R. C., Doody, R., Kurz, A., Mohs, R. C., Morris, J. C., Rabins, P. V., ... & Winblad, B. (2001). Current concepts in mild cognitive impairment. *Archives of neurology, 58*(12), 1985-1992.
- Robertson I. H. (2013). A noradrenergic theory of cognitive reserve: implications for Alzheimer's disease. *Neurobiol Aging,* 34, 298–308. 10.1016/j.neurobiolaging.2012.05.019
- Rodrigues, P. F., & Pandeirada, J. N. (2015). Attention and working memory in elderly: the influence of a distracting environment. *Cognitive processing, 16*(1), 97-109.

- Santiago, L. M., Graça, C. M. D. L., Rodrigues, M. C. D. O., & Santos, G. B. D. (2016). Characterization of the elderly health in a speech and language therapy perspective. *Revista CEFAC, 18,* 1088-1096.
- Stern Y. (2012). Cognitive reserve in ageing and Alzheimer's disease. *Lancet Neurol.* 11 1006–1012. 10.1016/S1474-4422(12)70191-6
- Thapliyal, G., Halder, S., & Mahato, A. (2016). Memory, verbal fluency, and response inhibition in normal aging. *Journal of Geriatric Mental Health, 3*(2), 145.
- Thompson, R. A., Lewis, M. D., & Calkins, S. D. (2008). Reassessing emotion regulation. *Child Development Perspectives, 2*(3), 124-131.
- Whalley, L. (2012). *The ageing brain.* Hachette UK.
- Willis, G. B. (2004). *Cognitive interviewing: A tool for improving questionnaire design.* sage publications.

* * *

LATE-LIFE DEPRESSION: AN OVERLOOKED REALITY

Megha Choudhary and Lakshmi Priya K.

CHAPTER OUTLINE

This chapter focuses on late-life depression by discussing the prevalence rates around the country and worldwide, exploring the symptomatology which differs from an adult form of depression, and how it is masked with other older age problems. Additionally, the chapter explores the risk factors, comorbidities, its implications and how it can be effectively assessed in various health care settings. This chapter uses case vignette to help explore possible treatment options and barriers faced to receive adequate help, ushering into its implication for further research and outcomes.

Introduction

Late-Life Depression is not a normal part of Aging: Late- life depression (LLD) or geriatric depression falls on the spectrum of mood disorder impacting people who are older than 60 years of age (Blackburn, 2017). Depression has been a cause of concern amongst the elderly for over decades now. Mental health professionals have had a tough time recognising and treating depressive symptoms in this population due to the various challenges. As opposed to what it may seem, depression in the elderly is not a normal part of aging; however, the changes they may endure as they age, including cognitive and physical decline, may risk them for depression. Studies show that regardless of physical illnesses or difficulties, geriatric adults feel content with themselves, considering it as a normal part of aging. It is often noticed that situational changes in the psychosocial realm of one's life is what makes one feel not okay and distressed. (National Institute of Aging, 2017).

Signs and Symptoms; Differentiating it from other Presentations

How Geriatric Depression may really look like: The way geriatric depression is presented in the elderly, it gets difficult to recognize if the individual is clinically depressed or not. Because of how we have believed as a society how old age should look like, the typical vegetative symptoms of adult depression is considered as 'normal part of aging', when present in older age groups. LLD affects millions of people worldwide; only fewer than 20% receive treatment for the same. The reason being difficulties in recognizing geriatric depression as a separate condition. Awareness into this aspect is important to understand that these signs be recognized and cared for early on.

Older adults do display the vegetative signs of depression as classified in ICD-10, however low mood is not something they report voluntarily. They are noticed to complain of reducing energy and motivation and complain more of physical symptoms as they are more generally accepted with older age. Some studies have shown that when an older adult often complains of chronic and consistent headaches or joint pains, a screening of LLD can be considered as well (Robinson, 2020). Some of the chronic physical conditions like cardiovascular difficulties, or cancer for example, due to the change in one's lifestyle can also have a comorbidity of depressive symptoms in older adults. These chronic physical conditions impact their quality of life significantly and often the diagnosis and treatment of depression is missed, considering the physical illness as primary (National Institute of Aging, 2017). They may also be taking medications which may as side effects can contribute to depression. Often the emotional signs of depression like irritability, lethargy in older adults are often confused with emotional difficulties related to changes in their psychosocial domains like retirement or children leaving home, and hence not considered significant enough for it to be catered to (National Institute of Aging, 2017). Confusion or attention problems caused by depression can sometimes look like Mild Cognitive Impairment (MCI), a progressive neurological or other brain disorder (Krans, 2008).

To help understand the difference in symptomatology better, the table below indicates some of the subtle differences in clinical presentation of depressive symptoms between young adults and the elderly (NIA, 2017; Joo, 2018; Robinson, 2020).

Symptom Domains	**Adult Presentation**	**Geriatric Presentation**
Mood	• Depressed • Anhedonia (reduced interest) • Suicidal thoughts	• Fatigue • Hopelessness • Anger, anxiety, irritability • Thoughts of death
Somatic	• Increased/Decreased Sleep • Increased/Decreased Appetite • Increased/Decreased Psychomotor Activity • Increased/Decreased Pain	• Increased Pain • Somatic symptoms that overlap with other medical conditions like gastritis, arthritis etc.
Cognitive	• Reduced concentration • Indecisiveness	• Reduced selective attention • Reduced working memory/retrieval • Reduced new learning • Reduced processing speed • Executive dysfunction

How to recognize Late-Life Depression: A reason why it may be so tough to diagnose LLD is that the presentation of symptoms varies from individual to individual. It becomes important to assess some longitudinal aspects of a person's behaviour before we can rule out depression. Assessing a person's behavioural changes over a span of time can help us understand if someone needs a professional consultation. Some of the changes to look for are (Krans, 2008; Stanborough, 2021):

- **Personality changes:** Suddenly becoming quieter, or more pessimistic about the world, or suddenly becoming irritable for a consistent period of time. Sudden loss of emotional expressions or over emotional expressions can be a sign of LLD.
- **Losing or gaining significant amount of weight:** Apart from the possible weight changes due to medical conditions or medications, and after having discussed with the practitioner, a considerable sudden change in weight is noticed along with a change in eating habits- like decline interest in eating, not getting adequate taste, or eating more in emotional situations can be a sign of depression.
- **Changes in energy levels:** Apart from the physical abilities to be active due to the various biological make up of an older person's body, just a general decline in feeling motivated to move about or expressing constant discomfort with activity, choosing to lay in bed for longer hours, slowed gait can also be a part of LLD.
- **Differences in social interactions:** Frequent excuses to be alone, or reporting feeling empty even with family members who would bring joy earlier can be some signs of depression to look for. Reduced interest in

suddenly not wanting to meet some regular people like people who they would go for walks with, or meet to chat with in the neighborhood.

- **Reduced performance and productivity:** Sudden reduction in quality of things they would do like change in taste of foods they have been preparing since years, making frequent errors in things they used to be particular about like paying bills, organizing etc. Unmindfulness and being forgetful about daily things may not necessarily only be a part of cognitive decline.

A case vignette given below further helps in understanding how the presentation of depressive symptoms in the elderly might be (Unützer, 1999; Frank, 2014):

S.P. is a 74-year-old retired schoolteacher with no previous history of psychiatric illness. She is referred by her primary care physician because of fatigue, and anhedonia, as well as complaints of memory loss. Her adult son and daughter accompany her to the visit. S.P. reports that although she loves her children, they get on her nerves and she does not like to do the things they want her to do. She complains of feeling fatigued and attributes it to pain in her back and knees. She is able to fall asleep without difficulty but awakens at 4 AM and is unable to go back to sleep. On further questioning, she admits, "I don't enjoy anything." She also complains of difficulty concentrating and keeping track of events, and of feeling tired all the time. She asks, "Do I have that 'old-timer's disease'?" She gives permission for her children to provide input. S.P.'s adult children report that their mother has been disinterested, withdrawn, and no longer wants to spend time even with her grandchildren. She no longer cooks, complaining of fatigue, and has been losing weight. They are concerned because S.P. wants to stay in bed for much of the day. They also note that she has been forgetful and requires reminders for birthdays and other events that she normally would not have trouble remembering. Family notes symptom onset 8 months ago, when she moved from out of state after her second husband's death. S.P. had been an avid gardener, and her family notes that she stopped 3 months ago, despite their encouragement.

S.P.'s medical history is significant for hypertension and coronary artery disease with a history of myocardial infarction 5 years ago, type 2 diabetes mellitus, vitamin D deficiency, and osteoarthritis. Her current medications include metoprolol, lisinopril, aspirin, metformin, hydrocodone-acetaminophen, and vitamin D. She also takes sertraline 100 mg daily and alprazolam 0.5 mg twice a day, which she states is for, "not sleeping well since my husband died." There is no history of substance use and family history is negative for mood disorders or other psychiatric illness. S.P. had a normal annual comprehensive physical examination and diagnostic work-up 1 month ago and her medication regimen has been stable for the last 3 months. On examination, S.P. appears dishevelled. Her clothing is clean but frayed. She describes her mood as, "Alright." Her affect is blunted and she becomes tearful when discussing her late husband. She denies suicidal or homicidal ideation. There is no evidence of psychosis. S.P. is alert and oriented to person, place, month, and year. She scores 24/30 on the MMSE examination. She refuses to complete the clock drawing.

Epidemiology

Depression as an illness that can be treated and is like any other physical ailment is a very new concept in Indian society. People are yet to accept this and come to terms with the prevalence of depression and the threats it poses. With the medical field making giant leaps, India as a country has seen an increase in life expectancy. This has resulted in an increasing number of elderly persons and it contributes to 7% of India's total population (Kamble et al., 2009). The increasing population in our country has been bringing to us the challenge of mental health of our elderly population. Mental health symptoms in the elderly population present themselves usually in the Primary Health Care settings, and are usually disguised as physical ailments. Epidemiological studies have been specifically difficult due to the differences in the definition of depression and a difference in population studied due to a selection bias. Studies have been able to find a prevalence rate from 1-4% for major depression in the general population (DSM-IV criteria), and from 8-16% for depressive symptoms which may require treatment (Helmer et al., 2004). An underestimate diagnosis and thereafter a lack of proper medical care has also been associated with the heterogeneous nature of the symptom presentation of depression in the elderly. In India, community-based studies involving 70 to 7,150 elderly subjects report prevalence rates varying from 8.9% to 62.16%. Clinic-based studies involving 50 to 5,260 participants report prevalence rates ranging from 42.4% to 72% (Grover & Malhotra, 2015). Studies have reported depression to be more common among females.

Late-Life Depression and the Indian Scenario

The research done in the area of geriatric depression in India and how it has impacted the population is very scarce. To be able to deal with this problem, we need to have a better knowledge of its presentation in our population. Having said that, some of the studies done show that depression is a growing concern amongst the elderly (Seby et al., 2011). The biggest challenge that a growing population of elderly is that it also brings with it an increase in the number of mental health concerns as well. Depression is one of them and our health care system often overlooks them because of a lack of awareness at the primary health centre level and the tendency to hide any mental health concerns one may be facing (Lodha & De Sousa, 2018).

Dementia and depression have a close relation and often in the Indian context, symptoms of depression are overlooked when there is a person presenting with symptoms of dementia (Muliyala & Varghese, 2010). In the Indian context, we also often overlook the need to have a primary care set up which can help in the old age homes as well. Often the primary health centres are not equipped to diagnose or identify the symptoms and refer the patient further. A factor adding to this is the lack of diagnostic tools in the Indian setting (Katiyar et al., 2020).

With the presence of multitude of such problems, the management of later life depression in India is in a very poor state and there is a lot of scope for improving this aspect of mental health in our country.

Factors Leading to Depression

The symptoms discussed along with the case vignette in the previous section gives us a clear picture of what Late-Life Depression looks like. Let's look into some of the possible factors leading to the same.

- **Economic:** Studies have suggested that after the age of 65, a large number of elderlies become economically unproductive. The transition one has to make from the role of a provider to someone who now becomes dependent on others is a tough one, and not everyone is able to negotiate through this transition in life.
- **Other Comorbid Conditions:** Depression is often seen to be comorbid with other illnesses in the elderly including long term lung infection, diabetes and myocardial infarctions (Cole, 2005; Barua et al., 2010). With these chronic illnesses, it becomes important that the patient takes care of his/her diet, physical fitness and engage in regular check-up, follow-up and revision

of medications. It was found that patients above 65 years of age were usually negligent of their health and would not adhere to treatment protocols in some cases. These lead to multiple complications and the development of comorbid depressive symptoms.

- **Longevity:** Improved health care services now promise longevity, but other socio-economic and socio-cultural factors like: poverty, breaking up of joint family systems and the lack of services, especially for the elderly prove to be a great threat to this group. Financial dependency and a sense of lack of support (as explained earlier) give rise to a multitude of problems, including depressive symptoms.
- **Dependence:** Elderly who were found to be dependent on others for their daily activities are often found to be depressed as compared to those who are able to carry on their daily activities without help.
- **Literacy and Education:** Education made it easier for the elderly to adapt to a newer lifestyle beyond an age and carry out their daily life activities. Instead, an uneducated person was found to be struggling with this aspect of their life and often end up having symptoms of depression.
- **Life Events:** Negative life events, especially the occurrence of multiple negative life events through the course of ones' lifetime are a significant factor to the development of depression in the elderly. These negative life events are often seen as predisposing and contributing factors to the development of mental health problems like depression (Kraaij et al., 2002).
- **Migration:** Depression has also been found in those who have migrated to a different country and have had

difficulties adjusting to the socio-cultural changes; acculturation playing a very important part (the concept of migratory grief) (Lee et al., 2005).

- **Social Support:** As compared to western tradition, eastern traditions depend heavily on social support, especially from ones' family. A lack of the same or the breaking away of the social support system was found to be a major contributing factor.
- Other socio-cultural factors that could be a cause for concern include- the female gender that has found to be more at risk. Widowed, divorced, unmarried and separated were found to be at a higher risk of having depression later in life (Barua et al., 2010).

Comorbidities with Geriatric Depression

As discussed before as well in this chapter, aging encompasses many chronic medical illnesses, biological changes, socio-developmental challenges which substantially make the diagnosis of depression difficult. In such cases it is better to look out for absence of positive symptoms and presence of conditions like anhedonia and avolition. Subsyndromal cases of depression that do not meet the diagnostic criteria for major depression are equally at risk of developing comorbidities like suicidal ideation, decreased quality of life, functional impairments and a risk for a full-blown depressive episode (Parker et al., 2011; Grover et al., 2018).

Comorbid physical illness is highly prevalent in elders with depression. Hypertension, diabetes mellitus, osteoarthritis, and cataract problems are most common conditions with underlying depression. Additionally, conditions like cardiovascular symptoms, pain symptoms, endocrinological symptoms also tend to cause anxiety, depression and somatic complaints which go undiagnosed (Grover et al., 2018). While depression treatment is helpful along with management of the chronic medical conditions, untreated symptoms prolong and further complicate the disease process, reduce the quality of life, increasing the duration of disability and functional difficulties. Medical conditions like dementia, cancer, sclerosis, etc., are life threatening, deteriorating and irreversible illnesses which due to its impact on one's life functioning can lead to symptoms of depression as well (Robinson, 2020; Hurley, 2021).

Medications for these chronic illnesses like the sedatives or chemotherapies or antiepileptic medicines, hormone medications, etc., can also cause depressive symptoms (Hurley, 2021). It is hence advisable that when primary care treatment is being provided for the elderly, a psychiatric follow up be also done to monitor and control for such symptoms early on.

Additionally, suicide is also a significant comorbid condition impacting at least 50% of older adults with completed suicide. As part of the clinical evaluation, it is essential to screen for suicidal ideation, which can range from passive (thoughts of hopelessness or that life is not worth living), in the absence of intent to self-harm, to active thoughts of self-harm or suicidal ideation. Access to weapons or other lethal means such as hoarding of medications should be ascertained as part of the assessment. Firearms are the most frequently used method of completed suicide in older adults (28%), followed by hanging (24%) and poisoning (21%). Unlike suicide risk factors, which are often static, warning signs can be variable and should be assessed frequently and on an ongoing basis. These signs include thoughts, feelings, and behaviors that indicate preparation for suicide. However, studies show that clinicians often miss opportunities for intervention. Luoma and colleagues (2002) found that 58% of individuals aged 55 years and older had contact with their primary care providers within 1 month of completed suicide, whereas 77% had contact within 1 year of completed suicide. This study also found that 11% of individuals aged 55 years and older had contact with a mental health professional within 1 month and 8.5% within 1 year of completed suicide. These figures underscore the need for thorough assessment of suicide risk and warning signs to facilitate prompt intervention (Kraaij, 2002; Noel, 2004; Blackburn, 2017; Hurley, 2021).

The geriatric population is more susceptible to cognitive deficits accompanied by depression; Differentiating with dementia:

Depression is categorized on a mood spectrum in the psychiatry classificatory systems, however, for older adults studies have shown that it qualifies well as a cognitive disorder as well. Potter et al.'s study in 2007 showed that depression and lasting cognitive impairment are comorbid in adults older than 70 years of age and have even higher chances of occurring for those who are 85 years and above. Since the chances of cognitive impairments and depressive symptoms is so high in the geriatric population, differentiating symptoms that appear due to increased age and shrinkage in brain size to those that occur because of the psychopathology has been difficult (Potter et al., 2007). Additionally, studies have shown that MCI is now also categorized as a part of LLD, as opposed to only a starting point in conditions that progress to dementia like Alzheimer's. The prevalence of MCI in geriatric depression ranges from 25% to 50%, which is higher than the prevalence of age related cognitive decline in older adults who do not have clinically depressive symptoms (Potter et al., 2007; Robinson, 2020).

Some older adults with LLD may exhibit a reversible dementia syndrome (previously termed "pseudo dementia"), i.e., a cognitive impairment that mimics dementia but diminishes upon remission of depression. When compared to AD patients with concomitant depression, 'reversible dementia' patients have more somatic anxiety, early morning awakening and loss of libido. It is important to note that a large percentage of these cases progress into irreversible dementia within 2-3 years (Morimoto et al., 2014).

Impact on Daily Living

Review studies have shown that depression in elderly is linked with their Quality of Life. The severe the depressive symptoms are, the poorer the quality of life is noticed to be. Additionally older adults who had depression along with other physical conditions, reported poorer quality of life than those without any comorbidities. Due to the impact of these conditions on role limitations at both individual and collectivist level, older adults reported a lower daily functioning abilities and quality of life. Based on various psychometric assessments, it was also assessed that as depressive symptoms improved for older adults, so did the rating on perceived quality of life. Studies propose that reduced quality of life in older adults could be due to acceptance of their ill health and fate of their age, along with reduced internal capacity to make things better for themselves and adjust to changing situations. Psychological resilience further declines the quality of life experienced. Furthermore, frequent hospital admissions, the length of stay at hospital, and post-discharge rehabilitation period further reduced the quality of life experienced by depressed older adults (Fiske et al., 2009; Lin et al., 2014; Sivertsen et al., 2015).

Assessment of Depression in the Elderly

Various studies over the years have found that Depression is the most common Psychiatric Disorder in old age. Yet, when it comes to the diagnoses and the treatment of Depression, the numbers of cases reported have been startlingly low. This trend is found world over and forces us to look into the possible factors that could be contributing to this. A study done by Sharma V.K & Copeland J.R.M, (1986) suggest that the 10-15% of the population above the age of 65 suffer from significant depressive symptoms in the UK as well as the US. Despite the high prevalence, it was found that only very small proportions of the elderly sought treatment and were being treated subsequently. The sighted the following as the possible reasons that could be contributing to these low figures:

- The elderly complained less about their symptoms.
- The symptoms were considered 'understandable' with regard to their physical and psychosocial status by those around them including their General Practitioner.
- Some of the symptoms have come to be accepted as a natural part of the ageing process.

The issues regarding the diagnoses of depression amongst the geriatric population remains to be a huge concern for the mental health practitioners the world over including in India. Having said that, it's essential that we look at some of the tools we have at hand to make a diagnosis and provide appropriate treatment to a person who is suspected of having depression. Some of the widely used scales have been listed out:

1. **Geriatric Depression Scale (GDS):** Self Report Inventory that can be easily administered. It fails to identify Depression amongst elderly with dementia (Adapted into multiple languages) (Yesavage, 1982).
2. **Short Geriatric Depression Scale (SGD-S):** Has high Face Validity and can be easily used in Primary Health Care Settings.
3. **The Psychogeriatric Assessment Scale (PAS):** Provides an assessment of clinical changes seen in dementia and depression. Easy to administer and can be used by lay persons after training (Jorm, Henderson et al., 1997).
4. **Centre for Epidemiological Studies-Depression Scale (CES-D):** A very good tool to assess major depression in elderly population. Loses its validity when it has to screen for mild to moderate depression (Radloff, 1977).
5. Indian version of WHO (five) Well-being index (1998 Version).

Treatment

Diagnosing late-life depression is challenging, especially when there are additional age related comorbidities (Frank, 2014). Caregivers, family members, and friends all play a big part in helping a loved one cope with depression. They can first talk to their loved one about their feelings and share their understanding and support. Next, they can discuss the importance of treatment and outline the possible options for care. A good starting point is the person's primary care physician. Older adults receive much of their medical care from their primary care doctor, who can also address depression treatment.

Pharmacological Management

Although depression is equally common in old and young adults, most of the drug trials exclude elderly subjects. In addition to the exclusion of elderly, most of the drug trials also exclude subjects with medical comorbid. Prior to 1995 there were no studies or occasional studies that evaluated the use of antidepressants in elderly. But fortunately, in the last 10 years many studies of use of antidepressants have been reported. The points below summarize some of the important pharmacokinetic and pharmacodynamic issues to be remembered while prescribing antidepressants in elderly. The principle of "Start low and go slow" should be followed (Frank, 2014; Avasthi, 2018; Grover, 2018).

1. Elderly are more sensitive to a given drug concentration
2. The body organs of elderly have decreased capacity to adapt
3. There is progressive loss of functional body tissues at the cellular level
4. Starting dose of an antidepressant must be lower (one third to half) for elderly compared to the starting dose used in young adults
5. The half- life of most of the antidepressants increases
6. Elderly require longer duration to achieve a steady plasma state
7. Side effects related to dose or concentration will take longer to resolve
8. Homeostatic mechanisms that function via central and peripheral feedback mechanisms are altered in the elderly and make them more susceptible to side effects.

The number of drugs used to treat elderly patients must be minimized to reduce the incidence of adverse reactions, potential drug-drug interactions, and adherence difficulties while at the same time minimizing costs associated to with pharmacotherapy. Elderly people are generally more susceptible to side effects, and hence, the newer antidepressants are preferred. Besides the common side effects seen with antidepressants elderly subjects are particularly prone to certain side effects like orthostatic hypotension and falls, hyponatremia, cardiac side effects, etc., (Park, 2011; Wiese, 2011).

Regardless of the medications used, the following advice applies when treating elderly patients with depression (Frank, 2014; Avasthi, 2018; Grover, 2018):

Start low. Because elderly people often have co-existing medical problems, and because they metabolize some drugs more slowly and are more at risk for drug interactions compared with younger people, the APA advises starting at a low dose, generally about half the normal starting dose for adults.

Consider alternatives. Try a drug for two to six weeks at the recommended dose to see if symptoms subside. If the drug doesn't work, or if side effects become bothersome, adjust the dose or consider another medication.

Maintain treatment. As many as 38% of elderly people who experience an initial bout of depression suffer from a recurrence in three to six years. For this reason, maintenance therapy is vital.

Electroconvulsive Therapy

Antidepressant medications don't work for everyone. Older people may quit taking antidepressants or repeatedly miss doses because of side effects, memory problems, or difficulty keeping track of complicated drug regimens. They are also more likely than younger patients to have medical complications, or psychosis in addition to depression. For all these reasons, electroconvulsive therapy (ECT) is another option to consider (Wiese, 2011).

ECT remains one of the most effective treatments for depression that is severe or accompanied by psychosis. It can be used safely in elderly patients, including those with cardiac pacemakers and implanted defibrillators. Initially, 6 to 12 treatments, given two to three times a week, may be necessary to bring the depression under control. If the patient relapses, or has treatment-resistant depression, ECT may be given periodically over six months, with treatments gradually becoming less frequent (Wiese, 2011).

Psychotherapy

Psychotherapy alone may help older patients whose depression is mild or has occurred because of a stressful life change, such as losing a spouse or starting retirement. Combining psychotherapy with medication may be helpful for those with more severe depression. Various psychotherapies have been used for the treatment of depression in elderly. Out of the various psychotherapeutic models, cognitive behaviour therapy (CBT), interpersonal psychotherapy (IPT) and supportive counselling have been commonly used in elderly.

CBT have received the most research attention of any psychotherapy for LLD and research suggests that CBT is a viable therapeutic option for older subjects suffering from major depression and to a lesser degree for dysthymia and minor depression. Although several types of interventions fall under this category of psychotherapy, CBT, and problemsolving therapy (PST) have been evaluated in older adults (although BT has been used primarily as a comparison condition with CBT).

There are few studies which have evaluated the efficacy of IPT alone in older subjects. In one study IPT plus pill-placebo was found to be better than pill-placebo alone in preventing the recurrence of major depression. In the same study it was also found that combined treatment of IPT and antidepressants produce best relapse prevention during the maintenance phase, whereas IPT plus placebo produce the worst rates. There it can be concluded that IPT may be most effective as a maintenance treatment for severely depressed older adults when administered along with antidepressants. Only one study has evaluated the efficacy of IPT against usual care for minor depression after 6 months of treatment and reported that IPT was superior to usual care in reducing the symptoms (Birrer, 2004; Blackburn, 2017).

Self- help skills are also employed for elderly to whom therapist services are not available, or cannot be approached due to stigma. Isolation during such a phase can worsen the illness trajectory. Support groups for people going through similar difficulties help in connecting with others to share, ventilate, encourage and empower (Robinson, 2020). Reaching out to loved ones through digital or personal means, volunteering in the neighbourhood, going for walks, joining clubs with other elderly and finding occasions to laugh can help in initiation of combating the isolation and loneliness. Instead of focusing on habits which are lost, things which cannot be done now due to physical constraints, focusing more on what can still be done despite the barriers, what new skills or revising of old skills is still possible and can be taken up (Robinson, 2020; Hurley, 2021).

Making family members and friends aware of the illness and the symptoms is also important to ensure effective care at home. Due to the presentation of depression as a condition, its symptomatology makes it difficult for older adults to seek help or apply the help given to them. Mental illness is still a taboo and only recently there has been an advocacy for mental well being. For older adults who are above the age of 60-70 years, they have always witnessed mental health struggles as being something one deals with on their own or something which is so called 'normal'. For them, it is even more challenging to believe they can have a clinical diagnosis of depression, let alone asking for and seeking help. The fear of becoming a burden, a fear of being judged are some of the psychosocial issues which make it difficult further. A difference in this approach can be achieved by offering emotional support, unconditionally, without judgment and with empathy (Robinson, 2020). Depression develops for many reasons in people who are elderly. While it may take some time to determine the best treatment strategy for a particular individual, the reward is often a better quality of life – whether that means being able to spend time with grandchildren or other loved ones, taking up a new hobby, or going on an extended road trip (Robinson, 2020).

Barriers to Treatment of the Elderly

As any disorder that requires treatment, depression too has its barriers in the process. But when it comes to LLD, the challenges have been found to be multi-fold. Identifying these barriers will help mental health professionals to provide better services to those in need.

A study done by Conner et al. in 2010 with elderly patients of African America origin suggested that, the beliefs surrounding mental health and mental illness in specific play a very important role in treatment seeking behaviour. The stigmas associated with the same prevent a lot of patients to timely seek advice or help. A lot of culturally sanctioned coping techniques come into play during that time, and most of.

Further, it has been found that misdiagnosis is a leading contributor to the barriers in treatment of depression in the elderly. It can be hypothesized that the misdiagnosis usually occurred due to the lack of scales made specifically for the older population as compared to the ones that have their norms developed based on a much younger demographic. This issue has been addressed in a way by the development of depression rating scales, particularly for the elderly.

As one grows older, one sees and experiences and lot of changes in their body and mind and understands them as a part of the natural part of ageing. Under the umbrella term of 'natural part of ageing', often depressive symptoms get ignored or side-tracked. An understanding of how symptoms could manifest differently amongst different age groups and a better understanding of depression affects the life of an elderly as compared to the life of an elderly without depression will definitely help in understanding, diagnosing and treating depression better in this population (Rabins, 1996).

Research also suggests some of the following factors as barriers to treatment of depression in the elderly:

- **Knowledge deficit:** Culturally, we are still trying to make sense of the concept of mental health and the need to reach out to professionals for the same. It is still a much-stigmatized topic and few people like to talk about it openly. While in the rural settings the population may not be aware of the same, in the urban setting it has been found that people- usually aware are hesitant to reach out to mental health professionals or even talk about the need for help (Unützer et al., 1999).

- **Losses and social isolation:** As has been mentioned many times in this chapter, as one ages, one encounter many more loses in life in the form of loss of family and friends. The elderly tends to get isolated with a reduction in their social support system and with lesser number of people they are willing to reach out to or can reach out to.
- **Multiple medical problems:** Often the symptoms of depression co-exist with other multiple illnesses. And the more the number of illnesses the higher the possibility that the symptoms of depression get masked or ignored. These get counted as the natural process of ageing or are considered as a natural consequence of having multiple illnesses. Also, with the consumption of multiple medications, people often get discouraged to venture into taking more medications.
- **Financial loses:** A very important aspect when it comes to seeking treatment especially in our country is the availability of financial support. Seeking any kind of health service which could possibly turn into a chronic routine becomes a huge financial burden and with lack of financial aid, the elderly find it difficult to reach out for help from trusted sources for a considerable amount of time.

What can we all do as a part of the Society

As has been discussed throughout this chapter and been identified through some of the research that has been done in this field, it can be safely said that Late-Life Depression is a major cause of worry amongst the elderly population. Keeping aside the multiple problems they face or could face because of their age, depression or good mental health in general becomes a major source of stress. A few things can be done by all of us- whether we are in the field of mental health, health in general or just concerned family members are:

- Talk more and spread awareness. The more we talk the more comfortable we get in discussing such issues. The more the people talk the more the condition of depression becomes a less stigmatized topic and more a topic of concern that needs to be addressed.
- Reducing the stigma around seeking professional help when it comes to mental health: If we see the merit in approaching a doctor for our physical symptoms, we may be able to see the merit in approaching a professional for our mental symptoms as well.
- Making mental health easily available for the elderly population.
- Spreading awareness of the symptoms amongst the elderly and their caretakers and encouraging them to talk about their difficulties.
- Using valid and reliable assessment tools not just by the mental health professionals, but also by primary health care professionals who happen to come in contact with the elderly population at the beginning itself. Assessing for symptoms will help these professionals to make the right decision to refer the patient to the right specialist for further treatment.
- Incorporating a psychiatric evaluation for elderly during general practitioner visits.

Conclusion

Late-Life Depression has a complex etiology and requires a sensitive and dual approach to treatment for old people: both mental and physical check-ups. These are important to reduce the devastating risks that follows geriatric depressive conditions. Depression in geriatric population is treatable, we as a society can be more mindful about the needs and concerns of older people, and help them in their last years. Overlooked conditions have much more damage implications than getting a diagnosis. With more researches being conducted in this population worldwide, it is possible to make a difference in the life of the elderly who may be silently suffering.

References

- Avasthi, A., Grover, S. & Bharadwaj, R. (2018). Clinical Practice guide-lines for management of depression in elderly. *Indian Journal of Psychiatry*; 60: 341-362.
- Barua, A., Ghosh, M. K., Kar, N., & Basilio, M. A. (2010). Socio-demographic factors of geriatric depression. *Indian journal of psychological medicine*, *32*(2), 87-92.
- Birrer, R.B., (2004). Depression in later life: A diagnostic and therapeutic challenge. *American Family Physician*; 69(10):2375-2382.
- Blackburn, P. (2017). Depression in Older Adults: diagnosis and management. *British Columbia Medical Journal*; 59(3): 171-177.
- Cole, M. G. (2005). Evidence-based review of risk factors for geriatric depression and brief preventive interventions. *Psychiatric Clinics*, *28*(4), 785-803.
- Conner, K. O., Copeland, V. C., Grote, N. K., Rosen, D., Albert, S., et al. (2010). Barriers to treatment and culturally endorsed coping strategies among depressed African-American older adults. *Aging and Mental Health*; 14(8), 971-983.
- Fiske, A., Wetherell, J.L. & Gatz, M. (2009). Depression in older adults. *Annual Review of Clinical Psychology*; 5: 363-389. doi:10.1146/annurev.clinpsy.032408.153621
- Frank, C. (2014). Pharmacological treatment of depression in the elderly. *Canadian Family Physician*; 60 (2): 121-126.
- Glover, J. & Srinivasan, S. (2013). Assessment of persons with late life depression. *Psychiatry Clinics of North America*; 36: 545-560.

- Grover S, Malhotra, N. (2015). Depression in elderly: A review of Indian research. *Journal of Geriatric Mental Health;* 2: 4-15.
- Grover, S., Avasthi, A., Sahoo, S., Lakdawala B. & Dan A. et al. (2018). Prevalence of physical comorbidity and prescription patterns in elderly patients with depression: A multicentric study under the aegis of IAGMH. *Journal of Geriatric Mental Health;* 5:107-114.
- Helmer, C., Montagnier, D. & Peres, K. (2004). Descriptive epidemiology and risk factors of depression in the elderly. *Psychologie&neuropsychiatrie du vieillissement;* 2, S7-12.
- Hurley, K. (2021, January 25). Depression in the elderly. *Psycom;* https://www.psycom.net/depression.central.elderly.html
- Joo, J, H. (2018, August 06). Identifying, treating depression in elderly patients. *Healio Primary Care;* https://www.healio.com/news/primary-care / 20180806 / qa-identifying-treating-depression-in-elderly-patients
- Jorm, A. F., Mackinnon, A. J., Henderson, A. S., Scott, R., Christensen, H., Korten, A. E. & Mulligan, R. (1995). The psychogeriatric assessment scales: a multidimensional alternative to categorical diagnoses of dementia and depression in the elderly. *Psychological medicine, 25*(3), 447-460.
- Jorm, A. & Mackinnon, A. (1995). The psychogeriatric assessment scales. *Canberra: National Health and Medical Research Council Social Psychiatry Research Unit, Mental Health Research Institute, Australian National University.*
- Kamble, S. V., Dhumale, G. B., Goyal, R. C., Phalke, D. B. & Ghodke, Y. D. (2009). Depression among elderly persons in a primary health centre area in Ahmednagar, Maharashtra. *Indian Journal of Public Health; 53*(4), 253-5.
- Katiyar, R. V., Ahmad, S., Beg, M. W. & Baqar, T. (2020). Geriatric Mental Health Challenges in India-A Review. *J Evol Med Dent Sci, 9,* 1787-1794.
- Kraaij, V., Arensman, E. & Spinhoven, P. (2002). Negative life events and depression in elderly persons: a meta-analysis. *The Journals of Gerontology Series B: Psychological Sciences and Social Sciences; 57*(1), P87-P94
- Krans, B. (2018, September 2). *Geriatric Depression (Depression in Older Adults).* Healthline. https://www.healthline.com/health/depression/elderly

- Lee, H. Y., Moon, A. & Knight, B. G. (2005). Depression among elderly Korean immigrants: Exploring socio-cultural factors. *Journal of Ethnic and Cultural Diversity in Social Work*; *13*(4), 1-26.
- Lin, J.H., Huang, M.W., Wang, D.W., Chen, Y.M., Lin, C.S., Tang, Y.J., Yang, S.H. & Lane, H.Y. (2014). Late-Life Depression and Quality of Life in a geriatric evaluation and management unit: an exploratory study. *BMC Geriatrics*; 14:77. https://doi.org/10.1186/1471-2318- 14-77
- Lodha, P. & De Sousa, A. (2018). Geriatric mental health: The challenges for India. *Journal of Geriatric Mental Health*, *5*(1), 16.
- Morimoto, S. S. & Alexopoulos, G. S. (2013). Cognitive deficits in geriatric depression: clinical correlates and implications for current and future treatment. *The Psychiatric clinics of North America*; *36*(4), 517–531. https://doi.org/10.1016/j.psc.2013.08.002
- Muliyala, K. P. & Varghese, M. (2010). The complex relationship between depression and dementia. *Annals of Indian Academy of Neurology*, *13*(Suppl2), S69.
- National Institute on Aging (2017, May 01). Depression and older adults. *U.S. Department of Health & Human Services*; https://www.nia.nih.gov/health/depression-and-older-adults
- Noel, P.H., Williams, J.W. & Hunkeler, E. (2004). Depression and comorbid illness in elderly primary care patients: Impact on multiple domains of health status and well-being. *Annals of Family Medicine*; 2 (6):555-562.
- Park, M. & Unutzer, J. (2011). Geriatric Depression in Primary Care. *The psychiatric clinics of North America*; 34 (2): 469-499. doi: 10.1016/j.psc.2011.02.009
- Potter, G. & Steffens, D. (2007). Depression and Cognitive Impairment in Older Adults. *Psychiatric Times*; 24 (13).
- Rabins, P. V. (1996). Barriers to diagnosis and treatment of depression in elderly patients. *American Journal of Geriatric Psychiatry*; 4(4 SUPPL.).
- Robinson, L., Smith, M. & Segal, J. (2020, September). Depression in older adults: signs, symptoms and treatment. *Helpguide*; https://www.helpguide.org/articles/depression/depression-in-older-adults.htm

- Seby, K., Chaudhury, S. & Chakraborty, R. (2011). Prevalence of psychiatric and physical morbidity in an urban geriatric population. *Indian journal of psychiatry, 53*(2), 121.
- Sivertsen, H., Bjorklof, G.H., Engedal, K., Selbaek, G. & Helvik, A.S. (2015). Depression and Quality of Life in Older Persons: A Review. Dementia and Geriatric Cognitive Disorders; 40: 311-339. https://doi.org/10.1159/000437299
- Stanborough, R.J. (2021, May 13). *How to recognize and help someone with hidden depression.* Healthline. https://www.healthline.com/health/depression/hidden-depression
- Unützer, J., Katon, W., Sullivan, M. & Miranda, J. (1999). Treating depressed older adults in primary care: narrowing the gap between efficacy and effectiveness. *The Milbank Quarterly; 77*(2), 225-256.
- WHO. (1998). Wellbeing Measures in Primary Health Care/The Depcare Project. WHO Regional Office for Europe: Copenhagen.
- Wiese, B. (2011). Geriatric Depression: The use of antidepressants in the elderly. *British Columbia Medical Journal;* 53(47): 341-347.
- Yesavage, J. A. (1988). Geriatric depression scale. *Psychopharmacological Bulletin; 24*(4), 709-711.

* * *

LONELINESS IN ELDERLY IN THE AGE OF SOCIAL NETWORKING

Akash Kumar Mahato and Susmita Halder

Introduction

It is an old saying that one can be lonely even in mid of a crowd, and one can feel connected even in solitude. With an increase in urbanization, increase in nuclear pattern of families, and younger members of the family moving out or migrating to distant places for job, the number of elderly leading solitary life is also increasing. However, living alone and loneliness could be different concepts each having its own implication for the elderly. While the means of communication have advanced many folds than before, it may or may not have achieved to connect people meaningfully to reduce loneliness. The present chapter discusses different perspectives of loneliness in the elderly in the age of social networking.

Loneliness is not merely being alone. It is defined as a distressing feeling that accompanies the perception that one's social needs are not being met by the quantity or especially the quality of one's social relationships (Pinquart and Sorensen, 2001). It refers to a state of solitude which might lead to physical and mental health deterioration (Cacioppo & Cacioppo, 2018) and has been pronounced as a hidden killer for elderly people. It is a subjective feeling of disconnectedness with others which has the potential to decrease the resilience of the individuals in old age. Loneliness is not a hallmark of old people. It may affect people in young age even in adolescence too; to the matter-of-fact younger people have been reported to have more loneliness compared to middle aged people, who in turn have reported more loneliness than older people (Barreto et al., 2021). However, the impact of loneliness could be more significant in elderly compared to younger population. Loneliness might have been used synonymously with the concept of isolation or social isolation but could be an independent process having its own impact on health (Nielson, 2019). In general, emotional loneliness refers to the absence of an attachment figure (together with feelings of isolation) and social loneliness as the lack of a social network, the absence of a circle of people that allows an individual to develop a sense of belonging, of company, of being part of a community. The terms, loneliness and social isolation have been used indistinctly and as different concept (Yanguas et al., 2018).

It could be a difficult task to arrive on a universal theory of etiology of loneliness, but studies across the globe are unanimous on certain risk factors of loneliness which include marital status, general health, long-term physical or mental health conditions, living alone or with others, housing conditions, age group (Pyle & Evans, 2018). These factors when combined with other variables, e.g., personal wellbeing, perception of life satisfaction, happiness, anxiety and perception of self-worthwhile yielded unique profile of most lonely people and included widowed older homeowners living alone with longterm health conditions among others. The loneliness model posited by (Cacioppo et al., 2006) suggest that social isolation is tantamount to feeling unsafe, and this sets off implicit hypervigilance for (additional) social threat in the environment. This surveillance for social threat which is unconscious in nature produces cognitive biases leading lonely people perceive the social world as a more threatening place, expect more negative social interactions, and remember more negative social information.

As people grow older, the number of close acquaintances being deceased also increases, and thus in late life elderly individuals are expected to have decreased social contacts (Matud et al., 2019). They might have increasing difficulties in association with others in terms of adjustments and adaptability. They usually feel lonely, and it is associated with negative feelings which decreases the quality of their social relationships (Golden et al., 2009; Creecy et al., 1985; Holmén et al., 2012). The growing risks of losing their partners and the people from whom they used to receive emotional support also leads to loss of social roles. In addition, limitations in mobility, ability to maintain social networks are consistent with the negative age stereotypes (Deimling & Bass, 1986). Older adults suffer from the experience of social deficits, and they perceive the absence of satisfying and meaningful social relationships which might be accompanied by psychological symptoms in relation to perceived absence.

Prevalence Patterns

Loneliness is not a diagnostic entity and possibly the reason specific epidemiological studies are very less. Despite this loneliness has been reported in different proportions in studies, as part of depressive phenomenon and risk factor of depressive symptoms (Caioppo et al., 2006) and associated with suicidal behaviour (Stickley & Koyanagi, 2016). There are different findings from different studies with sociocultural factors primarily playing a role in the differences. Barreto et al. (2021) report loneliness much more in younger population, while Anil et al. (2016) report increase in prevalence of loneliness proportional to age group and elderly people above

80 years of age being affected more than younger population. Hossain et al. (2020) in their systemic review of prevalence and correlates of loneliness in India report pooled prevalence to be 41% among the participants, it was higher in elderly compared to younger participants and aging, family structure, marital status, religious practices, group membership, educational attainment, source and level of income, psychological attributes, and comorbid physical and mental health conditions were associated factors of loneliness among the affected individuals. Barreto et al. (2021) used data from the BBC Loneliness Experiment and analyzed the frequency of loneliness reported by 46,054 participants aged 16–99 years, living across 237 countries, islands, and territories. Their findings suggest that loneliness increased with individualism, decreased with age, and was greater in men than in women. They also found that age, gender, and culture interacted to predict loneliness, although those interactions did not qualify the main effects, and simply accentuated them, and younger men living in individualistic cultures were most vulnerable to loneliness.

While the findings may suggest a difference in the pattern of prevalence of loneliness across the globe, it duly establishes the phenomenon of loneliness significantly present in elderly.

The risks as well as impact of the phenomenon are too large to ignore. As mentioned earlier, loneliness is not a hallmark of elderly and younger population are more at risk of having loneliness; however, the impact of loneliness could be grave for elderly as the cumulative impact of loneliness which they have accrued since their younger phase of life find least resistance in old age giving way to major ill health conditions, primarily increased rate of cardiovascular disease, depression, complications due to weakened immunity, blood pressure related complexities, and eventually increased mortality (Eaker et al., 1992; Olsen et al., 1991; Penninx et al., 1997; Shiovitz & Ayalon, 2010; Sugisawa et al., 1994; Hawkley et al., 2007). Thus, feelings of loneliness conclusively mark increased risk for morbidity and mortality (Hawkley & Cacioppo, 2010).

Loneliness, Social Networking, and the Elderly

Loneliness is subjective and different expectations and goals from a relationship increase the gap within the relationship which aggregate distress and pleasance in human being. In recent times, social media or networking is available to every age group (Pinquar et al., 2001). People tend to have casual or meaningful connection with others. The need for being in a constant connection with others and growing interest in their lives has also increased. Outside the virtual life, being updated and connected is quite tough but through social media, are constantly been updated about our known people as well as relatively lesser known people across the world. In old age, the perception of being isolated from family is higher, which increases their sense of loneliness. Lesser engagement in both work and relationship could lead to passivity and role reduction, but may also lead to increased use of social media or digital media even in elderly. To reduce social isolation and loneliness elderly people are motivated enough to find out ways to cope through social media. Social media tools help them to explore and practice their hobbies and interests they care and engage in those activities. Facebook, WhatsApp, Instagram, Twitter and other social networking sites have become a communication tool for seniors to stay in touch with family members and being updated about their lives. Social media improves their participation in communities, creating new social groups and encourages new relationships with others. Social networking decreases the feeling of loneliness as they are in constant touch with others. Even if they do not have direct conversations but receiving updates and sharing own experiences with others tend to increase subjective feelings of being connected with others. While the above propositions are with good intentions and expectations, scientific data may or may not be in congruence with this.

As per the Cambridge dictionary (2021), social networking is defined as the use of websites and other internet services to communicate with other people and make friends. The activity involves sharing information and communicating with groups of people using the internet through websites and applications specially designed for this purpose. The term is often used interchangeably with social media; while social media is actually the medium, e.g., YouTube, Facebook, Twitter, Instagram, WhatsApp which are used for social networking. The trend of social networking has increased phenomenally in last two decades and is equally popular among people of all ages including the elderly. As per available data around 72% of all adults in the US used some sort of social media. This included 40% of people aged 65 and older. YouTube and Facebook were amongst the most popular social media channels for older Americans (Brad, 2021).

But how does this data translate in ground reality. The use of social media and networking varies from country to country; however, they are equivocal on suggesting that elderly people are almost double to three times less active on these social media platforms (Synthesio, 2021). One interesting find in this study was almost similar pattern of use of social media and networking in elderly compared to younger generation in countries like China, Mexico and Brazil. On another note, a study by Luo and Waite (2014) on nationally representative sample of 14,072 adults aged 65 and older, report loneliness in about 35% of older Chinese people. These figures are compatible to those reported in Western countries. Even though both the surveys are totally different, the findings cast a doubt that even when people are actively engaged in online social networking, can it help thwart loneliness.

Social Networking Recommended to Counter Loneliness, but is it Online?

Considering the health risk of loneliness, social scientist and researchers do suggest different strategies to counter loneliness, and most of them agree on using or increasing social networking (Yanguas et al., 2018; Johnson et al., 2020). Hawkley and Cacioppo (2010) mention six qualitative reviews of the loneliness intervention literature published since 1984, that explicitly or implicitly addressed four main types of interventions that include enhancing social skills, providing social support, increasing opportunities for social interaction, and addressing maladaptive social cognition. All but one of these reviews concluded that interventions which targeted opportunities for social interaction met with success. This social networking may not be confused with using social media and actually refers to engaging the elderly more with their neighborhood, community, and people around including family and friends, though social media can be a medium for social networking.

Use of the Internet by seniors as a mode of communication may lead to rapid changes in pattern of social interaction with other and may play an important role in successful ageing. In general, many elderly people are perceived to be at risk of social isolation and may lose serious components of the specific social environment through retirement as they reduce the social interaction with friends and relatives due to medical illness or for physical and geographical distance. Social interaction through digital media may reduce the psychological gap and enhance the social ties. There is no denial that technology may play an important role in helping the elderly to keep these social connections. As a greater number of younger generations are shifting to other cities or different locations due to job obligations, regular contact and communication is an issue. In this scenario, technology used in social networking enables elderly to connect easily to distant family members through video calls, reducing their sense of isolation, and contribute to their psychological well-being and sense of empowerment, and supporting their relationships regardless of time and location. Information and communication technology (ICT), together with initiatives led by local communities or government agencies, can be used as a tool to help reduce feelings of loneliness and increase the mental well-being of older adults (Gustafson et al., 2015). In general, social media allows older adults to express themselves, participate in discussions and stay in contact with society. Participating in social networks can empower older people and provide them with a sense of connectedness and greater control and self-efficacy.

Contrasting Views

Irrespective of the scopes of social media of providing infotainment and easy connectivity with family and friends surpassing geographical boundaries, there is no denial of the fact that some elderly people do feel lonely even when they are within the securities of full-fledged family. Thus, prior personality predispositions, quality of interpersonal relationship, familial and psychosocial support have a big role on elderly feeling lonely. Social media content may have the potential to uplift mood, but the question is for how long?

The potential positive social effects on individuals and groups supports the notion that the Internet has expanded the ability to interact or communicate through encouraging establishing and maintaining social connections and relationships across geographical distance or boundaries. However, online interaction is inherently informal and impersonal, shallow, and sometimes unfriendly. Studies do also suggest that using the Internet for communication with unknown people was associated with greater levels of family loneliness and displacement (Gerst-Emerson et al., 2015).

In a systematic review exploring the effects of contemporary ICT interventions on reducing social isolation of the elderly, (Cheng & Schulz, 2016) reviewed twenty-five publications which suggest ICT use was consistently found to affect social support, social connectedness, and social isolation in general positively. But more importantly, the results for loneliness were inconclusive and some studies found a nonsignificant or negative impact. More importantly, the positive effect of ICT use on social connectedness and social support seemed to be short-term and did not last for more than six months after the intervention. The researcher concluded that ICT alleviate the elderly's social isolation through four mechanisms: connecting to the outside world, gaining social support, engaging in activities of interests, and boosting self-confidence and could be an effective tool to tackle social isolation among the elderly, but it is not suitable for every senior alike.

On similar lines, in a systematic review to assess the effectiveness of interventions designed to alleviate social isolation and loneliness in older people, Dickens et al. (2011) reviewed thirty-two studies and found substantial heterogeneity in the interventions delivered and the overall quality of included studies.

The important findings of this review suggest that over 80% of participatory based interventions produced beneficial effects compared with 44% of those categorized as non-participatory. 58% of interventions that explicitly targeted socially isolated or lonely older people reported positive outcomes, compared with 80% of studies with no explicit targeting. It appeared that common characteristics of effective interventions were those developed within the context of a theoretical basis, and those offering social activity and/or support within a group format. Interventions in which older people are active participants also appeared more likely to be effective.

While these studies are primarily structured and intervention focused, there are also ample of literature that suggest on adverse impact of social networking even in elderly. Social media has been touted as food that lack nutritional value. So, in moderation or little amount, its fine but an excessive intake of social media may be bad for health (Nobel, 2018). In fact, Hunt et al. (2018) in their study investigating the potential causal role of social media for poor well-being, strongly suggest that limiting social media use to approximately 30 minutes per day may lead to significant improvement in well-being. Even though participants of this study were undergraduates, the findings may have good generalization value across elderly population.

Elderly are also not free from addictive value of social media use and its adverse effects. Meshi et al. (2020) in their study investigating the possible association between social isolation and degree of social media use in older adults failed to identify a relationship between perceived social isolation and estimated daily time on social media. However, higher problematic social media use was associated with higher perceived social isolation in the studied elderly sample.

Challenges and Scope of Social Media and Networking for Elderly

Elderly people are already at the verge of cognitive decline. Engagement in social networking could be a cognitively challenging task for elderly having impaired attention, working memory and visuospatial skills, who may find it difficult to navigate through flooded information and flurry of advertisements. They may also not be aware of spurious links and at higher risk of financial fraud compared to younger generation when using social media. A considerable number of older adults also suffer from functional limitations which hinder them from using technology in a comparable way to younger adults. Limitations like blindness may, despite assistive technology, even prevent the use of online social networks if no further assistance is available (Kuerbis et al., 2017).

Older adults often cite a lack of digital literacy skills, or lack of confidence in their own skills, as reason to not engage with social media platforms (Wang & Wu, 2021). Because many older adults have extremely low levels of social media use, instructional and informational support enables them to build self-efficacy and skill in using these media more actively. (Wu et al., 2019; Mohta & Halder, 2020). A sizeable number of elderly people cite anxiety and lack of confidence in using devises viz. mobile, tablets or personal computer to use social media (Leist, 2013; Vaportzis et al., 2017, Marston et al., 2019).

We also need to see the possibilities what engaging in online social networking brings for elderly people. Social media and networking are definitely of some good use apart from its entertainment and information sharing utility.

As social engagement among older adults has been linked to higher levels of cognitive function and reduced levels of cognitive decline, the effects of social media use may have some cognitive consequences too. Prior studies have found that cognitive ability is a predictor of Internet use in older adults (Czaja et al. in Quinn, 2018) and that cognitive ability is associated with the amount and types of activities in which older adults engage. Study by Quinn (2018) highlights on positive effects of social media engagement on cognitive domains of attention, processing speed, working memory, and inhibitory control among novice adult social media users, aged 65 and older. Despite the setup in the study like a classroom, there lies scope of replication. Pinquart et al. (2001) too suggest that social interaction through social media helps older adults overcome age-related memory changes and somewhat there is dearth of researches related to social networking and non-social domains among users at later ages.

An interesting trend in the use of social media by elders is health care. It can be a good source of health support. Patients can locate and obtain health-related information and services; they can give and receive information to manage specific diseases; and establish relationships with health professionals for medical assistance. It can be used to advance health-related knowledge such as information on prevention, diagnosis, and treatment of specific conditions and disorders in elderly, though not at the cost of professional advice (Leist, 2013). Han et al. (2021) in their study of experiences of social media apps' use among older adults in Singapore and its impact on health-related outcomes, found that use of social media apps was perceived to positively impact health through its ability to keep older adults cognitively engaged, improve health communication, and increase social connectedness. However, opinions remained mixed on older adults' vulnerability to social media addiction.

Conclusion

Loneliness is a reality and global phenomenon. While the rise in elderly population indicates advancement of health facilities and enhanced life expectancy, it also comes with its own challenges. Occupational liabilities and changing familial patterns have led to rise of nuclear families, where an ever-increasing number of elderlies are left alone in rural as well as urban setups. Contrary to perception that loneliness is hallmark of elderly people, loneliness is experienced by younger and middle-aged people too, and strikingly depending on cultural background younger people are more at risk of feeling lonely. The very fact that an individual may feel lonely even in mid of social event suggests that there is much of subjectivity in loneliness phenomenon. The other determining variables, e.g., quality of familial and psychosocial support, interpersonal relationships, feelings of self-worth and satisfaction and premorbid personality play an important role in building up or thwarting feelings of loneliness. Social networking is a handy tool to overcome barriers of geographical distance and provide an easy and convenient way to connect with people. The technological marvel is within access of elderly too, but the proportion of elderly users vary across countries and culture and so does vary the extent or level of activeness on these social networking sites. Social networking could be a useful tool for cognitive engagement of elderly, with potential of maintaining cognitive reserve and helping elderly at risk of degenerative disorders. While online social networking has the potential to let elderly people connect and make friends with others; its actual impact on thwarting loneliness significantly needs to be explored further. It comes with its own challenges specific to elderly. Online social networking could be a tool of maintaining meaningful social network. However, a better approach of shifting focus from entertainment and virtual connect to community and neighborhood bonding through actual social networking is needed. There is a need of controlled studies focusing on impact of online social networking and social media use to counter loneliness in elderly.

References

- Anil, R., Prasad, K., & Puttaswamy, M. (2016). The prevalence of loneliness and its determinants among geriatric population in Bengaluru City, Karnataka, India. *International Journal of Community Medicine And Public Health*, 3(11), 3246-3251.
- Barreto, M., Victor, C., Hammond, C., Eccles, A., Richins, M. T., & Qualter, P. (2021). Loneliness around the world: Age, gender, and cultural differences in loneliness. *Personality and individual differences*, 169, 110066.
- Bell, C., Fausset, C., Farmer, S., Nguyen, J., Harley, L., & Fain, W. B. (2013). Examining social media use among older adults. In Proceedings of the 24th ACM conference on hypertext and social media (pp. 158-163).
- Brad, B. (2021). Seniors using technology and social media more amid pandemic. Retrieved 20.01.2020 from https://mylifesite.net/blog/post / seniors-using-technology-and-social-media-more-amid-pandemic
- Cacioppo JT, Hawkley LC, & Ernst JM, et al. (2006). Loneliness within a nomological net: An evolutionary perspective. *Journal of Research in Personality*, 40:1054–1085
- Cacioppo JT, Hughes ME, Waite LJ & Thisted RA. (2006). Loneliness as a Specific Risk Factor for Depressive Symptoms: Cross-Sectional and Longitudinal Analyses. *Psychol Aging*, 21(1):140–151.
- Cacioppo, J. T., & Cacioppo, S. (2018). The growing problem of loneliness. *The Lancet*, 391(10119), 426.
- Cambridge dictionary (2019). Social networking. https://dictionary.cambridge.org/dictionary/english/social-networking
- Chen, Y. R., & Schulz, P. J. (2016). The Effect of Information Communication Technology Interventions on Reducing Social

Isolation in the Elderly: A Systematic Review. *Journal of medical Internet research,* 18(1), e18.

- Chen, Y., & Feeley, T. H. (2014). Social support, social strain, loneliness, and well-being among older adults: An analysis of the Health and Retirement Study. *Journal of Social and Personal Relationships,* 31(2), 141-161.
- Creecy, R. F., Berg, W. E., & Wright, R. (1985). Loneliness among the elderly: A causal approach. *Journal of Gerontology,* 40(4), 487-493.
- Deimling, G. T., & Bass, D. M. (1986). Symptoms of mental impairment among elderly adults and their effects on family caregivers. *Journal of Gerontology,* 41(6), 778-784.
- Dickens, A. P., Richards, S. H., Greaves, C. J., & Campbell, J. L. (2011). Interventions targeting social isolation in older people: a systematic review. *BMC public health,* 11, 647.
- Domènech-Abella, J., Lara, E., Rubio-Valera, M., Olaya, B., Moneta, M. V., Rico-Uribe, L. A., ... & Haro, J. M. (2017). Loneliness and depression in the elderly: the role of social network. *Social psychiatry and psychiatric epidemiology,* 52(4), 381-390.
- Eaker ED, Pinsky J & Castelli WP. (1992). Myocardial infarction and coronary death among women: Psychosocial predictors from a 20-year follow-up of women in the Framingham Study. *Am J Epidemiol,* 135:854–864.
- Gerst-Emerson, K., & Jayawardhana, J. (2015). Loneliness as a public health issue: the impact of loneliness on health care utilization among older adults. *American journal of public health,* 105(5), 1013-1019.
- Golden, J., Conroy, R. M., Bruce, I., Denihan, A., Greene, E., Kirby, M., & Lawlor, B. A. (2009). Loneliness, social support networks, mood and wellbeing in community-dwelling elderly. *International Journal of Geriatric Psychiatry: A journal of the psychiatry of late life and allied sciences,* 24(7), 694-700.
- Gustafson, D. H., McTavish, F., Mahoney, J. E., Johnson, R. A., Lee, J. D., Quanbeck, A., ... & Shah, D. (2015). The effect of an information and communication technology (ICT) on older adults' quality of life: study protocol for a randomized control trial. *Trials,* 16(1), 1-12.
- Han, M., Tan, X. Y., Lee, R., Lee, J. K., & Mahendran, R. (2021). Impact of Social Media on Health-Related Outcomes Among Older Adults in Singapore: Qualitative Study. *JMIR aging,* 4(1), e23826.

- Hawkley LC & Cacioppo JT. (2007). Aging and loneliness: Downhill quickly? *Current Directions in Psychological Science*, 16:187–191.
- Hawkley, L. C., & Cacioppo, J. T. (2010). Loneliness matters: a theoretical and empirical review of consequences and mechanisms. *Annals of behavioral medicine : a publication of the Society of Behavioral Medicine*, 40(2), 218–227.
- Holmén, K., & Furukawa, H. (2002). Loneliness, health and social network among elderly people—a follow-up study. *Archives of gerontology and geriatrics*, 35(3), 261-274.
- Hunt, M.G., Marx, R., Lipson, C., & Young, J. (2018). No More FOMO: Limiting Social Media Decreases Loneliness and Depression. *Journal of Social and Clinical Psychology*, 37 (10).
- Johnson, J. K., Stewart, A. L., Acree, M., Nápoles, A. M., Flatt, J. D., Max, W. B., & Gregorich, S. E. (2020). A Community Choir Intervention to Promote Well-Being Among Diverse Older Adults: Results From the Community of Voices Trial. *The journals of gerontology. Series B, Psychological sciences and social sciences*, 75(3), 549–559.
- Kuerbis, A., Mulliken, A., Muench, F., Moore, A. A., & Gardner, D. (2017). Older adults and mobile technology: Factors that enhance and inhibit utilization in the context of behavioral health.
- Luo, Y., & Waite, L. J. (2014). Loneliness and mortality among older adults in China. The journals of gerontology. *Series B, Psychological sciences and social sciences*, 69(4), 633–645.
- Marston, H. R., Genoe, R., Freeman, S., Kulczycki, C., & Musselwhite, C. (2019). Older adults' perceptions of ICT: Main findings from the technology in later life (TILL) study. In Healthcare (Vol. 7, No. 3, p. 86). Multidisciplinary Digital Publishing Institute.
- Matud, M. P., & García, M. C. (2019). Psychological distress and social functioning in elderly Spanish people: A gender analysis. *International journal of environmental research and public health*, 16(3), 341.
- Meshi D, Cotten S.R. & Bender A.R. (2020). Problematic Social Media Use and Perceived Social Isolation in Older Adults: A Cross-Sectional Study. *Gerontology*, 66:160-168.
- Mohta, R., & Halder, S. (2020). Elderly Population and New Age Technology. *Journal of Psychosocial Research*, 15(1).
- Neilson, L. (2019) Social isolation, loneliness in older people pose health risks. Retrieved 20.01.2022 from https://www.nia.nih.gov/news/social-isolation-loneliness-older-people-pose-health-risks

- Nobel, J. (2018). Does social media make you lonely? Retrieved 21.01.2022, from https://www.health.harvard.edu/blog/is-a-steady-diet-of-social-media-unhealthy-2018122115600
- Olsen RB, Olsen J, Gunner-Svensson F & Waldstrøm B. (1991). Social networks and longevity. A 14-year follow-up study among elderly in Denmark. *Soc Sci Med*, 33:1189–1195.
- Penninx BW, van Tilburg T, & Kriegsman DM, et al. (1997). Effects of social support and personal coping resources on mortality in older age: The Longitudinal Aging Study Amsterdam. *Am J Epidemiol*, 146:510–519.
- Pinquart, M., & Sorensen, S. (2001). Influences on loneliness in older adults: A meta-analysis. *Basic and applied social psychology*, 23(4), 245-266.
- Pyle, E., & Evans, D. (2018). Loneliness-what characteristics and circumstances are associated with feeling lonely. Office for National Statistics.
- Qualter, P., Vanhalst, J., Harris, R., Van Roekel, E., Lodder, G., Bangee, M., ... & Verhagen, M. (2015). Loneliness across the life span. *Perspectives on Psychological Science*, 10(2), 250-264.
- Quinn, K. (2018). Cognitive effects of social media use: A case of older adults. *Social Media + Society*, 4(3), 2056305118787203.
- Shankar, A., McMunn, A., Banks, J. & Steptoe, A. (2011). Loneliness, social isolation, and behavioral and biological health indicators in older adults. *Health Psychology*, 30(4), 377.
- Shiovitz-Ezra S & Ayalon L. (2010). Situational versus chronic loneliness as risk factors for all-cause mortality. *Int Psychogeriatr*, 22:455–462.
- Stickley, A. & Koyanagi, A. (2016). Loneliness, common mental disorders and suicidal behavior: Findings from a general population survey. *Journal of affective disorders*, 197, 81–87.
- Sugisawa H, Liang J & Liu X. (1994). Social networks, social support, and mortality among older people in Japan. *J Gerontol*, 49: S3–13.
- Sum, S., Mathews, R. M., Hughes, I., & Campbell, A. (2008). Internet use and loneliness in older adults. *Cyber Psychology & Behavior*, 11(2), 208-211.
- Synthesio (2021). Social media usage statistic around the world. Retrieved 20.01.2020 from http://synthesio.wpengine.com/blog/social-media-usage-statistics / ?utm_medium = blog & utm_source = mktg&utm_campaign=socialmediausage

- Wu, Y. H., Lewis, M., & Rigaud, A. S. (2019). Cognitive function and digital device use in older adults attending a memory clinic. *Gerontology and Geriatric Medicine*, 5, 2333721419844886.
- Yanguas, J., Pinazo-Henandis, S., & Tarazona-Santabalbina, F. J. (2018). The complexity of loneliness. *Acta bio-medica: Atenei Parmensis,* 89(2), 302–314. https://doi.org/10.23750/abm.v89i2.7404
- Zhang, K., Kim, K., Silverstein, N. M., Song, Q., & Burr, J. A. (2020). Social Media Communication and Loneliness Among Older Adults: The Mediating Roles of Social Support and Social Contact. The Gerontologist.

* * *

SUICIDE AND SELF-INJURIOUS BEHAVIOURS IN ELDERLY

Susmita Halder, Shinjini Samajdar and Akash Kumar Mahato

Introduction

Suicide has been one of the most discussed public health concerns because it is a behaviour which might end the life of a person. This behavior is associated with various psychosocial problems but the act of suicide can be differentiated from a disease or disorder. Suicidal behaviour includes the ideation and the attempt in a continuum which can cause fatal damage to the wellbeing (Cattell & Jolley, 1995) and the statistics reveal that the curve of attempting suicide each day is in upward flow (Minayo & Cavalcante, 2010). The prevention of suicide has been primary focus of health care system and nation as a whole and thus minimal presence of suicidal ideation draws attention of physician and therapists. Suicidal ideation might not be identified easily and the person with such ideation might put out of sight of the therapist because of his or her psychological conditions. While taking in-depth interviews, the clinicians are become cautious and usually the focus is on the causal factors and belief related to it. Clinicians are involved in understanding various factors associated to suicidal risks and gaining comprehensive knowledge of suicidal behaviours. It has been seen that more than 20% cases who attempted suicide can lead to death. Research on suicide behaviour is growing and the integration and interpretation of the multifaceted components are associated with suicide are being acknowledged in comprehensive way. The highest incidence rate of suicide can be seen within the age group of 15-24 years. Studies show that, the adolescence suicidal behaviours are driven by impulsivity whereas in elderly population, the suicidal behaviours are manifested with strong intend to die or end one's life. In fact older people are more successful age group with approximately 1 in every 4 attempts resulting in deaths. Hence, it increases the suicide rate in the elderly population. Studies indicate higher prevalence of suicide among the young and middle adults, but the number of people engaging in suicidal acts is increasing among older adults as well. Despite increasing rates of suicidal acts in elderly, they seem to not get adequate reporting in the media compared to young adults or middle aged adults. The identification of suicidal thoughts and inclination in elderly might have been less recognized compared to young and middle adults (Kumar et al., 2015). Prevalence of geriatric depression and suicidal acts are common, and it should get into the light as well. Identifying and understanding the suicidal risk factors in elderly population can improve the comprehension of acts and its corresponding consequences. Still there is no clarity regarding prevalence data and nature of suicidal risk in elderly population. Thus suicide in elderly is complex, as early identification may be difficult, further the ratio of suicide attempt turning fatal is relatively high and their general health status may not be strong enough to recover from an attempt. Importance to classifying and exploring the signs and symptoms must be given regardless of age group. In literature the prevalence of suicidal acts has been reported to be focused on the younger age groups, but if it is considered, highest suicide rate can be seen in > 60 years of age (Waern et al., 2002). The scenario which are shown through discussions in all these years might be quite different from the actual one.

Contrary to the common perception that elderly people suffer from hopelessness, despair and depression, fact is they show less pathological reactions and psychological symptoms even in difficult situation. They normally cope better with multiple stressors. However, coping as a continuous process may fail when perceived stress is huge and one is apprehensive of his or her inner strength to deal with it. Studies suggest that for elders, demographic risk factors, mode and nature of suicide differ from young population. For example, compared to younger ones elderly 'successful' or completed suicides are more in numbers than attempted suicide. Also they choose more lethal mode to commit suicide to make it successful. (Osgood, 1985; Alexopoulos, 1996).

Prevalence of suicidal death, is higher among the elderly population and one of the reason behind this could be the little attention this group usually get in case of intervention because public health measures, medical research, and media attention tend to get more focused on younger age groups. Epidemiological studies on suicide in elderly population are inadequate whereas, the incidence of suicide in this group is increasing globally (Tsoh et al., 2005). Understanding of profile of suicide attempts can lead to the strategies to prevention of suicidal attempts and acts itself.

Suicide is identified as vital public health concern for the elderly population. Worldwide data suggest approximately one-sixth of suicide are reported to happen after the age of 40 (Yu et al., 2021). Suicidal acts in older adults are more lethal than in young adults; consequently, more consideration is required among the geriatric populace. The aged population appear as a significant member of the population, and with the elderly population raising the suicides pose a serious issue for global societies.

Young adults who are in the age range of 18-25 years are recognized with highest risk in suicidal acts and thoughts along with self-harm behaviours (Crosby et al., 2011); whereas adults within the age group of 45 to 64 have more in numbers of death from suicides than other age groups (Venkoba, 1991; Curtin et al., 2016). Moreover, the death rate by suicide in elderly is considerably greater than before over the years and it is higher than any other age group. This enhancement is noticeable for both genders. The proportion of adults within this age group report severe thoughts of suicide and attempted suicide (Braden et al., 2017). Males who are aged 75 and over have the uppermost rates of suicide in nearly all developed countries, and among numerous of these nations suicide rates rise with growing old (Cutright et al., 2000). However, many countries have documented the decreased rates among the elderly in recent years. However, in India, the suicide rate among older individual is more than the national rate of suicide. Statistics given by the Government of India has added more concern as the data indicates suicide in the elderly population is increasing and depressive episodes are the leading indication of suicide following comorbid physical conditions and financial concerns (Rao, 1991).

There are number of studies, as well as many subjective account of self-injurious behaviour in the elderly population. About 5% of all self-harm cases in a general hospital occurred in individuals over the age of 65 (Parks & Feldman, 2006). When Self-Injurious Behaviours (SIB) are observed in the elderly, it is more closely associated to efforts to be in touch with others, seizure commotion, labors to lessen physical ache, excessive forms of self-stimulation, or displays of disappointments. SIB in elderly with depression revealed that those who were depressed and engaged in SIB were more likely to have poorly incorporated societal arrangement and were more discouraging. Dementia is an additional threat factor for SIB, although the studies on SIB in this population highlighted the need for future research (de Jonghe-Rouleau & de Jonghe, 2005). Dementia is mainly associated to difficulties with memory functioning, particularly, the capability to discover new information or proficiency. In adding together to difficulties with memory, persons with dementia often experience from expressive and receptive communication discrepancy potentially ensuing from strokes or the sequence of their dementia. People who go through from the difficulties in dementia—and who formerly used to communicate competently but now are not capable to either understand verbal communication or fruitfully articulate themselves—are more vulnerable to episodes of frustration or annoyance. This may be expressed all the way through SIB. In addition, because of the lack of ability to learn new information or skills, learning compensatory behavior to converse with others is difficult, which may only further aggravate their frustration (Patel & Hope, 1992).

Numerous research have revealed multi-domain reasons linked to suicidal ideation or suicidal behaviors. Quality of life (QOL) has been originated to be allied with the possibility of suicidal ideation or suicidal behaviors in the older adults (Ponte et al., 2014; Kim et al., 2012). In psychological evaluation, many cases with suicidal death had a wish to die (WTD) (Palacio-Acosta et al., 2005), which was also found to be associated with all-cause death (Raue et al., 2010). Furthermore, there are other risk factors related to suicidal ideation and suicidal behaviors, which include clinical depression (Liu et al., 2009), substance use or mishandling (Awata et al., 2005), poor awareness of health, monetary problems, relationship dilemma or crisis, poor societal support, marital status, living alone, impaired cognitive functioning, history of the burden of physical illness, and traumatic events (Chen et al., 2008). More consideration should be paid to elderly inpatients with medical illness because they are more likely to have a suicide attempt and suicide death because of old age, trouble of physical diseases, and an increased consensus of depression (Shah et al., 2000). Thus, to sort out elderly inpatients with suicidal ideation in the beginning stage and giving opportune sufficient conduct in a general hospital, may reduce rates of suicidal behaviors and related mortality (Shah et al., 2000).

It is easier said than predicting precisely, and it has plenty of allied aspects which may have biopsychosocial perspectives and it plays role in emerging suicidal thoughts and behevaiour (Raue et al., 2010). Nevertheless, the suicidal ideation and active suicidal attempts repeatedly take place on a continuum. Thus, suicidal ideation are commonly the primary pace in the procedure of ultimate suicide (Liu et al., 2009), and older adults having suicidal ideation may be more likely to proceed out their suicidal intentions in the course of more indomitable and mortal techniques (Yen et al., 2005). Consequently, suicidal acts such as plans and ideation have variously been well thought-out as pointers to forthcoming suicide (Awata et al., 2005). An older adult is less communicable with people around them in case of having suicidal intentions. (Yip et al., 2003). Even if objective of suicide might be communicated, they are often complicated to acknowledge or to deal with. Prevalence studies may present useful facts about the predictors of suicidal intentions and the alteration from one behaviour to other. Older adults are most susceptible and helpless to health problems due to an assortment of factors: depression, anxiety, neurocognitive disorders, dementia, social isolation, loss of relatives, pain, and chronic physical diseases. These stated factors amplify the possibility for suicidal behavior. So, these possibility factors should be in use into explanation in suicide prevention strategies.

Self-harm is the main possibility factor for suicide, which has uppermost rates amongst older adults (WHO, 2014). Nonetheless, self-harm is also presented in the nonexistence of suicidal intent (i.e., non-suicidal self-injury). Amongst older adults, self-harm is additional in women, people with bodily and/or mental health state and those with preceding self-harm record (Troya et al., 2019; Morgan et al., 2018). Contrast to younger populations, self-harm rates are fewer prevalent in elderly. Nevertheless, self-harm rates might be underestimated as of shame and seeming or felt stigma (Long, 2018), be short of disclosure and intricacy in working with older adults (Troya et al., 2019). Furthermore, amongst older adults, evidence suggests there to be increased lethality connected with self-harm (Troya et al., 2019). This augmented invasiveness often results in higher reserve and action costs due to medical complications caused by frailer health.

Self-injurious behaviours or self-harm can be facilitated by multiple factors, and it has been seen that the major identified vulnerability factors can be different among the group of elderly people. These factors can be grouped by medical, psychological and social dynamics. The most prevalent medical conditions which are identified as the predisposing factors are chronic diseases, critical illnesses, sudden changes in health conditions. Personality disorders, depression, anxiety, OCD, adjustment disorders and eating disorders can cause maintenance of SIB or self harm. Psychosocial factors which are dominating the acts of self harm are identified as the sudden financial loss, existence of mental illness in family, early childhood trauma, experience of multiple family member loss, partner bereavement, massive changes in environment can evident self harm or SIB among elderly people (Hong et al., 2021).

Passive suicidal ideation is the part of suicide related behaviour which can symbolise the early stage and probable target to start the intervention for the course of suicidality. Suicidal ideation starts from passive ideation and manifests as active suicide plans and attempts. However, in elderly population passive ideation is more prevalent as prodromal phase and clinicians identify the indicator for psychological distress which may lead to active suicidal thoughts. In case of older adults, it is not well characterised and understandable for suicidal risk assessment. Self neglect and refusal to take care and protect of own self in the areas of nutrition, clothing, maintenance of hygiene, taking proper medicines and precautionary safety are some of the indicators. Factors which are enhancing the risk associated with self neglect are identified as education, economic background, cognitive impairment, physical disability and psychological distress (Dong et al., 2009).

There are numerous myths and misconceptions regarding the suicidal acts and behaviour of older adults in society. Clarification and objectification of myths are required to promote awareness and knowledge of suicide in elderly. Some of them can be identified and others might have indirect impact over the wellbeing of older adults. One of the most well active myth is, it is normal to get depressed or having death wishes when one is getting older. But in reality, depression is not a normal part of ageing and psychological wellbeing generally increases with age because of the experiences and perspectives. Whereas, people with suicidal ideation or depression might have went through loneliness, isolation, other physical or psychosocial distress. It is important to address that, there is significant distinction between feeling lonely or grieving loss and clinical depression. Another myth or misconception, which can be addressed is elderly people deciding to commit suicide is a logical choice because they are choosing death from the viewpoint that, they don't want to live a life with decreased QOL and wellbeing. Here also, we have to address the fact that, an older adult with suicidal ideation and thoughts might have underlying maintaining factors which could influence the behaviour. They usually seek help to get out from the negative thoughts which are causing them distress and identifying the signs of having suicidal thoughts are important to prevent the act (Segal, 2001).

By the side of misconceptions and risk factors of suicide in elderly population the preventive measures are required to organize and make it applicable to the target population. There are suicide prevention programmes in countries and they have the responsibility to promote awareness among the native people. In this kind of programmes, a team is assigned to monitor and discover the attitude towards the act and behaviors. This way of preventive programmes is named as universal prevention by Mrazek & Haggerty (1994). Another level of prevention, selective prevention, that focuses on high-risk groups which are not showing any advance signs of suicidal thoughts or actions but are exposed to important life transitions and loses which can make the person vulnerable to depression or suicide to improve resilience and reducing risk factors. Indicated prevention is for the individuals who are having active suicidal thoughts and ideation. It is essential to address that the primary caregivers of the population has the vital role in prevention and they are needed to be more active than anyone else. They are needed to be educated properly and the awareness among the family members can reduce the chances of engaged into the act. The role of clinician or general physician is to identify the presence of suicidal ideations or vulnerability factors. Once the screening procedure is completed the pharmacotherapy and psychotherapeutic interventions are indicated. Preventing the act of suicide and encouraging them to maintain a meaningful life is indicated through psychotherapy. Restricting the thoughts of suicide, collective ideas of suicidal act and the cumulative conduct through media is remained important in preventive measures.

The main causal factors associated with suicide in elderly population can be described as follows:

Stress and Coping: It has been seen that, internal source of emotional strength can be disturbed, and equilibrium might vary with ages. Coping and resilience can be buffer and that enhance the vulnerabilities to perceived stress. Intolerance and irritability might be taken place which can indulge self-neglect, self-harm behaviour. Being isolated, being disconnected with others and not able to adapt with changing situations cause perception of oneself as maladaptive which influence the social isolation and self-sabotage.

Decision Making and Suicide: Impaired decision-making has been recognized as a impending factor accountable for suicide attempts in older adults. With ageing the capacity to functioning executively become difficult which can limit problem solving capacity of older adult. It encourages the rumination and self blaming after any hassle which lead to suicidal behavior.

Chronic Illness: Chronic physical illness and disability restrict the physical capacity and increases the dependence on others that produce worthlessness and they usually wish to die than living with intense pain and sufferings.

Grief: Bereavement following loss of near ones due to unusual incident can be markedly difficult to accept at the age where the change is usually difficult to cope with. Demise of spouse leads to intense unhappiness and the life become seized by loneliness. It impacts over the meaning and purpose of life. In old age, many deaths take place which is intolerable. Grief arises as the life comes to an end which exacerbates the death wishes and suicidal ideation comes through.

Financial Difficulties: Person in old age might be dependent on the family members for the financial requirements. Even if the individual is having monetary fund for his necessities but because of physical restrictions and declination of cognitive functioning, they need to be dependent on others. It implies the worthlessness within them and leads to sadness and helplessness. In other elderlies having serious financial crises, try to limit their expenses, medical bills as well as basic expenses like good food. This invokes thoughts of ending their own life as they perceive themselves as burden to their family.

Role of Society

Misconceptions and prejudices in society regarding ageing process has restricted the exploration of psychological symptoms in elderly population. In eastern societies, it has been seen that, people do believe that talking about suicide can increase the risk of suicidal attempts among elderlies. In societies today, older adults seem to have less valuation due to individualistic nature of society, self-reliance and tendency to be independent. Societal ageing is impacting economic growth, patterns of work and retirement which might increase the probability of emotional distress among elderlies. Active involvement in society is less in old age, which naturally decreases social interaction and challenges related to ageist comments, and discriminations increasing the risk of suicide. As a social being elderly people need proper care and attention to evolve positively.

Warning Signs of Suicide in Elderly Population:

Affective/Psychological	Behavioural	Others
Depressive symptoms	Apathy	Sudden demise of close family member (i.e., Spouse, Child)
Rumination	Asocial	Critical illness
Symptoms of psychosis: active hallucination and delusional ideas	Anger outbursts	Certain life changing events (i.e., Financial loss, Disaster, Public health concerns)
Preoccupied with death wishes	Being alone for prolonged period of time	Physical disability

Psychological Intervention

One of the limitation in management of suicidal behaviour of elderly people is their primary care physicians are often unable to identify the signs and symptoms of suicidal ideation. Often the suicidal ideations are difficult to discriminate with death wishes which come along with prolonged illness or changed meaning of life with ageing. In more than 50% of cases primary care physicians are not aware of the aggressive trait of depressive symptoms which might intensify the suicidal acts. Recognition of late life depression and planning for the treatment is required as early possible. Evidences show that, education to primary caregivers can decrease suicidal rate and educational programmes concerning diagnosis of depression is needed to be prepared. Acute risk of suicidal behaviour has become difficult because the underlying symptoms of depression might be masked by different somatic complaints especially in women. In elderly population, they are less intended to express their suicidal intentions which limit the early identification. Older people generally use methods of suicide which are lethal in nature. Restricting the access of those can decrease the chances. After recognizing the suicidal risks among elderly, he or she should be enquired about their intentions regarding the mode or weapon of suicide. Negotiating the removal of those weapons from home will diminish suicide risks. The quantities and possible toxicities of prescribed medications which might be used by overdosing should be considered. Re-examining suicidal risks and severity of depression is the most important effort of a clinician to prevent suicidal acts (Halder & Manot, 2020).

Patients with critical medical illnesses might have intense death wishes and disappointments can be reflected as self neglect, denying medicines and foods and involving in risk taking behaviour. Regular physical check up for maintaining the record of changes in weight, physical appearances and sleep pattern might help in screening along with validated screening tools. Passive suicide must be identified and the insight regarding the pattern should be discussed with the patient and caregivers.

Regarding psychological management of individuals with suicidal ideations or thoughts in their old age, the intervention target would be identifying the preliminary warning signs of suicide. Clinician should focus on the screening process of suicide. It would be prolonged, but the procedure should be comprehensive. Detailed case history by the side of with presence of underlying psychological disturbances and susceptibility are required to be illustrated before the treatment preparation. Screening and diagnostic tools are in use of recognition of pattern of suicidal thoughts and ideations. Presence of depression is supposed to be known by the clinician. It is recommended by the clinicians that elderly individuals should have physical checkup regular. If the individual is having underlying physical illness which might have contributed to the course of suicidal thoughts is needed to be in consideration and treated accordingly. It is essential to address that the primary caregiver of the population has the vital role in prevention and they are needed to be more active than anyone else. They are needed to be psycho-educated and the awareness among the family members can reduce the chances of getting into the act. Communication and being in touch with the elderly person can dissolve the preoccupied negative thoughts and perceived loneliness of the person. Elderly individuals are usually having helplessness as their physical restrictions and ideas of hopelessness are also perceptible among them. Providing support, listening to them, giving expectation to look forward and reassurance are the vital role of family members. Those who have went through demise of spouse and living alone need more attention because in this case loneliness become the most noticed risk factor of suicidal acts. With increasing age, the tendency to be isolated and being alone has been seen to be prominent which decreases the standard of living and indulge death wishes and suicidal ideations. So, involvement in various societal activities and community involvement are required to include in daily schedule of elderly people. It will help in improving communication with neighbors and native people which can reduces risk factors of suicide.

In the section of intervention of suicide, here we present a case study for better understanding the course of symptoms and intervention procedure to target the suicidal thoughts and behaviour.

Case Details

The indexed client is 74 years old, male, married, retired bank officer, lives with wife, he has no children. He is having negative apprehensions, low mood and suicidal ideation as reported by his wife. He denied to admit that he is having suicide intentions. He reported to have death anxiety and apprehensions regarding financial crisis. He is apprehensive about future and it was revealed that the client is having depression.

The course of illness

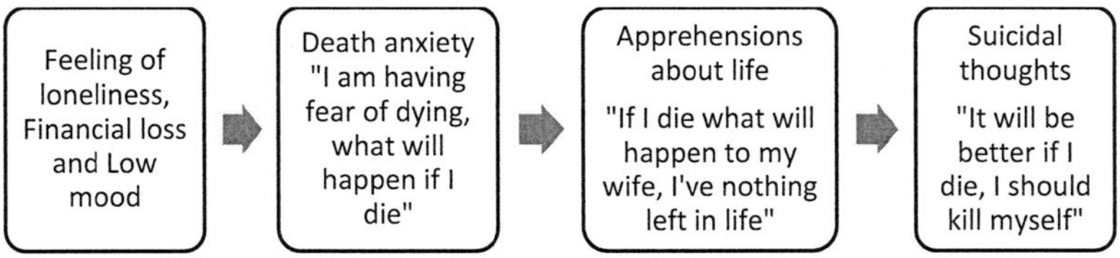

Targeted Behaviour and Therapeutic Plans:

Target Behaviour	**Intervention**
Awareness of presence of suicidal thoughts	Labeling the thoughts of suicide
	Orient the patient
	Psychoeducating the patient and family members regarding the course of illness
Acceptance of presence of suicidal thoughts	Providing understanding that the remedies are present
	Preparing the connection between the thoughts and acts
Disorganized daily routine	Activity scheduling including interest areas and occupying with different activities

Negative thoughts and behaviour	Cognitive Behavioural Therapy
Improving family engagement	Family counseling
Relapse prevention	Follow-up sessions
Total sessions: 8-10 session Follow-up sessions: 4 sessions Total time for each sessions: 45 minutes approximately	

Stabilization of patients and resolution of instant crises are typically essential before go on board on a full course of Cognitive Behavioural Therapy (CBT) with suicidal elders. On the other hand, explained CBT strategies, e.g., behavioral agreement or pessimistic thought stopping may be predominantly suitable throughout a emergency if used in combination with direct crisis intervention techniques put into practice in consultation with principal caregivers. In most authority, privacy and confidentiality should be broken down if patients are at risk to themselves or to others and, as a consequence, contributor must receive steps to notify family members and/or smooth the progress to hospitalization. Medication and other sign reduction method, both for the duration of and after crisis intervention, may also be apposite and need to be collective with cognitive and behavioural treatments.

Conclusion

The elderly age group is less explored by the clinicians and epidemiologists to target as a group to be identified for suicidal thoughts and self-injurious behaviours. Suicidal behaviour in elderly people are not impulsive and more thoughtful actions compared to younger adults due to significant changes in life, isolation, familial support, health status and sense of no hope in improvement of conditions. People in their 60s might have despair and loneliness in regard to their lack of occupying activities and being apart from loved ones. The preventive factors should focus on the pre-established roles of family members towards the wellbeing of older adults. Early identification of signs of suicide and evaluation is vital to bring down suicidal actions and self harm in the elderly.

References

- Almeida, O. P., Draper, B., Snowdon, J., Lautenschlager, N. T., Pirkis, J., Byrne, G., ... & Pfaff, J. J. (2012). Factors associated with suicidal thoughts in a large community study of older adults. *The British Journal of Psychiatry, 201*(6), 466-472.
- Awata, S., Seki, T., Koizumi, Y., Sato, S., Hozawa, A., Omori, K., & Tsuji, I. (2005). Factors associated with suicidal ideation in an elderly urban Japanese population: A community-based, cross-sectional study. *Psychiatry and clinical neurosciences, 59*(3), 327-336.
- Baca-Garcia, E., Perez-Rodriguez, M. M., Oquendo, M. A., Keyes, K. M., Hasin, D. S., Grant, B. F., & Blanco, C. (2011). Estimating risk for suicide attempt: Are we asking the right questions?:Passive suicidal ideation as a marker for suicidal behavior. *Journal of affective disorders, 134*(1-3), 327-332.
- Braden, J. B., Edlund, M. J., & Sullivan, M. D. (2017). Suicide deaths with opioid poisoning in the United States: 1999–2014. *American journal of public health, 107*(3), 421-426.
- Cattell, H. (2000). Suicide in the elderly. *Advances in Psychiatric Treatment, 6*(2), 102-108.
- Cattell, H., & Jolley, D. J. (1995). One hundred cases of suicide in elderly people. *The British Journal of Psychiatry, 166*(4), 451-457.
- Chen, C. S., Yang, M. S., Yang, M. J., Chang, S. J., Chueh, K. H., Su, Y. C., ... & Cheng, T. C. (2008). Suicidal thoughts among elderly Taiwanese aboriginal women. *International Journal of Geriatric Psychiatry: A journal of the psychiatry of late life and allied sciences, 23*(10), 1001-1006.

- Choi, N. G., Kim, J., & Asseff, J. (2009). Self-neglect and neglect of vulnerable older adults: Reexamination of etiology. *Journal of Gerontological Social Work, 52*(2), 171-187.
- Coon, D. W., DeVries, H. M., & Gallagher-Thompson, D. (2004). Cognitive behavioral therapy with suicidal older adults. *Behavioural and Cognitive Psychotherapy, 32*(4), 481-493.
- Crosby, A., Gfroerer, J., Han, B., Ortega, L., & Parks, S. E. (2011). Suicidal thoughts and behaviors among adults aged ≥18 Years--United States, 2008-2009.
- Curtin, S. C., Warner, M., & Hedegaard, H. (2016). *Increase in suicide in the United States, 1999-2014* (No. 2016). US Department of Health and Human Services, Centers for Disease Control and Prevention, National Center for Health Statistics.
- Cutright, P., & Fernquist, R. M. (2000). Effects of societal integration, period, region, and culture of suicide on male age-specific suicide rates: 20 developed countries, 1955–1989. *Social Science Research, 29*(1), 148-172.
- de Jonghe-Rouleau, A. P., Pot, A. M., & de Jonghe, J. F. (2005). Self-injurious behaviour in nursing home residents with dementia. *International Journal of Geriatric Psychiatry: A journal of the psychiatry of late life and allied sciences, 20*(7), 651-657.
- Dong, X. (2017). Elder self-neglect: research and practice. *Clinical interventions in aging, 12*, 949.
- Dong, X., Simon, M., De Leon, C. M., Fulmer, T., Beck, T., Hebert, L., & Evans, D. (2009). Elder self-neglect and abuse and mortality risk in a community-dwelling population. *Jama, 302*(5), 517-526.
- Forsell, Y. (2000). Predictors for depression, anxiety and psychotic symptoms in a very elderly population: data from a 3-year follow-up study. *Social psychiatry and psychiatric epidemiology, 35*(6), 259-263.
- Halder, S., & Manot, S. (2020). Identifying suicidal risk and its association with depression in the elderly population. *Journal of Geriatric Mental Health, 7*(1), 29.
- Hong, Z., Zhang, H., Xu, L., Zhou, J., Kong, F., Li, J., ... & Gao, Z. (2021). Negative life events and self-harm among the elderly: Result from a survey of 7070 people aged ≥ 60 in China. *Psychiatry research, 298*, 113727.

- Kumar, P. S., Anish, P. K., & George, B. (2015). Risk factors for suicide in elderly in comparison to younger age groups. *Indian journal of psychiatry, 57*(3), 249.
- Kwon, J. W., & Kim, J. H. (2012). The impact of health-related quality of life on suicidal ideation and suicide attempts among Korean older adults. *Journal of gerontological nursing, 38*(11), 48-59.
- Liu, I. C., & Chiu, C. H. (2009). Case-control study of suicide attempts in the elderly. *International psychogeriatrics, 21*(5), 896-902.
- Long, M. (2018). 'We're not monsters... we're just really sad sometimes:'hidden self-injury, stigma and help-seeking. *Health Sociology Review, 27*(1), 89-103.
- Minayo, M. C. D. S., & Cavalcante, F. G. (2010). Suicide in elderly people: a literature review. *Revista de saude publica, 44*, 750-757.
- Morgan, C., Webb, R. T., Carr, M. J., Kontopantelis, E., Chew-Graham, C. A., Kapur, N., & Ashcroft, D. M. (2018). Self-harm in a primary care cohort of older people: incidence, clinical management, and risk of suicide and other causes of death. *The Lancet Psychiatry, 5*(11), 905-912.
- Mrazek PJ, Haggerty RJ, editors. *Reducing the risk for mental disorder: Frontiers for prevention intervention research.* Washington, DC: National Academy Press, Institute of Medicine; 1994
- Palacio-Acosta, C., García-Valencia, J., Diago-García, J., Zapata, C., Ortiz-Tobón, J., López-Calle, G., & López-Tobón, M. (2005). Características del suicidoen Medellín, Colombia. *Revista de SaludPública, 7*, 243-253.
- Parks, S., & Feldman, S. (2006). Self-injurious behavior in the elderly. *The Consultant Pharmacist®, 21*(11), 905-910.
- Patel, V., & Hope, R. A. (1992). Aggressive behaviour in elderly psychiatric inpatients. *Acta Psychiatrica Scandinavica, 85*(2), 131-135.
- Ponte, C., Almeida, V., & Fernandes, L. (2014). Suicidal ideation, depression and quality of life in the elderly: study in a gerontopsychiatric consultation. *The Spanish journal of psychology, 17.*
- Raue, P. J., Morales, K. H., Post, E. P., Bogner, H. R., Ten Have, T., & Bruce, M. L. (2010). The wish to die and 5-year mortality in elderly primary care patients. *The American Journal of Geriatric Psychiatry, 18*(4), 341-350.
- Rudd, M. D., Joiner, T. E., & Rajab, M. H. (2001). *Treating suicidal behavior: An effective, time-limited approach.* Guilford Press.

- Scocco, P., & De Leo, D. (2002). One-year prevalence of death thoughts, suicide ideation and behaviours in an elderly population. *International journal of geriatric psychiatry, 17*(9), 842-846.
- Segal, D. L. (2001). Levels of knowledge about suicide facts and myths among younger and older adults. *Clinical Gerontologist, 22*(2), 71-80.
- Shah, A., Hoxey, K., & Mayadunne, V. (2000). Suicidal ideation in acutely medically ill elderly inpatients: prevalence, correlates and longitudinal stability. *International journal of geriatric psychiatry, 15*(2), 162-169.
- Silverman, M. M., Berman, A. L., Sanddal, N. D., O'carroll, P. W., & Joiner Jr, T. E. (2007). Rebuilding the tower of Babel: a revised nomenclature for the study of suicide and suicidal behaviors. Part 2: Suicide-related ideations, communications, and behaviors. *Suicide and Life-Threatening Behavior, 37*(3), 264-277.
- Szanto, K., Reynolds III, C. F., Frank, E., Stack, J., Fasiczka, A. L., Miller, M., ... & Kupfer, D. J. (1996). Suicide in elderly depressed patients: is active vs. passive suicidal ideation a clinically valid distinction?. *The American Journal of Geriatric Psychiatry, 4*(3), 197-207.
- Troya, M. I., Babatunde, O., Polidano, K., Bartlam, B., McCloskey, E., Dikomitis, L., & Chew-Graham, C. A. (2019). Self-harm in older adults: systematic review. *The British Journal of Psychiatry, 214*(4), 186-200.
- Tsoh, J., Chiu, H. F., Duberstein, P. R., Chan, S. S., Chi, I., Yip, P. S., & Conwell, Y. (2005). Attempted suicide in elderly Chinese persons: a multi-group, controlled study. *The American journal of geriatric psychiatry, 13*(7), 562-571.
- Van Orden, K. A., & Conwell, Y. (2016). Issues in research on aging and suicide. *Aging & mental health, 20*(2), 240-251.
- Waern, M., Rubenowitz, E., Runeson, B., Skoog, I., Wilhelmson, K., & Allebeck, P. (2002). Burden of illness and suicide in elderly people: case-control study. *Bmj, 324*(7350), 1355.
- World Health Organization (WHO) WHO; 2014. Preventing suicide: A global imperative.http://www.who.int/mental_health/suicide-prevention/world_report_2014/en/
- Yen, Y. C., Yang, M. J., Yang, M. S., Lung, F. W., Shih, C. H., Hahn, C. Y., & Lo, H. Y. (2005). Suicidal ideation and associated factors among

community-dwelling elders in Taiwan. *Psychiatry and clinical neurosciences, 59*(4), 365-371.

- Yip, P. S., Chi, I., Chiu, H., Chi Wai, K., Conwell, Y., & Caine, E. (2003). A prevalence study of suicide ideation among older adults in Hong Kong SAR. *International journal of geriatric psychiatry, 18*(11), 1056-1062.
- Yu, R., Chen, Y., Li, L., Chen, J., Guo, Y., Bian, Z., ... & Fazel, S. (2021). Factors associated with suicide risk among Chinese adults: A prospective cohort study of 0.5 million individuals. *PLoS medicine, 18*(3), e1003545.

* * *

SUBSTANCE USE DISORDER IN ELDERLY POPULATION: A REVIEW OF BIOPSYCHOSOCIAL FACTORS

Sampurna Chakraborty and Shridhar Utagi

ABSTRACT

Very little clinical and research interest has been directed at substance use disorders among older adults. Age-related biases like substance use disorders may partly explain the lack of interest and neglect that occurs mainly in young and middle-aged people. However, a growing body of epidemiologic evidence has indicated that substance use and alcohol use disorders are far more prevalent in older populations than previously recognized. Projections have suggested that the number of substance misusers globally will have doubled from 2006 to 2020 and onwards. Therefore, better detection and treatment methods must consider older adults' distinctive biological and psychosocial characteristics contributing to addictive behaviour. Additionally, problems related to substance addiction are possibly more significant and likely to be an important cause of morbidity in the population aged 65 years and above, primarily because of the ageing process and declining health. There is an evident dearth of research on the impact of addiction and tailored treatment options for the ageing population. This chapter will discuss the factors related to and contributing to addiction, assess its impact and preventive measures, and focus on appropriate and effective treatment modules tailored to improve addiction-related physical and mental health issues.

Keywords: Substance use, Elderly population, Biopsycho-social issues, Intervention.

Introduction

Ageing is an essential factor in health and disease. Old age has often been viewed as a time of physical and mental decline and infirmity. Whenever we talk about substance use in the elderly/geriatric population, the first thing that rings the bell is the process of ageing and its impact on the metabolism of the substance, the changes in the brain and its harmful effects. To date, substance use disorders (SUDs) among older or elderly patients have received relatively very little attention in clinical and research initiatives. Prevailing cultural biases may partly explain this apparent neglect of a particular age range of individuals affected by addiction among family members and practitioners, which minimizes the perceived extent of the problem among older adults. Ageism contributes to a pattern of underdiagnoses that is considered a problem in younger adults does not qualify the same urgency and importance for care in older adults (SAMHSA, 1998). Primary health care practitioners and addiction specialists do not routinely address or screen older adults for SUDs (Rothrauff et al., 2011). Additionally, research evidence for various assessment and treatment practices best suited for the older population is lacking. Most clinical research trials specifically exclude participants above 65 years of age for age-related constraints. Thus, the literature existing to identify SUDs in the older population mainly relies on extrapolating data and resources (assessment and interventions) from younger cohorts. Therefore, our target should be to develop diagnostic assessment instruments and personalized treatment and preventive strategies focused on the demographic and biopsychosocial characteristics of the elderly with SUDs or addictive behaviours.

Demographic Characteristics

The historical and current trends with future projections of population demography demonstrate significant changes concerning people above 65 years of age. It is estimated that over the last 50 years and in the next 50 years, there has been and will be a fundamental shift in the distribution of the human population (Population Division, UN, 2009). Different world areas display different shift patterns in the demographics, but despite these different demographic patterns, already 64% of the older population (aged 60 and over) are living in developing countries. By 2050 nearly 80% of those aged 60 and above are expected to be living in developing countries (Population Division, UN, 2006).

Psychiatric conditions in the older population are likely to be underreported to a great extent. This can be explained by overlapping symptoms like decreased appetite, sleep disturbances, fatigue, difficulty in concentration, memory deficits in geriatric depression and anxiety with the normal ageing process and physical illnesses. Death certificates often do not mention the presence of any major psychiatric diseases such as dementia or depression, despite its probable presence or it being known to be a significant contributing factor to the death of an older person. Moreover, there is a high likelihood that the routine data to record the health and, in particular, the mental health statistics of the older population is not conducted routinely. Therefore, the existing data may be insufficient and unreliable (Matthews & Savva, 2010).

Among mental health problems and burden for the elderly, SUDs play a significant contribution as it is likely to produce multiple physical problems (Degenhardt & Hall, 2012) in addition to the usual ones associated with the ageing process (Vos et al., 2010; Wittchen et al., 2011).

There are two categories of substance use problems that are the main concerns among older adults: alcohol and prescription drugs, mainly benzodiazepines (BZD). Although the use of illicit drugs is low in this age group, it seems to be an emerging issue currently. It has been noted that individuals who have had more exposure to alcohol, tobacco and illegal drugs in their youth tended to be more lenient about substance use in later life. Additionally, they often use it to cope and deal with anxiety, pain, and stress in response to life's pressures and rationalize the use pattern in terms of 'use for healing purpose'. When more people abuse alcohol and drugs in their later years, it is likely to be associated with more problems and needs for treatment (Blow & Barry, 2012; Hallgren et al., 2009). Recently, a rise in the admission and treatment-seeking behaviour among the elderly for addiction or associated physical and mental conditions has been noticed (Chhatre S et al., 2017). This is effective to raise a survey to understand the demographic trend of substance use and accordingly develop appropriate means of assessment, intervention, and prevention of the said problem in the elderly group. Research is also warranted in this domain to validate or negate the existing models of psychopathology related to substance use and identify the contributing factors and develop new relevant models. This research is necessary for planning personalized treatment models for the elderly.

Neurobiological Perspective of Addiction in the Elderly

Substance use and use of drugs are generally lower among older adults when compared to the general population. However, recent trends suggest a significant presence and rise in substance use among the geriatric population (Kuerbis et al.,

2014). Substance use among the older population presents with specific risks of harm especially considering even the minimal amounts causing harm.

Some of the brain changes that occur due to ageing and may additionally affect the elderly due to substance use includes (Comprehensive textbook of psychiatry 10th edition, 2017):

1. Age-related factors decrease the strength of norepinephrine or dopamine circuits.
2. Increased sensitivity of receptors.
3. Increased vulnerability to develop adverse cognitive side effects because of medications.
4. Structural changes such as the decline of brain weight, neuron loss, neuronal atrophy, synaptic loss and pruning of dendritic trees, nucleolar atrophy, white matter changes, and gliosis.
5. Reduced neuroplasticity or the ability to adapt and strengthen connections or form new connections between neurons and circuits.

Considering these changes, an attempt to understand how individual substances, mainly alcohol, BZD, tobacco (the most used substance among the elderly), may affect the cohort and their impact on general health and disease.

Alcohol: Alcohol (Ethanol) is an organic compound generally used as a recreational drug or substance, which, when used in a dependence pattern, has a harmful physical and neurobiological impact. It is metabolized by the liver, and its physical impact on the body in late life is unique compared with young to middle-aged adults (Oslin, 2000). As one age, the lean body mass and total body water decrease; the liver's ability to process alcohol is also diminished; and the permeability of the blood-brain barrier and sensitivity of the neuronal receptors to alcohol in the brain increase (Kennedy, 1999; Blazer & Wu, 2009). These changes result in older adults experiencing increased impairment compared to younger adults at equivalent consumption levels and higher blood alcohol concentrations with less awareness of their impairment; hence they are more vulnerable to the ill effects of alcohol even in moderate amounts (Gilbertson et al., 2009; Sklar et al., 2012). Neuronal growth and executive functions added with ageing-related changes might accelerate the process of ageing, making the person more vulnerable to diseases (Bachi et al., 2017). Along with these changes, the elderly with comorbidities such as diabetes and hypertension have a higher risk of adverse cardiovascular events, liver dysfunction, and reduced cognitive functioning accentuated by alcohol use.

Benzodiazepines: Benzodiazepines are fat-soluble drugs. As older adults have less lean muscle mass and more body fat, these drugs have a longer duration of action, combined with heightened receptor sensitivity, resulting in a more profound effect of the drug. The use of BZD is associated with the risk of dependence, cognitive deficits, falls resulting in fractures, motor vehicle accidents, delirium, respiratory distress, paradoxical reactions, and overall mortality (Garrido et al., 2014). The rising BZD misuse in the elderly occurs despite current knowledge about the increased sensitivity of this age group to serious side effects, including falls and cognitive decline (Neutel et al., 2012). The continued use of BZDs in the elderly additionally may cause reversible cognitive effects such as impaired attention, verbal learning, executive function and working memory. However, the association of long-term cognitive impairment with BZD use has given conflicting results and needs further exploration (Dell'osso & Lader, 2013).

Concerning neurodegenerative disorders, the use of BZDs has been linked to an increased risk of Alzheimer's dementia in a large cohort study (De Gage et al., 2014). However, there have been conflicting results in the last couple of decades (Verdoux et al., 2005). Risk factors for the use of BZDs in the elderly include female gender, multiple prescribers and poly-pharmacy, chronic pain, physical disabilities or reduced mobility, cognitive impairment, social withdrawal, and presence of suicidal ideation (Kuerbis et al., 2014).

Tobacco: Tobacco use is the highest among all the substances in all age groups, including the elderly used in dependent patterns. The long-term use of tobacco has been implicated in an increased risk of cardiovascular diseases

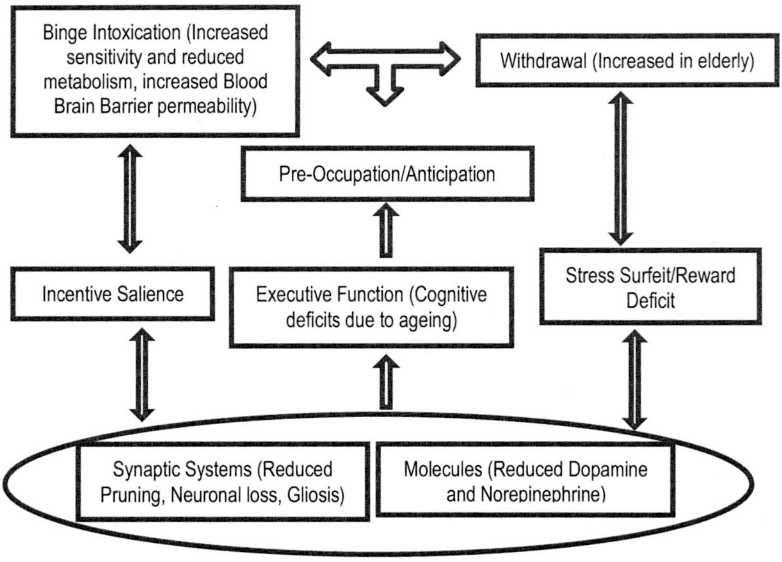

Figure 1: The Neurocircuitry of addiction

(hypertension, atherosclerosis), cerebrovascular diseases (stroke), respiratory ailments (chronic obstructive pulmonary disorder, reduced lung capacity, chronic bronchitis) and several types of cancers. Tobacco use in the elderly continues from initiation in use started at a young age. As explained earlier, it is associated with increased oxidative stress and free radical generation, which results in brain changes.

Psychosocial Perspective of Addiction in the Elderly

Drug dependence is explained as an individual's attempt to cope with his or her internal emotional state and external social and physical environment. From the classical and contemporary psychoanalytic perspective, drug use and dependency are best understood as a person's ego disorganization and failed coping attempts. The psychoanalytic formulation of addiction postulates that ego disorganization leads to poor coping, resulting in underlying depression, tension, and distress that motivates or drives the addictive behaviour.

From a different perspective, behavioural tradition suggests that when an intense, noxious, threatening, or harmful stimulus situation remains relatively unchanged, it will inevitably be followed by anxiety. In behaviour theory, anxiety reduction is a secondary reinforcement after using some addictive substance since attaining the goal object (drug) possesses its reinforcing properties at a neurobiological level. This occurs because, through experience, drug ingestion has become associated with a primary drive state to reduce the anxiety or imbalance. According to this perspective, drug abuse is a learned behaviour. The following response is likely to become progressively more prominent as the ensuing tension reduction from the drug brings relief and reinforcement of the act that induced the administration of the drug in the first place. As this process is repeated, the sequence of events is shortened in time because the decrease in tension reduction becomes so powerfully reinforced, and every point in the sequence becomes an associative cue for the ultimate relief. With each reinforcement, the act of substance abuse becomes strengthened, and the likelihood of its recurrence under similar conditions is increased.

Drug use and dependence have social consequences. The process of substance use comes with social judgements and dysfunctions in the surrounding environment. The individual dependent on the substance has to face the reproaches of the spouse and other members of the family, the quarrels, the disdain and withdrawal of friends and acquaintances, the tensions and conflicts in the occupational sphere, and, finally, the dropping out from society. The sequelae of events become dysfunctional and, finally, result in a complete disintegration from the social groups. This isolation and rejection engender negative feelings in the subject, which foster an attitude of letting oneself go into the state of being an addict.

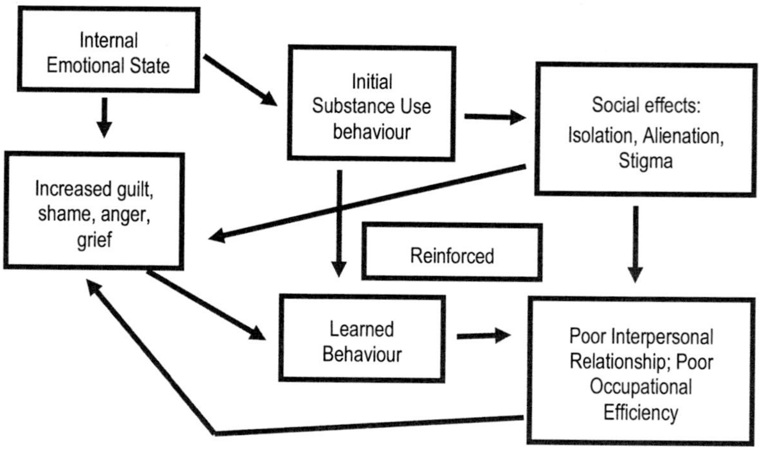

Figure 2: Schematic representation of Psychosocial Factors contributing to Substance Use and Dependence Behaviour in the Elderly

The psychodynamic, behavioural and social factors, therefore, may prompt a fixation of the learned behaviour to deal with the disturbed internal states like anxiety, shame, guilt and distress resulting from the various social impact of addictive behaviour such as isolation, bias, rejection, poor interpersonal and occupational efficacy and gradual decrease in self-esteem and self-worth that in turn maintains the vicious cycle. It is important to note here that this pattern of vicious and interrelated behaviour may be a long and intense pattern for the elderly and therefore becomes a more reinforced, resistant to change and stubborn pattern of behaviour.

Impact of Substance Use in Elderly

The chronic effects of alcohol, cigarettes, and prescription medication on the adult population are well established and dealing with their health consequences is part of daily medical work. The impact of associated cardiovascular disease, cancer, and alcoholic liver disease is recognized as a public health priority and becomes increasingly significant as individuals age. In addition, to the direct effects of intoxication, overdose and withdrawal, the physical complications of substances of abuse are numerous and manifest in almost all organs. Severe medical disorders among older adults who misuse alcohol are much more common than among the overall population of a similar age, with prevalent physical, psychological, social, and cognitive health impairments (Rigler, 2000).

Instability falls, and immobility: Falls in the elderly are a major cause of concern, with unintentional injury currently the fifth leading cause of death in older adults (Vos et al., 2012). Decreased attention, altered motor coordination, and cognitive dysfunction with impaired judgment combine in older adults to increase the risk of falling. Apart from the impact on a person's health, falls may reduce confidence and instil a fear of further falls in previously mobile adults. This results in constriction of activities and socialization, leading to isolation, inactivity, greater substance intake, precipitating family concern, and eventually ending in institutionalization. Reducing substance use is one of the essential factors to reduce falls in the elderly.

Elderly alcoholics also have a higher prevalence of alcohol-related medical conditions than the elderly population at large. Such conditions include alcoholic liver disease, alcoholic cardiomyopathy, hypertension, chronic obstructive pulmonary disease, neurological diseases (including cognitive disorders and peripheral neuropathy), malnutrition, osteopenia, psoriasis, peptic ulcer disease and various cancers.

Substance use in the elderly is harmful and brings upon the wrath of comorbidities and thus requires to be taken as a significant issue of public health to identify, treat, and improve the quality of life and longevity.

Assessment of Addiction and Associated Behaviours

A large gap in knowledge and research exists on how substance use and the behaviours of the affected cohorts are to be screened and identified. When tasked with creating diagnostic definitions and criteria for substance abuse, the scientific and research committees usually envisage an average patient who is usually socially active, young or a middle-aged adult of normal physiology with no existing health complications. The medical, psychological and social frailties of an older adult are rarely considered. The Diagnostic and Statistical Manual of Mental Disorders, 5th Edition (DSM-5), describes SUDs as '...a cluster of cognitive, behavioural, and physiological symptoms indicating that the individual continues using the substance despite significant substance-related problems. Criteria for diagnosis include impaired control, social impairment, risky use and pharmacological responses such as tolerance and withdrawal. However, these criteria are often inapplicable for those who may not be employed, do not drive, and have limited social networks. The symptoms associated with intoxication, craving and withdrawal are often atypical. Among older adults, approaches to identifying substance misuse, dependence patterns, and physiological and psychological impact assessment are lacking. The tools used are similar to those employed in younger cohorts. However, these methods may be inappropriate or even misleading and suggest a need to develop standardized scales and tools to assess addiction behaviour among the elderly that consider the elderly characteristics relevant to addictive behaviour.

Commonly used tools for screening and assessment of addictive behaviour are the CAGE (Cut - Down, Annoyed, Guilty, Eye-opener) questionnaire, Drug Abuse Screen Test (DAST), Tobacco, Alcohol, Prescription Medication, and other Substance Use (TAPS), The Alcohol Use Disorder Identification Test (AUDIT), Addiction Severity Index (ASI). However, these tools are primarily insensitive when applied to older people and do not consider other medical comorbidities resulting from substance use. One scale that proves appropriate for the elderly is MAST-G (Michigan Alcoholism Screening Test - Geriatric version). When assessing substance use among the elderly, a detailed assessment of health impacts and occupational impact is necessary. Comprehensive Geriatric Assessment (CGA) could prove to be a valuable framework for assessment. This tool can assess an older person's medical comorbidities, mental health status, day-to-day functioning and continuing social circumstances. The detailed finding of the tool can help professionals involved in care anticipate and treat complications, identify potentials for rehabilitation, offer social care support and determine the follow-up plans. Therefore, the elderly person has a likelihood of receiving a holistic treatment approach.

Physical Risk Factors	Psychiatric Risk Factors
• Female sex (for prescription drug) • Chronic pain • Male sex (for alcohol), • Physical disabilities or reduced mobility • Transitions in care/living situations • Poor health status • Chronic physical illness/polymorbidity • Significant drug burden/polypharmacy	• Poor coping style • Previous substance use disorder • Previous or concurrent psychiatric illness • Interpersonal difficulties • Perceived/Actual occupational failure • Trauma • Family conflicts • Poor social support

Figure 3: Risk Factors for Substance Use in the Elderly

Treatment Considerations and Overview

There is a substantial body of evidence that brief motivational interventions delivered by various healthcare providers can reduce alcohol consumption among older adults (Fleming et al., 1999; Lin et al., 2010; Moore et al., 2011). Lin and colleagues found that reductions in alcohol use were associated with older adults' concerns about impending outcomes and health risks, reading educational materials, and the positive perception of physicians and practitioners providing advice to reduce drinking (Lin et al., 2010). Two large-scale effectiveness studies have examined the implementation of such brief intervention trials in older adults: the Primary Care Research in Substance Abuse and Mental Health for the Elderly study (PRISM-E; Oslin et al., 2006) and the Brief Intervention and Treatment for Elders (Florida BRITE) project (Schonfeld et al., 2010). Both the trials identified several barriers to the implementation of these brief interventions. The limitations identified are as follows: (1) stigma from the perspective of older patients; (2) lack of training for healthcare professionals in screening and brief interventions for elderly; (3) chronic medical conditions in older adults, which may make it more challenging to identify the role of alcohol use or SUD in decreased functioning or quality of life (Blow & Barry, 2012). Therefore, brief intervention motivational interviewing may be effective, but keeping in mind a powerful empathetic, non-judgmental and supportive stance of the therapist may be of great help.

Certain modifications to a standard pharmacotherapy regimen may need to be made when treating older adults. For instance, detoxification from alcohol or drugs may need to be carried out over a more extended period. The incidence of medical principles (e.g., myocardial ischemia, arrhythmias, orthostatic hypotension) and neurological (e.g., delirium tremens, dizziness, seizures) being higher in elderly patients than in their younger counterparts may make the process even more challenging (Letizia & Reinbolz, 2005).

A study conducted using nationally representative cross-sectional data from 346 private substance treatment centres in the USA, Rothrauff et al. (2011) found that only 18% of these centres could provide age-specific services. It has been noted that in both inpatient and outpatient settings, older adults could relate more to groups of their peers who have experienced similar challenges, such as the death of a spouse, shrinking of the social network, loss of physical vigour and agility, and declining cognitive and sexual function. Therefore, support groups and especially psychological intervention in a group format may be particularly effective.

An expert panel commissioned by SAMHSA (1998) offered specific SUD treatment approaches with older adults. These include:

- Engaging in non-confrontational treatment;
- Focusing on (re)building self-esteem;

- Teaching skills to cope with depression, loneliness, and loss;
- Focusing on (re)building social networks;
- Tailoring content and pace of presentation toward older adults;
- Hiring staff who are interested in and experienced with working with older adults;
- Providing linkages with medical services and community-based services.

Conclusion

The myth that older adults do not use substances and do not use substances problematically as much as adolescents and adults are essentially dispelled by the current statistics and demographic trends. Older-adult substance users may not present with the same symptoms as their younger counterparts and, therefore, may be more challenging to identify. Treatment options generally remain limited, as few programs or health care settings offer tailored interventions for older adults. Health care professionals need to do thorough assessments and enlist evaluation of the medical status and comorbidities, mental health status, and day-to-day functioning. The assessment also needs to focus on the continuing occupational and social circumstances. Knowledge about older-adult substance use and the issues that contribute to the late-onset or maintained addiction in late life will need to be continually updated through clinical and fundamental research.

Furthermore, the advancement and development of interventions that may be more effective for and desired by the generation of older adults need to be tailored and modified to meet the needs of the elderly. Brief interventions blended with supportive psychotherapy, support groups, group psychotherapy can be found beneficial. Newer technologies such as mobile and technology-based interventions need to be made feasibly accessible to the older generation and reduce the adequate assessment and treatment gap.

References

- Bachi, K., Sierra, S., Volkow, N. D., Goldstein, R. Z., & Alia-Klein, N. (2017). Is biological ageing accelerated in drug addiction? *Current opinion in behavioural sciences, 13*, 34-39.
- Blazer, D. G., & Wu, L. T. (2009). The epidemiology of substance use and disorders among middle aged and elderly community adults: national survey on drug use and health. *The American Journal of Geriatric Psychiatry, 17*(3), 237-245.
- Blow, F. C., & Barry, K. L. (2012). Alcohol and substance misuse in older adults. *Current psychiatry reports, 14*(4), 310-319.
- Chhatre, S., Cook, R., Mallik, E., & Jayadevappa, R. (2017). Trends in substance use admissions among older adults. *BMC health services research, 17*(1), 1-8.
- De Gage, S. B., Moride, Y., Ducruet, T., Kurth, T., Verdoux, H., Tournier, M., & Bégaud, B. (2014). Benzodiazepine use and risk of Alzheimer's disease: case-control study. *BMJ, 349*, g5205.
- Degenhardt, L., & Hall, W. (2012). Extent of illicit drug use and dependence, and their contribution to the global burden of disease. *The Lancet, 379*(9810), 55-70.
- Dell'osso, B., & Lader, M. (2013). Do benzodiazepines still deserve a major role in the treatment of psychiatric disorders? A critical reappraisal. *European Psychiatry, 28*(1), 7-20.
- Dorahy, M. J. (2014). The Diagnostic and Statistical Manual of Mental Disorders–5th edition (DSM-5).
- Fleming, M., & Manwell, L. B. (1999). Brief intervention in primary care settings: A primary treatment method for at-risk, problem, and dependent drinkers. *Alcohol Research & Health, 23*(2), 128.
- Garrido, M. M., Prigerson, H. G., Penrod, J. D., Jones, S. C., & Boockvar, K. S. (2014). Benzodiazepine and sedative-hypnotic use among older seriously ill veterans: choosing wisely? *Clinical therapeutics, 36*(11), 1547-1554.

- Gilbertson, R., Ceballos, N. A., Prather, R., & Nixon, S. J. (2009). Effects of acute alcohol consumption in older and younger adults: perceived impairment versus psychomotor performance. *Journal of studies on alcohol and drugs, 70*(2), 242-252.
- Hallgren, M., Högberg, P., & Andréasson, S. (2009). Alcohol consumption among elderly European Union citizens. *Health effects, consumption trends and related issues. Stockholm: Swedish National Institute of Public Health.*
- Kennedy, G. J., Efremova, I., Frazier, A., & Saba, A. (1999). The emerging problems of alcohol and substance abuse in late life. *Journal of Social Distress and the Homeless, 8*(4), 227-239.
- Kuerbis, A., Sacco, P., Blazer, D. G., & Moore, A. A. (2014). Substance abuse among older adults. *Clinics in geriatric medicine, 30*(3), 629-654.
- Letizia, M., & Reinbolz, M. (2005). Identifying and managing acute alcohol withdrawal in the elderly. *Geriatric Nursing, 26*(3), 176-183.
- Lin, J. C., Karno, M. P., Tang, L., Barry, K. L., Blow, F. C., Davis, J. W., & Moore, A. A. (2010). Do health educator telephone calls reduce at risk drinking among older adults in primary care? *Journal of General Internal Medicine, 25*(4), 334-339.
- Matthews, F. E., & Savva, G. M. (2010). Ageing: International Statistical Trends and Prospects. *Principles and Practice of Geriatric Psychiatry*, 83-89.
- Moore, T. M., Elkins, S. R., McNulty, J. K., Kivisto, A. J., & Handsel, V. A. (2011). Alcohol use and intimate partner violence perpetration among college students: Assessing the temporal association using electronic diary technology. *Psychology of Violence, 1*(4), 315.
- Neutel, C. I., Skurtveit, S., & Berg, C. (2012). What is the point of guidelines? Benzodiazepine and z-hypnotic use by an elderly population. *Sleep medicine, 13*(7), 893-897.
- Oslin, D. W. (2000). Alcohol use in late life: disability and comorbidity. *Journal of Geriatric Psychiatry and Neurology, 13*(3), 134-140.
- Oslin, D. W., Grantham, S., Coakley, E., Maxwell, J., Miles, K., Ware, J., & Zubritsky, C. (2006). PRISM-E: comparison of integrated care and enhanced speciality referral in managing at-risk alcohol use. *Psychiatric Services, 57*(7), 954-958.
- Rigler, S. K. (2000). Alcoholism in the elderly. *American Family Physician, 61*(6), 1710-1716.

- Rothrauff, T. C., Abraham, A. J., Bride, B. E., & Roman, P. M. (2011). Substance abuse treatment for older adults in private centers. *Substance abuse, 32*(1), 7-15.
- Rothrauff, T. C., Abraham, A. J., Bride, B. E., & Roman, P. M. (2011). Occupational turnover intentions among substance abuse counsellors. *Journal of Substance Abuse Treatment, 40*(1), 67-76.
- Sadock, B. J., Sadock, V. A., & Ruiz, P. (2017). Comprehensive textbook of psychiatry 10th edition.
- Schonfeld, L., King-Kallimanis, B. L., Duchene, D. M., Etheridge, R. L., Herrera, J. R., Barry, K. L., & Lynn, N. (2010). Screening and brief intervention for substance misuse among older adults: the Florida BRITE project. *American journal of public health, 100*(1), 108-114.
- Sklar, A. L., Gilbertson, R., Boissoneault, J., Prather, R., & Nixon, S. J. (2012). Differential effects of moderate alcohol consumption on performance among older and younger adults. *Alcoholism: Clinical and Experimental Research, 36*(12), 2150-2156.
- UN-DESA. (2009). Population Division of the Department of Economic and Social Affairs of the United Nations Secretariat, World Population Prospects: the 2008 Revision and World Urbanization Prospects: the 2009 Revision.
- United Nations. (2006). United Nations Population Division: World Population Prospects, 2006 Revision.
- US Department of Health and Human Services. (2000). Substance Abuse and Mental Health Services Administration 1998 National Household Survey on Drug Abuse. *Washington, DC: HHS.*
- Verdoux, H., Lagnaoui, R., & Begaud, B. (2005). Is benzodiazepine use a risk factor for cognitive decline and dementia? A literature review of epidemiological studies. *Psychological medicine, 35*(3), 307-315.
- Vos, T., Flaxman, A. D., Naghavi, M., Lozano, R., Michaud, C., Ezzati, M., & Harrison, J. E. (2012). Years lived with disability (YLDs) for 1160 sequelae of 289 diseases and injuries 1990–2010: a systematic analysis for the Global Burden of Disease Study 2010. *The Lancet, 380*(9859), 2163-2196.
- Wittchen, H. U., Jacobi, F., Rehm, J., Gustavsson, A., Svensson, M., Jönsson, B., & Steinhausen, H. C. (2011). The size and burden of mental disorders and other disorders of the brain in Europe 2010. *European Neuropsychopharmacology, 21*(9), 655-679.

* * *

DEATH AND DYING: PERCEPTION IN OLD AGE

Ajaz Ahmad Sofi

Introduction to Death Anxiety

Death is an inevitable subject and serious aspect of human life. The presence of death is relatively natural and common. Death cannot be eliminated and it holds weight in everyone's life, but the way it is perceived by an individual or group may differ. Everyone will be confronted with the end of his or her own life or the loss of a loved one, but although death is inevitable, no one can get ready to deal with the loss due to death and the grief or sorrow that follows (Okechi, 2017).

According to Kesebir (2014), death anxiety is a conscious or unconscious psychological state resulting from a defense mechanism that can be triggered when people feel threatened by death. Death anxiety is all about the fear and anxiety associated with the expectation, and awareness of dying, death and nonexistence. There are several cognitive, emotional as well as motivational factors related to death anxiety and it differs for every person depending upon different factors (Lehto & Stein, 2009).

Death anxiety is considered a basic fear underlying the development and maintenance of numerous psychological conditions (Iverach et al., 2014). This condition is characterized by extreme fear of dying that increases with exposure to an anxiety-provoking situation, e.g., some people might experience increased level of fear in hospitals or near cremation places (American Psychiatric Association, 2013). The American Psychiatric Association does not officially recognize thanatophobia as a disorder. Instead, the anxiety someone may face because of this fear is often attributed to general anxiety (Schroeder, 2019).

Introduction to Perception of Death and Dying

Most of the people have dealt with the death of a loved one at some point of time, but the way how death is perceived by each individual differs depending on their emotionality and coping strategies (Marques, 2019). The different ways in which death is perceived by different individuals, what they think and feel about it actually, is dependent on how they understand life and their distinctive personality. It is exclusively dependent upon how they see life whether it is looked upon from any perspective like scientific, cultural and religious (Okechi, 2017).

If an individual perceives life from a scientific perspective, then they may end up preparing themselves for death prior to the occurrence based on a doctor's report and other scientific evidence. Those who perceive death from the religious end of the pendulum are more or less interested in other injunctions of death. These factors include the enemies causing misfortune by using spiritual powers, deities striking people who offend God, and other spiritually connected forces bringing end to human life. Religion, though, offers an existential framework to answer different questions related to death and dying, but it is the attitude and belief of every single individual that acts as the tracing element to define the impression someone has in the face of death (Okechi, 2017).

People also tend to perceive their death and that of others according to the values of the culture in which they were raised and are living in. While some find the prospect of death to be very frightening, they are not able to contemplate it and possess a strong resistance to it. On the other hand, some perceive death as a natural, usual or tranquil conclusion to their long and productive life. The perception of an individual also depends on how people around them perceive death and react to grief. Socio-psychological, economic and age differentiation are also some of the factors that play an extensive role in defining how different people interpret death. According to Jung, differences in age and experience with life undermines the perception of death (Marques, 2019). According to Frank, divergence in culture, spiritual belief and level of civilization attained by an individual come to play a significant role in shaping their perception and beliefs related to death (Marques, 2019).

The people of advanced nations have accepted death to be a necessary end and have come to terms with it, believing it to be a part and stage of life that will come irrespective of context and time. In the past where death was natural, familiar and a part of everyday life, friends and relatives surrounded the person who was dying, with coffin being buried in the public places without any concerns (Marques, 2019). However, with the passage of time, people started associating death with a feeling of fear and detachment. Hence, it has been transformed into a taboo and forbidden subject in our society. It is especially because of the fact that it exposes human frailty, raises the idea of human mortality while diminishing the defensive fantasies that are built by the people as a wall around the idea of their own death.

The transformation of death from a domestic and familiar idea to a cold, isolated and hidden idea has given rise to unbearable fear and the desire to get away from it. This situation also gives rise to the difficulties faced by many individuals in accepting death as well as coping with the death of their loved ones. The word by which an individual refers to death, whether it is referred to as "passing away", "moving on", or "going to a better place", determines their perception on death (Prater, 2018).

Gender differences have been found to play an important role in death anxiety. According to different researchers, significant findings have been revealed on gender differences in death anxiety. For example, De Paola et al., (2003) observed that elderly women have high level of death anxiety in comparison to elderly men. In India, researchers have observed similar findings among the elderly population (Saini et al., 2016; Madnawat & Kachhawa, 2007).

Death Wishes among Elderly People

Sometimes, people may wish to die due to one or the other reason. A death wish refers to a desire for one's own death. It may be expressed in one's verbal communication or through behaviour that is self-destructive and dangerous. Death wishes are usually found among people who suffer from psychological disorders like depression and anxiety. Most of the time, death wish is developed due to severe or long term suffering related to physical or mental health. However, some older persons can develop a continuous wish to die without having any serious illness. This condition is commonly known as "tiredness of life" or "completed life" (Hartog et al., 2020).

Condition of physical health, psychological wellbeing, social support, and financial security, all can determine the development of death wishes among the people especially the elderly population. If an elderly person is suffering from persistent physical pain that has not be cured, they might wish to die in order to get rid of the pain. Death wishes in the geriatric population may also develop because of psychological complaints like extreme anxiety, worries, disturbing thoughts, restlessness or persistent sadness. Similarly, if an elderly person lacks proper social support from their family members or friends, they might also wish to die. Likewise, the elderly people who have no sufficient financial support from people or authorities around them, they might also develop death wishes, as they might not be in a condition to take care of their regular expenses. Researchers have observed death wishes among 9.5% of the elderly people aged 65 and older who were assessed for health care services provided at home (Harmer et al., 2021).

How the Perception of Death and Dying may Lead to Death Anxiety among the Geriatric Population

Anxiety is one of the common mental problems among the older generation, majorly because of the prevalent feelings of deficiency and disability during this stage of life. Although death is a biological fact but thoughts about death can be dreadful, and most people prefer to avoid such thoughts. Being anxious about death is common among people, but the degree of death anxiety differs from person to person. According to the previous studies conducted on the impact of death anxiety, it was ascertained that women, less religious people and older people have higher death anxiety compared to other individuals (Okechi, 2017). Older adults have been found to be more prone to develop anxiety. It is also because of increased physical and financial dependence, reduced self-confidence, restricted number of friends, chronic illnesses as well as increased susceptibility to physical pain.

Death anxiety is a common phenomenon in all cultures and religions. However, across the different age groups, the older adults have been found at high risk of developing death-related fear and anxiety in comparison to the younger ones. This is because as people age, their experiences with death keep on increasing. This phobia, referred to as thanatophobia, can be described as a feeling of anxiety, fear or dreadfulness that accompanies the thought of death or dying. According to Freud, this phobia is a result of the unconscious belief of individuals about them being immortal (Mohammadpour et al., 2018). Thus, it becomes evident that death anxiety is an integral part of old age and relieving it in older generations might improve their quality of life as well as their psychological health in old age.

The different characteristics of death anxiety include conscious fear of death, fear from the process of dying, a fear for the body after death, a fear of time that will be lost, a fear from the sufferings accompanied by the process and loneliness. Death is closely associated with old age, as by this time, life prepares many people psychologically for leaving the world. The aging population and older adults have to face the prospect of death. Therefore, as they approach it, they are likely to experience anxiety, which results from a strong fear of death and a minimized sense of safety (Wysokinsi et al., 2016).

This fear of death is an ultimate result of having made death a taboo subject, giving rise to people's unwillingness to discuss it or even mention it. Just the thought about death may result in anxiety, fear and uncertainty. Attitude towards death is highly individualized, and the variation in death anxiety depends on how one perceives death and several factors, including gender, religiosity, age, environmental conditions, lifestyle, access to health services and psychological state.

Psychological states such as generalized anxiety disorder can lead to higher death anxieties in several older adults.

Death anxiety of an individual is closely related to their perception of death. According to Tjernberg & Bökberg (2020), the elderly people who perceived death as a natural occurrence as well as a component of life were less worried about the incidence that is yet to take place. They were more interested in trying to live the present moment optimistically and wholeheartedly. They accept death, are more at peace with the concept of death and are ready to die. Others who are highly religious and devoted to their cultural practices and traditions are not much welcoming towards death and live in an unconscious belief. They tend to deny death consciously and they believe that death is a destruction. They are surrounded with extreme fear and worries about their family and friends. This negative attitude towards death connects the instance of death to both mental as well as physical loneliness. Some are anxious and worried about the process of dying; fearing it to be very painful, no matter how old they are or how many deaths they have witnessed in their life. They desire for a peaceful and painless death, preferably while sleeping (Fleming, 2017).

There is another group of people who are tired of their lives and the sufferings accompanied with it and are desperate to reach the end. They desire to meet death as soon as possible, because according to them, if death is near, there is no point in surviving even a single day more (Fleming, 2017). The group of individuals who readily accept death are also willing to discuss about it with their family members; they take it as a humorous topic. While there is another group of people: no matter what, they are not ready to accept that their life will come to an end very soon, they also ignore this topic and never tend to be interested in discussing about it.

The perception of death also depends on the impact of death on the physical health of an individual, and how the death will feel like in the physical body that depends on the reason of death, how long it takes, whether pain or any other symptom is caused and how the body appears during the process of dying. In certain cases, like accidents, the physical process of death is relatively quick and virtually painless compared to cancer, where the death is a prolonged process that requires constant medical attention to manage the pain (Wyeokinsi et al., 2016). Although the physiological process of death is consistent across individuals, the timeline and experience can differ (Kumar & Cavallaro, 2017).

Effects of Perception of Death and Dying on Elderly People

Though people try to adapt and adjust to the loss as part of the grieving process, but there are certain factors on which the emotional, psychological, behavioural and physical response of individuals depends, including the age of the bereaved individual, personality traits, ethnicity, religiosity, resilience, relationship with the deceased person and support received. The bereavement of a close friend renders a significant negative impact on the physical health, mental health, role limitations and social functioning. The most frequent immediate response to bereavement is shock, numbness and a sense of disbelief, especially because the reality of death has not yet entered awareness (Katzenmeyer, 2001).

Anxiousness or anxiety towards death may result in various mental health conditions, including depression, isolation and generalized anxiety disorder. In some cases, when the person is likely to die very soon, they isolate themselves from others, believing that they will soon lie in the bed of death; hence isolating themselves now can be better, and they start reflecting on their past life. They also restrict movement, stay in one part of the house and contact less frequently with others. These people are mostly surrounded by negative thoughts about death, themselves and the people around them. The deterioration in mental health, social functioning and impaired emotional role also depends on the extent of social involvement of the individual. Socially inactive individuals are more likely to face the issues than socially active people. Moreover, social support plays an important role in maintaining overall health of aging people (Geller, 2017).

The prevalence of depression increases with age making it one of the prevalent conditions among the older generation, which hampers their quality of life and well-being. Depressive symptoms not only indicate psychological well-being but also predict longevity and functional health. Depression also forms a link to several other physical, psychological and social problems. The sufferers are not able to cope up with the situation themselves and require professional help in order to minimize their feeling of grief, loneliness and sadness. According to Lander et al., 2000, clinical depression is more often overlooked among the elderly population.

Role of Mental Health Professionals to Deal with the Issues that may arise because of Different Perceptions of Death and Dying

By already being aware that death will touch everyone's life one or the other day, people can be proactive about learning new mechanisms to cope up with the process of dying and grieving. However, the real experience of grief cannot be felt, but a support system can be kept intact, along with learning all the necessary skills that are required to take care of one's mental health to minimize the suffering.

All the complaints of an older adult must be shared with a primary care physician, as they will diagnose the condition along with the possible causes. The diagnosis will help determine whether the individual is suffering from an anxiety disorder or mental health condition, or both. They can also distinguish serious health problems such as Parkinson's disease and Alzheimer's disease. In order to treat the death anxiety, both provider and patient must work as a team.

The mental health workers spend time with older adults, taking care of them and helping them minimize the feelings of loneliness and grief. They also adopt various strategies to reduce the impact of these issues. Treatment options for anxiety involve medication, therapy, coping skills, stress reduction and support of family members. Mental health professionals provide therapies to the older people when they face difficulty managing their emotions with the transition of age. These therapies help them find meaning in their lives, new sources of enjoyment and new support systems. Therapies also help identify the actual cause of anxiety and how to deal with the symptoms. Along with managing the emotions, these therapies also help elderly people cope up with the fear of death and grief if they have witnessed the death of a loved one or are surrounded by anxieties related to their own death.

Cognitive-behavioural therapies given to older adults help them change their thinking patterns that are the main reason for their fear, along with altering the way they react to anxiety-provoking circumstances. Therapy resolves the problem of anxiety and underlying reasons that lead to anxiety by teaching several relaxation skills and coping mechanisms to the people (Liu et at., 2019). Therapies make a patient ready to face their fears, and when they are ready, different techniques of exposure are imparted to them for desensitizing the patients to circumstances, which were the trigger points for them to feel extremely fearful.

Medication does not eliminate the symptoms or cure anxiety but helps the person to be in control while they are receiving therapy. The main medicines prescribed for anxiety disorders to control some of the symptoms include antidepressants, beta-blockers and anti-anxiety drugs. Death being a naturally occurring phenomenon that demands retiring formality from humans, religion helps individuals to abate the anxieties and overwhelm those who are not able to accept death.

Psychological Intervention for Anxiety related to Death and Dying

Relaxation: Relaxation exercises can be very helpful for dealing with anxiety issues related to death and dying. Different kinds of relaxation exercises can be used to overcome anxiety and bring calmness in mind and body. Different relaxation exercises like deep breathing and visualisation exercises can be very useful in doing away with anxiety related to death and dying (Cadman, 2018).

Mindfulness: Mindfulness is all about being in the present and being aware of the surroundings. It is contrary to the idea of getting involved in unrealistic worries related to the future and probable regrets related to the past. The process of mindfulness involves focusing actively on the present by deliberately attending to the details in the environment while using different sensory organs. According to the review of a research, being mindful can defuse the fear of death and dying (George Mason University, 2011).

Exposure Therapy: Exposure techniques aim at the confrontation of the sources of unrealistic fears. It means instead of running away from talking about death and dying, if a person would confront the matter in a more adaptive way, the anxiety would not be overwhelming for the person. The process involves acknowledging one's concerns and then facing different anxiety-provoking situations or conversations. For example, if an elderly person avoids visiting a hospital for routine checkup because of their death anxiety, they would need to visit this anxiety-provoking place in order to reduce the anxiety. According to a research, in vivo exposure can reduce death anxiety while developing helpful adaptive strategies to deal with emotional reactions (Furer & Walker, 2008).

Palliative Care Techniques that can help the Elderly to Deal with Death and Dying

Palliative care is an approach of medical care that enhances the quality of life of the patient who is suffering from lifethreatening illness as well as their families (Singh, 2019). It eliminates and minimizes the suffering of the patient by identifying the correct assessment and treatment procedures for pain and other problems, including physical, spiritual and psychosocial issues. Palliative care includes addressing the practical needs of the patient and availing them with bereavement counselling. It supports the patients, gives them a new energy and helps them to live an active life until death. Palliative care also includes various techniques to minimize the pain with enhancing their breathing.

Comfort care tends to be an essential part of medical care for the old age people who are on the verge of death. It is the only care that might help or provide relief to a person who is dying (Stibich, 2020). The ultimate goal of the care is to eliminate or relieve the suffering as much as possible and enhance their quality of life with prioritizing the wishes of the dying person. A dying person might require both emotional as well as physical attention. Being surrounded by their loved ones along with getting adequate support from health care providers at the last moment is apt for some people who want to end their life peacefully.

Elderly people might be having certain physical complaints like chest discomforts, body pain, breathing-related issues, restlessness, temperature-sensitivity, issues related to digestion and fatigue or physical tiredness. Therefore, some techniques to relieve the pain of dying people need to be adopted. Providing adequate comfort to enhance their breathing, appropriate medicines and lotions to minimize skin irritation and digestive problems might also be helpful.

According to Mohanti (2009), effective communication between health care professionals and the caretakers of the elderly people plays a key role when it comes to ethical palliative support. The needs of the elderly must to be communicated well to the health care providers. Family members must take care of what an elderly person is trying to communicate verbally. They also have to look into what the elderly people communicate non-verbally through gestures or facial expressions. Health care providers need to be well trained in understanding what the elderly people are trying to convey even when they are not able to communicate verbally.

Complete end of life care also includes helping the dying individual cope up with their emotional and mental distress. In order to handle this distress, conversations about how the person is feeling currently must be encouraged, or one might contact a counsellor who can provide proper care and help the person in their last days. The family members of the dying person must behave appropriately. They must not start grieving in front of the person as it might deteriorate their condition since they already have fears, worries and concerns about the family members and friends whom they will be leaving behind in coming time.

Do not keep the person isolated; a simple act of physical contact might also soothe the person to some extent. A comforting and cheered up environment can pump up the mood of the dying person and it can facilitate to make death easier. Therefore, people in the family should try to maintain a comforting surrounding. Playing soft music in low sound might also help the person as music improves mood, enhances relaxation while minimizing the pain. Though just being present with the dying person is enough, but family members might also share some of the good memories of the person and the good deeds of the person to help them relax.

Some of the dying people might give their spiritual needs the utmost priority, so resolving all the unsettled disputes with friends or family might be useful. The individuals, who find solace in their faith might also be provided with the environment to talk about their religious community, pray or listen to religious music. It will give them a very comfortable death while their mind is kept away from all the worldly affairs. Researchers have observed that years of spiritual solace plays an important role in reducing fear of death. This shows the importance of the religious practices in managing terror related to death (Maheshwari & Mukherjee, 2019).

Implications

Although we saw that different researchers have found significant observations regarding perception of death and dying among the elderly, many people are still unaware about the implications of these findings. Since the perception of death and dying is not formed overnight, the developmental progression of the same among the elderly needs to be analysed on time. Role of the family members of the elderly population cannot be ignored. Family plays a very important role to care the elderly (Das, 2012). Family members of the elderly need to be careful in order to facilitate the communication between the patient and the health care providers. Psychological intervention needs to be given due importance whenever the need arises. Psychological evaluation of the elderly need to be conducted on regular basis. Psychological requirements need to be explored so that the elderly can be helped on time.

Conclusion

Death is inevitable and this fact makes it an inseparable part of our life. The perception of death and dying varies from person to person. There are different factors, which influence the perception of death and dying. Some of these factors include age, gender cultural norms, threatening disease, spirituality, life experience, and social support (Kisvetrová & Kralova, 2014). Although, death anxiety is very common among people, it is because of different factors that the feeling becomes overwhelming.

An unfavourable perception of death and dying can have an adverse effect on the psychological, physical and social aspects of the life of elderly people. The elderly people can face psychological disorders, physical complaints and social problems very commonly. Mental health professionals play a key role for the care of the elderly people. Different psychological tools including supportive counselling, relaxation exercise, mindfulness and different types of psychotherapies are employed by mental health professionals to help the elderly deal with death anxiety.

Palliative care techniques are aimed at helping the elderly people to improve their quality of life in the last days. The collective approach of a team of physicians, psychologists, physical therapists, nurses and other health care professionals focuses on employing various techniques for the good of the geriatric population.

References

- American Psychiatric Association. (2013). Diagnostic and Statistical Manual of Mental Disorders (Vol. 5). *American Psychiatric Publishing.*
- Cadman, B. (2018). What to know about the fear of death. *Medical News Today.*
- Das, S. (2012). The role of Family in Health and Healthcare utilization among Elderly.
- Fleming, J. (2017). Here's what People in their 90s really think about Death. *The Conversation.*
- Furer, P., & Walker, J. (2008). Death Anxiety: A Cognitive-Behavioral Approach. *Journal of Cognitive Psychotherapy.*
- Geller, H. (2017). The Importance of Socialization in Aging. *Elder Care Alliance.*
- George Mason University. (2011). Being Mindful can neutralize Fears of Death and Dying. *Science Daily.*
- Harmer, B., Lee, S., Duong, T. & Saadabadi, A. (2021). Suicidal Ideation. *PubMed.*
- Hartog, I.D., Zomers, M.L., & Thiel, G.J. et al. (2020). Prevalence and characteristics of older Adults with a persistent Death wish without severe Illness: A large cross-sectional Survey. *BMC Geriatr.*
- Iverach, L., Menzies, R.G. & Menzies, R.E. (2014). Death Anxiety and its role in Psychopathology: Reviewing the status of a transdiagnostic construct. *Clinical Psychology Review*, 580-593.
- Katzenmeyer, L. M. (2001). Adolescent Bereavement and Social Support Perception of need according to Gender.

- Kesebir P.A. (2014). A quiet Ego quiets Death Anxiety: Humility as an existential Anxiety buffer. *Journal of Personality and Social Psychology.*
- Kisvetrová, H. & Kralova, J. (2014). Basic factors influencing Death Anxiety. *Ceskoslovenska Psychologie.* 58.
- Kumar, S., & Cavallaro, L. (2017). Researcher self-care in emotionally demanding research: A proposed conceptual framework. *Qualitative Health Research.*
- Lander, M, Wilson, K. & Chochinov, H.M. (2000). Depression and the dying Older Patient. *PubMed.Gov.*
- Lehto, R.H., & Stein, K.F. (2009). Death anxiety: An analysis of evolving concept. *Research and Theory for Nursing Practice: An International Journal.*
- Liu, W.M., Forbat, L. & Anderson, K. (2019). Correction: Death of a close friend: Short and long-term impacts on physical, psychological and social well-being. *PLOS ONE.*
- Madnawat, A. V. & Kachhawa, P. S. (2007). Age, Gender, and Living Circumstances: Discriminating Older Adults on Death Anxiety. *Research Gate.*
- Maheshwari, S. & Mukherjee, T. (2019). Role of Social detachment in Coping with Death Anxiety: A Case of elderly Hindu pilgrims. *OMEGA-Journal of Death and Dying.*
- Marques, D. T. (2019). Perceptions, Attitudes, and Teaching about Death and Dying in the Medical School of the Federal University of Acre, Brazil. *Revista Brasileira de Educaco Medica.*
- Mohammadpour, A. et al. (2018). Investigating the role of Perception of Aging and associated factors in Death Anxiety among the Elderly. *ClinInterv Aging.*
- Mohanti, B. K. (2009). Ethics in Palliative Care. *Indian Journal of Palliative Care.*
- Okechi, O. S. (2017). Culture, Perception/Belief about Death and their implications to the Awareness and Control of the Socio-Economic, Environmental and Health Factors Surrounding Lower Life Expectancy in Nigeria. *Acta Psychopathologica.*
- Prater E.S. (2018). Perceptions of Death and the effects of Emotion. *Mckendree.Edu.*
- Saini, P., Patidar, A.B., Kaur, R., Kaur, M., & Kaur, J. (2016). Death Anxiety and its associated factors among Elderly Population of Ludhiana City, Punjab. *Indian Journal of Gerontology.*

- Schroeder, S. (2019). Everything you should know about Thanatophobia. *Healthline.*
- Singh, A. & Mishra, N. (2009). Loneliness, Depression and Sociability in Old Age. *Industrial Psychology Journal.*
- Stibich, M. & Goldman, R. (2020). How to Deal With Death and Dying as You Age. *Very Well Mind.*
- Tjernberg, J. & Bökberg, C. (2020). Older Persons' Thoughts about Death and Dying, and their Experiences of care in end-of-life: A qualitative Study. *BMC Nurs.*
- Wysokinski, M. et al. (2016). Elderly People's Acceptance of Death: A Study of a Polish Cohort. *International Journal of Environmental Research and Public Health.*

* * *

SPIRITUALITY AND MENTAL HEALTH IN GERIATRIC POPULATION

Sahithya B.R. and Rithvik S. Kashyap

Introduction

Religion and spirituality are two important social and psychological factors in the lives of most people, especially the elderly. While religion is more structured, institutionally based, and involves traditional rituals and practices; spirituality is a more general term, not associated with a particular group or organization, and refers to the intangible and immaterial. It can refer to feelings, thoughts, experiences and behaviours related to the soul, or to a search for the sacred or truth . Traditional religion involves accountability and responsibility; whereas, spirituality has fewer requirements. Even when individuals reject traditional religion, they might consider themselves to be spiritual.

Spirituality is a broad concept, usually associated with searching for the meaning and existence of life (Chattopadhyay, 2007). Spirituality is often referred to the self- introspection and reflection on one's meaningful life, with the intention to instill positive attitude, hope, coping ability, and thereby reducing stress. Spirituality has a strong parallel to Maslow's (1970) 'Self-actualization' as described in 'hierarchical theory of human motivation'.

According to Fisher (2011), spirituality is multi-faceted and can be divided into four domains: personal, communal, environmental and transcendental. He described spiritual health as a dynamic state of being, reflected in the quality of relationships that people have in all the four domains of spiritual well-being: (i) Personal domain where a person intra-relates with self; (ii) Communal domain, with in-depth interpersonal relationships; (iii) Environmental domain, connecting with nature; and finally (iv) Transcendental domain, relating to something or someone beyond the human level. Spirituality is gaining importance in recent years, and much research is now focusing on spiritual health. In fact, the World Health Organization and its member countries are exploring spirituality as the fourth dimension of health (Chaves, Gil, Chaves & Gil, 2015). A number of studies suggest that religious or spiritual involvement is associated with better outcomes in both physical and mental health (Chattopadhyay, 2007).

Indian Religion and Spirituality

India is a culturally rich country with several languages and religions. Although India's national census does not officially recognise any racial or ethnic categories, there are several languages, religions, and cultural practices, making India one of the most diverse populations in the world. In India, religion is the foundation for most areas of life for most individuals and families. According to the 2011 census (Government of India), 79.8% of the population of India practices Hinduism, 14.2% adheres to Islam, 2.3% adheres to Christianity, 1.7% adheres to Sikhism, 0.7% adheres to Buddhism, and 0.3% adheres to Jainism. India is the birthplace of Buddhism, Jainism and Sikhism. In India religion is more publicly visible than it is in most Western countries mostly due to pomp and celebrations of various festivals, as well as temples, monasteries, and several sacred spaces people visit for pilgrimage.

Hinduism originally known as Sanatana Dharma, which means "eternal law" in Sanskrit, is one of the oldest organized religions in the world, tracing its roots back to 5000 BC. Due to its evolutionary development over a long period, Hinduism created diverse spiritualities that are dependent on timely needs. The unique features of this ever changing, socio-cultural-religious tradition are acceptance of diverse ideas, their eclectic adaptation, and skilful creation of a new syncretic spirituality (Junghare, 2016). Hindus follow a range of customs and practices most of which have been verbally transmitted from generation to generation, hence Hinduism can be interpreted diversely. Therefore, pinpointing what constitutes Hinduism is difficult, with some suggesting that it is an umbrella term that encompasses various religions and traditions within it. Nonetheless, in all its forms and variations, Hinduism has been particularly influential in Indian society. It affects everyday life and social interactions among people through the many Hindu-inspired festivities, artistic works and temples. Since Hinduism is a major religion practiced by almost 80% of the nation's population, the focus of this chapter is mostly on spirituality derived from Hinduism.

Hinduism's philosophical core is rooted for the most part in the three fundamental Hindu scriptures: the Vedas , the Upanishads , and the Bhagavad Gita (Goswami, 2014). Hinduism is not a monothetic religion, rather is a collection of teachings from several religious scholars from various schools of philosophy. Nonetheless, the various schools share several basic concepts. All the schools differentiate between matter and spirit. Spirit is understood within two main categories: eternal soul (the atman), and the supreme self or God (the paramatman). Most Hindus believe that the real self (atman) is distinct from the temporary body made of matter (prakriti). The eternal soul identifies with matter and is entrapped by maya (illusion). A soul undergoes numerous rebirths, until it is purified of all illusions and desire, and then it finally unites with that of the paramatman. The two principles that dictate a Hindu person's life are "karma" (action) and "dharma" (the righteous way to do the work)—the concept that every action leaves an imprint on one's Atman (soul or spirit). Karma refers to a universal law which dictates good actions to produce good results and bad actions to produce bad results for the doer. This theory of Karma greatly influences the people's view of life, suffering and death. Many Hindus therefore may come to believe that pain and suffering (both physical and psychosocial) are perhaps the result of bad karma, and not essentially of medical or mental illness (Aery, Das & Dharma, 2008; Thakrar, Das & Sheikh, 2018).

Later, yoga guru Patanjali advocated eight-fold path of yoga to purify the soul and attain Moksha, which could be achieved through adopting a lifestyle including 8 steps of yoga: (i) Yama (self control) with five rules, i.e., non-violence, truthfulness, not stealing, chastity and the avoidance of greed; (ii) Niyam (observance) through purity, contentment, austerity, study of Vedas and devotion of God; (iii) Asana (posture); (iv) Pranayama (control of the breath); (v) Pratyahara (restraint); (vi) Dharana (steadying of the mind); (vii) Dhyana (Meditation); and (viii) Samadhi (deep meditation). Other Indic regions such as Buddhisms and Jainism also have similar philosophies. For instance, Buddhism teaches its disciples to lead a well-ordered life by opting for a middle course between self-indulgence and extreme simplicity. Jainism emphasizes non-violence, vegetarianism, warmth and human sympathy. Another Indic religion Sikhism advocates spiritual devotion and reverence of God at all times while practicing the ideals of honesty, compassion, humility and generosity in everyday life.

Indian Spirituality and Ageing

Indian schools of philosophy also regulated the stages of life. Depending upon physical, psychological, familial, social and spiritual needs of an individual, life was divided into four stages: (i) Brahmcharya (studentship), (ii) Grihastha (householder), (iii) Vanprasth (forest dweller), and (iv) Sanyasa (ascetic). *Brahmcharya* includes all round developments (including formal, informal education) of the child from birth to facilitate the individual to stand on his/her own feet in later stages of life. The second stage, *Grihastha* (householder life) is a phase to perform all the duties according to dharma (right functioning). In this phase of adult life, an individual focuses on proper upkeep, stability, growth and development of human race, enjoying worldly life, earning money, having children, taking care of the family and its welfare, while also performing various duties required by family and society. During the *Vanprasth* stage, the individual, who is much older now handsover the household duties to one's successor, and leave the worldly life, luxuries and enjoyments. In the final *Sanyasa* (ascetic) stage of life, the individual gives up everything and exclusively perform intense "sadhana" (deep meditation), with the intention to reach the final goal of human life: "moksha" (Tiwari & Pandey, 2013).

Things have changed in the modern world, with the arrival of other religious practices, cultural and economic changes brought to India from the Mughals and British, and as well as due to influence of industrialization and globalization, the ancient way of living have changed significantly. However, despite these changes, elders in India are respected within the family as well as in the community for their wisdom and life experience, and are often sought for advice. They are considered as custodians of the civilisation and are given special status in the society and are seen as a valuable asset to the community (Cox & Newtson, 1993). Unlike in the Western country, in India, the grown children while taking care of their normal family and social responsibilities are also obliged to provide for the long-term care of their parents in the prime years of their lives (Kumari & Sharma, 2018). Therefore, it is uncommon for Indians to send their elderly parents to old age home like their Western counterparts, and it is quite normal for elderly to stay with their children and grandchildren in a common household.

While the present-day Indians may not rigidly practice the religious teachings, old age which is also a period of retirement, is mostly spent in spiritual pursuits, such as visiting temples, conducting community religious events, and travelling to holy places. In addition to their family, the religious community is the largest source of social support to the elderly, and involvement in religious or spiritual organizations is one of the most common type of voluntary social activity in India.

Spirituality and Mental Health among the Elderly

Spirituality, which roughly translates to search for truth and an attempt to attain Moksha can offer individuals a sense of meaning and purpose in life, which in turn can affect health behaviours and social and family relationships. For instance, an exploratory study by Kumari and Sharma (2018) on 20 elderly people living in Delhi, found that most elderly were engaged in spiritual practices in their day-to-day life to derive their meaning and purpose, exploring their own selves, looking to the answers of fundamental questions of their lives by the means of spirituality. Although their practices were different, they all believe in spirituality as a meaningful engagement leading towards their active and happy ageing.

In another study, Chokkanathan (2013) examined religiosity and well-being of older adults through face-to-face interviewing of 321 randomly selected older adults in Chennai, India. The direct-effect model posited a direct inverse relation between religiosity and psychological distress. In a recent study, Singh et al. (2019) used a mixed methods study to assess the associations between a culturally tailored intervention and pre-existing religious/ spiritual practices with indicators of well-being and factors which contribute to happiness among elderly rural women from Haryana state, India. The study consisted of three groups: field experimental group, practitioners of pre-existing religious or spiritual practices for at least 6 weeks, and non-practitioners of religious or spiritual practices. All the three groups completed self-report measures of overall happiness and life satisfaction, global health, quality of life, and health status. Results revealed that field experimental group participants improved significantly on physical health, body balancing, and self-care post religious or spiritual practices. Researchers also found that practitioners of pre-existing religious or spiritual practices were found significantly different from the non-practitioners on some indicators of health, quality of life, and well-being. These findings stress the importance of religious or spiritual practices among elderly rural women.

The impact of spirituality on the health of older persons specifically has been a growing concern and there are a number of empirical and theoretical reviews on the topic (Zimmer et al., 2016). There is also strong evidence of a connection between religiosity and mental health particularly among older persons. For example, Portnoff, McClintock, Lau, Choi and Miller (2017) investigated the association between spirituality and depression in three culturally diverse countries : the United States, China, and India. Their study sample included 5,512 participants in the age range of 18–75 years. They found that a high level of personal spirituality decreased by half the relative risk of moderate depression across all 3 countries. Spirituality in phenomenological terms was found to be protective against suicidal ideation across all 3 countries. The researchers concluded that phenomenological spirituality was protective against depression in the population aged 18-75 years. In another study, Mhaske (2013) examined the relationship between spiritual beliefs and mental health among 200 elderly persons living in institutions or old age homes in Pune city. All the participants belonged to middle socio-economic status, were aged between 60-85 years, and were staying for at least one year in the institution or old-age home. The researchers found negative and significant correlation between spiritual beliefs and mental health, suggesting that spiritual beliefs were protective against mental illness. In similar lines, Udhayakumar and Ilango (2012) studied 30 elders practising spiritual meditation in Tamil Nadu. The researchers found that higher levels of spiritual belief were associated with better quality of mental health among the elders practising spirituality. In the same year, Udhayakumar and Ilango (2012) explored the influence of spirituality in reducing the level of stress and improving the quality of wellbeing among the elderly practicing spirituality. The findings demonstrated that spirituality reduces stress, and has a positive effect on mental and physical health of the practitioners.

Singh and Kedare (2014) assessed the prevalence of depression in medically ill elderly patients, coping strategies used by them, and spirituality as a way of coping. The researchers found that non depressed patients had better coping with stressful situations, they used more of task oriented and avoidance-based coping, and were more spiritual when compared to depressed patients. These results suggest that perhaps spirituality may mediate coping styles and lead to better mental health. Tiwari Singh and Chand (2016) assessed and compared the level of spirituality and psychological wellbeing of elderly from institutionalized and non-institutionalized settings. They found that spirituality and psychological wellbeing were positively correlated, and concluded that elderly who have higher levels of spirituality have higher levels of psychological well being.

In recent years, Kapri and Kathpalia (2019) examined the impact of spirituality on well-being of the elderly persons. Result of this study showed that all elderly persons recognized the importance of spirituality in their lives, and its relationship with old age is in the capacity to bear the limitations, losses and difficulties that are inherent to the process, confronting the suffering involved. The researchers concluded that the influence of this capacity on Quality of life is perceived, principally, in the psychological health domain, favouring the development of positive thoughts and feelings which give them high levels of satisfaction with their lives.

All these studies cited above suggest a strong relation between spirituality and mental health. However, unlike other aspects of mental health such as psychosocial variables like cognitive biases, etc., empirical research on spirituality and its effect on mental health of the elderly is plagued by several problems. First and foremost, spirituality is not a specific term, and it is difficult to measure it. Spirituality means several things to different people, and is highly subjective. There is also a lack of validated tools to measure spirituality that have been standardized for the Indian population. Adding to the problem of measurement are different religions, philosophies and belief systems that make spirituality a diverse term that is difficult to measure. Hence having a single questionnaire to measure it can be very challenging for researchers. Perhaps it is due to these shortcomings, that there are very few researches done in this domain in India. Most of the studies on spirituality and mental health are conducted in Western countries with the assumption that the findings may be generalized to the population world over. However, Eastern practices of spirituality, especially in culturally rich countries such as in India are very different from the West. For instance, individuals in the West may believe death is the end of life, whereas Indians believe in life after birth, and that death is not really the end, but a new beginning. Hence, while the possibility of inevitable death may cause death anxiety in Western countries, it may not have the same impact in India, as the spiritual meaning attached to death is quite different. Further, within India, there are several religions and schools of philosophy that differ drastically from one another. Hence, it is imperative that researchers develop valid instruments to measure spirituality as practised by Indians across different religions and cultures.

Potential Mechanisms of Spirituality

Empirical research has gathered strong evidence connecting spirituality with better mental health among the elderly. However, the mechanisms driving the relationship are not well researched and remain unexplained. Zimmer et al. (2016) outlined some of the mechanisms through which spirituality may offer therapeutic effects on mental health of the elderly. They deliberated on social support; health promoting behaviours; stress reduction; and psychological factors as some of the mechanisms through which spirituality promotes better mental health.

Social Support: Quite often, spirituality is closely associated with spiritual or religious institutions, which often become a focal point for interaction, exchange and support. This is where the elderly get an opportunity for social interaction, and meet friends with similar interests. They get to share their problems, discuss existential crises and gather understanding.

Health Promoting Behaviours: Spirituality often encourages healthy lifestyle and health promoting behaviours. Behaviours that put health at risk such as drugs, alcohol, etc., are discouraged, while encouraging practices such as meditation, yoga, plant based diet, etc. Recent research also suggests that spirituality associated with activities such as meditation and yoga, promote both physical and mental health (Ross & Thomas, 2010).

Coping with Stress: Spirituality also exerts influence on how the individual copes with stressful life events. One of the characteristic features of spirituality is to make sense of adversity and to face adversity (Pargament & Raiya, 2007). This is especially important for the elderly who are trying to cope with many adverse life events such as loss of loved ones, retirement, loss of identity, physical illness and death anxiety (McFadden, 1995). By prompting a meaning to life, spirituality can bolster optimism, which helps in reducing the impact of stressful life events (Krause, 2003).

Psychological Factors: Spirituality helps individuals look at other people, life situations and ageing in a different perspective, give a new meaning that they have not thought of before. Spirituality not only promotes traits such as forgiveness, empathy, gratitude, compassion and altruism, but reduces anger and hostility. By promoting forgiveness, and reducing feelings of hostility and anger, spirituality has shown to be beneficial for health (Schaie, Krause & Booth, 2004).

Incorporating Spirituality into Geriatric Mental Health Care

Given the significant positive impact spirituality can have on the mental health of the elderly, which has been demonstrated by research findings, it is not far fetched to suggest that elements of spirituality should be incorporated by therapists and clinicians treating the elderly. Having knowledge of different religions, philosophies and spiritual practices and help clinicians establish rapport with the elderly persons, and enable them to trust the therapists. For instance, elderly may want to discuss different aspects of spirituality with their therapists, especially on sensitive topics such as death, life after death, etc. It is therefore important that the treating team be abreast these so that they may discuss the same with their patients (Lodha & De Sousa, 2018). While, religion and spirituality are recognised as effective coping resources, they have been largely ignored in favour of traditional psychotherapy. Therefore, it is important that we figure out how to integrate them into clinical practice. Further, incorporating these elements during the training can sensitise clinicians on the spiritual need of the patients, and explore spirituality as an alternative therapy for the elderly patients.

Implications and Conclusion

As evidence by several research findings, spirituality is an important determinant of physical, emotional, and social health among the elderly. Spirituality can affect mental and physical health. It is an important factor that enables the elderly to cope with retirement, isolation, physical health problems and life stresses. Spirituality offers social support, promotes healthy behaviours, helps cope with stress and makes an individual hopeful and positive. Studies have suggested that spiritual elderly people have better mental health and are less likely to develop depression and anxiety than those who do not. Given such immense benefits of spirituality, it is important that health professionals understand, acknowledge and address the spiritual needs of the patients, which may make the practice of medicine more holistic, ethical and compassionate. It is worthwhile to mention that clinicians such as psychiatrists, psychologists, social workers and nurses who cater to mental health needs of patients are trained in different aspects of religions, schools of philosophy and spiritual practices, so that they can use these sensitive components when addressing mental health issues of the elderly.

References

- Aery, V., Das, R., & Dharma, K. (2008). Hinduism: the tradition speaks for itself. *Caring for Hindu Patients,* 1.
- Chattopadhyay, S. (2007). Religion, spirituality, health and medicine: Why should Indian physicians care? *Journal of Postgraduate medicine, 53*(4), 262.
- Chokkanathan, S. (2013). Religiosity and well-being of older adults in Chennai, India. *Aging & mental health, 17*(7), 880-887.
- Cox, H. & Newtson, R. (1993) 'History of social gerontology', Sociological Practice: Vol. 11, No. 1, Article 4.

- Fisher, J. (2011). The four domains model: Connecting spirituality, health and well-being. *Religions, 2*(1), 17-28.
- Goswami, S. (2014). Spiritual dimensions of Indian culture. *Journal of Sociology and Social Work, 2*(1), 241-256.
- Government of India (2011). Census of India 2011 provisional population totals. *New Delhi: Office of the Registrar General and Census Commissioner.*
- Junghare, I. Y. (2016). Hindu Spirituality: A Theory for Everything. *International Journal of Religion & Spirituality in Society, 6*(3).
- Kapri, A., & Kathpalia, J. (2019). Impact of spirituality on well-being of old aged people. *Indian Journal of Health & Wellbeing, 10.*
- Krause, N. (2003). Religious meaning and subjective well-being in late life. *The Journals of Gerontology Series B: Psychological Sciences and Social Sciences, 58*(3), S160-S170.
- Kumari, S., & Sharma, A. (2018). Spirituality: a tool for learning, change and adaptation of elderly in changing Indian family. *International Journal of Learning and Change, 10*(1), 33-53.
- Lodha, P., & De Sousa, A. (2018). Geriatric mental health: The challenges for India. *Journal of Geriatric Mental Health, 5*(1), 16.
- Maslow, A. H. (1970). Motivation and Personality (2nd ed.). New York: Harper and Row.
- McFadden, S. H. (1995). Religion and well-being in an aging society. *Journal of Social Issues, 51*(2), 145-160.
- Mhaske, R. S. (2013). Spiritual Beliefs and Mental Health among Institutionalized Aged. *Journal of Psychosocial Research, 8*(1).
- Pargament, K. I., & Raiya, H. A. (2007). A decade of research on the psychology of religion and coping: Things we assumed and lessons we learned. *Psyke & logos, 28*(2), 25-25.
- Portnoff, L., McClintock, C., Lau, E., Choi, S., & Miller, L. (2017). Spirituality cuts in half the relative risk for depression: Findings from the United States, China, and India. *Spirituality in Clinical Practice, 4*(1), 22.
- Ross, A., & Thomas, S. (2010). The health benefits of yoga and exercise: a review of comparison studies. *The journal of alternative and complementary medicine, 16*(1), 3-12.
- Schaie, K. W., Krause, N., & Booth, A. (Eds.) (2004). Religious influences on health and well-being in the elderly. Springer Publishing Company.

- Singh, D., & Kedare, J. (2014). A study of depression in medically ill elderly patients with respect to coping strategies and spirituality as a way of coping. *Journal of Geriatric Mental Health, 1*(2), 83.
- Singh, K., Junnarkar, M. O. H. I. T. A., Singh, D., Suchday, S., Mitra, S., & Dayal, P. (2019). Associations between religious/spiritual practices and well-being in Indian elderly rural women. *Journal of religion and health*, 1-22.
- Thakrar, D., Das, R., & Sheikh, A. (2018). Hinduism: the tradition speaks for itself. In *Caring for Hindu Patients* (pp. 17-36). Routledge.
- Tiwari, S. C., & Pandey, N. M. (2013). The Indian concepts of lifestyle and mental health in old age. *Indian Journal of Psychiatry, 55*(Suppl 2), S288.
- Tiwari, S., Singh, R., & Chand, H. (2016). Spirituality and psychological wellbeing of elderly of Uttarakhand: a comparative study across residential status. *Journal of Psychology, 7*(2), 112-118.
- Udhayakumar, P., & Ilango, P. (2012). Spirituality and mental health among the elderly practising spirituality. *Journal of Research, Extension and Development, 1*(2), 8-13.
- Udhayakumar, P., & Ilango, P. (2012). Spirituality, stress and wellbeing among the elderly practicing spirituality. *SamajaKaryadaHejjegalu, 2*(10), 37-42.
- Zimmer, Z., Jagger, C., Chiu, C. T., Ofstedal, M. B., Rojo, F., & Saito, Y. (2016). Spirituality, religiosity, aging and health in global perspective: A review. *SSM-population health, 2*, 373-381.

* * *

TRANSITIONAL ACCEPTANCE TOWARDS AGING

Debolina Roy and Madhurima Dey Sarkar

Introduction

One of the dichotomies of life is that we want to transition towards betterment in our life, we want to move on with our lives but inevitably, we are also nearing the end stages of our life. Man wants to move forward and also stay status quo. This is also true when we are transitioning from one stage to another in our life. But the most difficult transition is from adulthood to old age and the various challenges which come with it. But researches mostly focus on the challenges and difficulties of this stage and not how old people can actually have a peaceful life and use their strengths acquired over the years for this successful transition.

In a study by Nilsson et al. (2000), data analysis of old people revealed four major characteristics of feeling old:

- Being able to date the beginning of feeling old
- Fear of helplessness and of being unable to manage one's life situation
- Not recognising one's former self
- Feeling different from others

The understanding from the above characteristics leads to the fact that old people feel that their life is now marked by disequilibrium. This leads to anxiety, a sense of disrupted reality and loss of identity where earlier conditions no longer are valid due to the experienced changes in health (Schumacher & Meleis, 1994; Selder, 1989).

However, as laid out of by Erickson in his theory of psychosocial development (1982), the conflict which people face from the age of 60 years is that of integrity versus despair, but if it is resolved, then the core strength which develops is that of wisdom. Wisdom as defined by Meynen (2012), is:

- Understanding how to get to the bottom of an issue, and having explored it in depth, being able to provide certainty and stability.
- Being familiar with border zones, understanding how to steer one's ship through shallows like a helmsman, and being able to cross over borders with assurance
- Understanding how to hold one's course in rough and difficult terrain and being able to deal with others whose courses are different.

Applying the strength of wisdom in various domains of one's life can alleviate the stress and can make the transition to old age a calmer and peaceful process.

Concept of Self through Transition

As people grow older, there is a change in their activities, their behaviour and the social interactions in which they engage. This change has significant influence in the concept of self, or to be precise in the understanding of self through this transition.

Carl Jung, a prominent psychologist once said that "The afternoon of life is just as full of meaning as the morning; only, its meaning and purpose are different.... What youth found and must find outside, the man of life's afternoon must find within himself".

The Self-concept in an interpretive sense is a symbolic, social, and linguistic phenomenon which can be understood as a contextualized and multidimensional network which constitutes of dynamic cognitive structure and interrelated beliefs and ideas about the self. Self-concept has both knowledge and evaluative components which are important adaptive and self-regulatory functions that contain traits, values, episodic, and semantic memories about the self.

During the transition to the final stage in adulthood, individuals tend to review their pasts and evaluate whether or not their lives had been meaningful and the product of their own making. In this level an individual puts his life together in some reflective way. His major achievements are behind him now and he must sum it all up, viewing it with a sense of integrity or if there have been major flaws with a possible sense of despair.

The ability of a retiring person to reappraise and redefine his worth helps him to draw a clear boundary between the past, present and future. If the retiring individual still has preoccupation related to his work he may be unable to foster a varied set of valued activities and he may fail to find a sense of self-worth beyond one's own job. Throughout the transition, other valuable virtues which matter are the capacity to shift emotional investments from one person to another and ability to enjoy life greatly despite the painful physical unease of a deteriorating body without preoccupation in terms of intact physical well-being. The self-concept indicates a positive transition when a positive adaption to the prospect of death, with an investment in the present and future are present, whereas in presence of preoccupation with passive recognition or denial of death and a clinging to one's separate identity with little investment in others can make the changing self-concept difficult to process and accept.

Older adults can engage in "Self-concept immunization" related activities by which they can make realistic assessments of changes in their self-perceived skills to promote continuity of the self.

Successful Adaptation to Work Life

One of the domains which get impacted during this stage is the work life. As the workforce continues to age, stereotypes of older workers become more prevalent and affect more workers, which could discourage them from staying in the workforce (Posthuma & Campion, 2009). Older workers need to stay longer in the workforce to plug the shortage of skilled workers (Burke & Ng, 2006) and to reduce the strain on our retirement system (Baldwin, 2009; MacDonald et al., 2011). We many a times try to dissociate work with old age as if both cannot go hand in hand and as a result, many of the researches have focused on the decline of work life among older adults and how physical and psychological changes can create a negative impact in an older person's work life. Yet despite declining resources associated with age, there is little link between age and work performance; instead, adaptation and skills acquisition may protect older workers from declining productivity (Charness et al., 2007). For example, Brooke (2003) conducted a cost-benefit analysis focusing on older and younger workers, and concluded that investments in older workers (e.g., recruitment, training) were well worth their costs (e.g., absenteeism, workplace injuries) when compared to similar investments made in younger workers. Older workers want to remain longer with an employer when they are treated fairly and if their contributions are valued because such attitudes foster a sense of belonging with the organization (Armstrong-Stassen & Schlosser, 2011).

A strategy which can be used to reinstate older adults into work life and help them leverage their potential to the fullest is the SOC model given by Baltes (2002). This model was proposed to help navigate successfully through the stage of old age across various domains. The model proposes 3 stages and these can be helpful even when applied to work domain:

1. **Selection:** When a person has to achieve a goal, the first strategy is to select and allocate his resources appropriately. Baltes' SOC model suggests that to maintain positive work functioning, workers select goals that promote a fit between resources and needs (Freund & Baltes, 2002b; Freund, 2006). With old age, there is declining physical health as well as a decline in cognitive functioning. The loss of resources necessitated that individuals construct a goal hierarchy or set more-realistic goals – for example, individuals may concentrate their energy on a few priorities (Freund & Baltes, 1998, as cited in Ng and Law, 2013).

2. **Optimization:** It involves strategies that are aimed at strengthening skills and capabilities to achieve the selected goals. This may include such things as enhancing current skills or putting extra time and effort into a task (Freund, 2006; Yeung & Fung, 2009). Older people over the years have accumulated skills and wisdom which can be helpful in the long run. In a study by Ng and Law (2013), the elderly workers focused on the gains they had made through aging, and they tapped into that accumulating resource to enhance their work functioning. The workers simply shifted their focus from declining resources to areas of gain to enhance their usefulness in the workplace. They were able to identify a lack of experience among their younger co-workers as a resource gap, and to make the case that knowledge and

experience can make a valuable contribution to the workplace, including training the younger workers.

3. **Compensation:** It refers to the use of alternative strategies to accomplish goals to counteract or make up for losses that interfere with goal attainment (Freund & Baltes, 2002). This was often accomplished with the assistance of support systems from both the employer and co-workers. In the study by Ng & Law (2013), some of the workers in their study reported receiving assistance from their employers to offset declining physical health with the provision of the appropriate tools and equipment (e.g., use of technology, flexible work arrangements). Others relied on and received social support from co-workers, either in terms of maintaining a common positive attitude or through direct assistance from co-workers with the demands of the job.

Thus, to reinstate older people in the work domain, it is important to let them have a sense of hope and to help them realize that skills can never go to waste; the timely and rightful allocation of it along with leveraging resources, without it being a tedious task on the mental and physical health, should be the foremost goal.

Transitioning to Old Age: A Cultural Perspective

Today, ageism is likely the most socially accepted form of prejudice (Nelson, 2002). However, how we view old age depends on our culture as well. In Western countries, which believes in individualistic culture and is mostly youth dominated, aging is viewed as negatively, where people are dependent on others (North & Fiske, 2015). Western cultures appreciate self-enhancing tendencies that then stem to success, separateness, internal attributes, and uniqueness of individuals (Pethtel, 2010). But with old age comes dependency and this usually goes against the attributes of individualistic culture. On the other hand, in Eastern countries, which believes in collectivist culture, aging is viewed mostly positively. They value interdependence within families where the emphasis is on connectedness, social context, and relationship harmony (Zhou, 2007). Elders claim seniority in East Asian cultures because collectivistic societies constructed an image of wisdom and prestige that elders gain through normative aging (Lee, 2011).

However, this does not mean that being a member of an individualistic society, elderly people are only facing challenges. In a study by Chen et al., (2018), aging index was calculated by taking into consideration 5 domains: Productivity and Engagement, Well Being, Equity, Cohesion and Security. It was observed that countries like United States scored higher on productivity, engagement and cohesion and low on equity and security. This shows that older people in these countries have a need to maintain a sense of autonomy and that can be one of the reasons that their rate of productivity and engagement is higher. The high performance of the United States in productivity and engagement also reflects the highest labor force participation rates at older ages, high effective retirement age, and high rates of volunteerism. These findings are likely driven by low unemployment rates and the adoption of flexibility in work hours and pension eligibility rules to reduce constraints to continued employment (Börsch-Supan et al., 2017). Japan, on the other hand, scored higher on the domain of well being. They show a higher life expectancy and better life satisfaction (Onishi et al., 2010). Uchida et al. (2004) argue that life satisfaction for East and South East Asians tends to be strongly premised on social fulfilment in the form of healthy relationships, social acceptance, and approval from loved ones, on top of self-satisfaction. These contrasts with Anglo-Americans and Europeans, whose life satisfaction appear to be derived more strongly from the self (Boehm et al., 2011).

Developing countries like India, consider the phase of old age as a time when there is decline in economic growth and employment opportunities. Once a person retires, they think that they don't serve any purpose now in their family or in the society. Consequently, this implies that the economy's capacity to sustain the elderly would decline over the period. However, productivity does not always involve a growth in economic well being of the society; it can be self-engagement as well. Roy (2019) in his study pointed out that in India, a section of the elderly gets involved in religious activities and tries to free their mind from the shackles of the family bondage by following the age-old path of Vanaprastha. However, there are other activities for which this grey population can be engaged. Old people, especially who belong to the 'third age' category can be motivated to work as volunteers in public and private sectors, social workers or may be in community services. They can also contribute to human development if they are motivated to donate organs after death and bring smiles to their future generations.

In India, it is very common to hear from elderly people that 'Oh! My days are numbered now' or while bidding good bye, one may say 'If I live then we will meet again' or may comment 'I have come out from all the bindings of family and waiting for the call from the Almighty'. These snapshots suggest that people of the Indian subcontinent relate ageing with death or detachment from familial bonding. It may appear that people living in Indian subcontinent consider ageing from a pessimistic view (Lamb, 2014). But one can also argue that these snapshots actually reveal taking death from a positive view. A study by Pandya (2016) showed that ageing was a state of mind, something that could be modified with, and was contingent on, the quality of one's thought processes and thinking, and death was a process that led to proximity with God. The study concluded by saying that spirituality and religiosity are protector variables as well as aspects promoting wellness and transcendence for older adults is thus substantiated.

Successful Navigation through the Transition

Growing old means letting go and letting go can be both hopeful and apprehensive.

Senior people have lived through many transitions throughout his or her lifetime already but this transition is one more in a long line of life-changing events. However, even though older adults are resilient, they still need help with the transition to a senior living community. That's often true even if they are open and accepting to the upcoming change.

Western world encourages individualistic society, a sense of control and independence under the guise of being financially self-sufficient and living alone are seen as desirable for both men and women, on the other hand, many eastern countries place greater value on collectivistic society which includes long-term associations with local communities and family. In such cultures, the older generation are cared for by younger members of the family and community throughout the entire process.

In general, it is most people's wish to remain independent in all possible domain as long as possible. However, it is known that at some point in life this may no longer be an appropriate option. During those transitive phases, an open invitation to this beautiful time of transition with accepting mind and a positive attitude can make all the difference in the experience. Acceptance of the vulnerability is required and courage can help the in this acceptance phase during the aging process. Clear, direct and thoughtful communication with family, friends and professionals are also an important part for the successful navigation. By embracing the limitless opportunities for personal growth during old age, the senior people can begin to shift from fear to welcoming the experience with open hearts.

Fear of losing control on oneself is one of the prominent barriers in the path of a successful navigation through the transition. Letting people care for the older generation can help alleviate the level of fear attached to the aging process. In this way, aging provides the older generation with a wonderful opportunity for learning and personal growth by finally letting go of their need to control situations and be self-reliant in other ways; and it can happen only when one opens up to accepting help from other people, and let life naturally run its course.

Older people who are being able to be more accepting of flaws in others, stimulate emotional growth age appropriately. Their show of acceptance and support and contribute to guide the younger generations.

For many seniors, such type of transitions are welcomed and an anticipated natural change. They prepare themselves to look forward to having the essentials of daily living taken care of for them. Many older adults anticipate enjoying the array of activities they could not take part during their professional lives and events offered in their new community.

Finally, the opportunity for social engagement is another attractive feature of senior living communities for many older people. As people age, they often lose contact with their former friends and family members due to loss, mobility issues, or cognitive impairment that makes socialization difficult. Being surrounded by peers who share similar struggles can provide the emotional support a senior often needs.

Recent studies have shown that satisfaction with life, having a purpose in life and subjective perception towards the process of ageing process contribute to ageing successfully, and therefore importance of psychological awareness of transitional adaptation in later life is an important part of successful ageing. Quality of aging has become synonymous with successful ageing. Good and adequate social functioning is often seen as a predictor in successful ageing, especially by older adults themselves. It reflects a wish to contribute and retain a role in society and being involved with people.

In era of 21st century, the community support is growing at a fast rate. Community services including professionals and other members can help the senior citizens to successfully navigate through the physical, mental, emotional and spiritual transitions successfully and maintain a good quality of life.

Implications of Successful Aging

Aging is an irreversible process and although medical science has worked in leaps and bounds to delay the process of it, it is still an inevitable phase. However, transitioning towards it successfully is something that our society should help and strive for. A clear self-concept helps to maintain the identity of elderly persons, which will help them have a positive outlook towards life and accepting the various changes which they have to embrace with age. Also living in the present moment is a crucial factor in the successful transition to old age. In terms of contributing to workplace, it is important for us to understand how to properly select and capitalize the resources which elderly people bring on to a work foray. Proper compensation for imparting their skills should also be made along with instilling a sense of hope in them.

Engagement in various recreational activities can also be beneficial for successful transition to aging. The recreational activities can be active and passive, depending on the level of movement and amount of energy expended in the task. A lot of studies reveal that engagement in such recreational activities has an effect on the quality of life, subjective wellbeing and coping in general.

Finally, transitioning to old age differs from person to person. It is tailor made and one size does not fit all. However, if we focus on the different predictors and moderators to successful aging, it would help us focus our attention to that phase of life, which is often neglected by researchers. All in all, it will foster the concept of inclusive well being.

Future Trends in Adaptive Aging

The National Statistical Office (NSO)'s report on Elderly in India in 2021 predicted that the India's elderly population (aged 60 and above) is projected to increase a 41% over a decade from 138 million in 2021 to 194 million in 2031.

This report evidently indicates a notable growth in the elderly population in India. According to nature's law, both the elderly and juvenile population require more overall support from caregivers to society for a successful adaptive transition.

The Indian Council of Medical Research (ICMR), The Rehabilitation Council of India (RCI) along with administrative bodies of government of India are planning and executing several research based strategies for overall support, growth and development for the elderly population in India.

The Ministry of Social Justice and Empowerment (Gov. of India) had launched National Policy for Senior Citizens in March 2011 to implement policy and plans for the welfare of older persons.

As time and technology are advancing, so is the need for the type of care and support. People no more look at the Old Age Care Homes as prisons, but more of a place of independence and contemporary social support. Maintaining the level with international standard, India is coming forward with a special care centre for a common disease of old agedementia. Asia's first Dementia Village is established in Karnataka and is functional since April 2021.

The new generation elderly population is seeking more beyond basic life support and care. They are more open to learn and adapt to the fast changing world. So, a technology based support care specially designed for elderly population can be the answer, where independency will be prioritized more than dependency on the caregivers.

People tend to see old age/elderlyhood as a pause from life. People plan and adapt to the transition towards adulthood to retirement where everything is more or less preplanned or forethought. A similar pre-planned elderlyhood focused plan can come handy post retirement. This may ensure that the transition towards the older age will be as smooth as it has always been without a pause.

References

- Baltes PB & Baltes MM. Psychological perspectives on successful aging: The model of selective optimization with compensation. Successful aging: Perspectives from the behavioral sciences. In: Baltes P. B, Baltes M.M, editors. New York: Cambridge University Press; 1990.

- Baumeister RF. Self-concept, self-esteem, and identity. In: Derlega VJ, Winstead BA, Jones WH, eds. Personality: Contemporary Theory and Research. 2nd ed. Chicago, IL: Nelson-Hall; 1999:339–375.
- Bergeron, C. D., & Lagacé, M. (2021). On the Meaning of Aging and Ageism: Why Culture Matters. *University of Toronto Quarterly, 90*(2), 140-154.
- Chen, C., Goldman, D. P., Zissimopoulos, J., & Rowe, J. W. (2018). Multidimensional comparison of countries' adaptation to societal aging. *Proceedings of the National Academy of Sciences, 115*(37), 9169-9174. https://doi.org/10.1073/pnas.1806260115.
- Costa PT, & McCrae RR. (2002). Looking backward: changes in the mean levels of personality traits from 80 to 12. In: Cervone D, Mischel W, eds. Advances in Personality Science. New York, NY: Guilford Press, 219–237.
- Diehl M, Hastings CT, & Stanton JM. (2001). Self-concept differentiation across the adult life span. *Psychol Aging*, 16(4):643–654.
- Hooker K, & McAdams DP. (2003). Personality reconsidered: a new agenda for aging research. *J Gerontol B Psychol Sci Soc Sci*, 58(6): 296-304.
- Irshad, C. V., & Dash, U. (2021). Healthy aging in India: evidence from a panel study. *Journal of Health Research*. https://doi.org/10.1108/JHR-09-2020-0395.
- Jeste, D. V., Depp, C. A., & Vahia, I. V. (2010). Successful cognitive and emotional aging. *World Psychiatry, 9*(2), 78. http://doi.org/10.1002/j.2051-5545.2010.tb00277.x.
- Karttunen NM, Turunen J, Ahonen R, & Hartikainen S. (2014). More attention to pain management in community-dwelling older persons with chronic musculoskeletal pain. *Age Ageing*, 43:845–850.
- Kobylarek, A. (Ed.). (2012). Aging: Social, biological and psychological dimensions. Agencja Wydawnicza.
- Lynch, R. (2013). Social work practice with older people: a positive person-centred approach. SAGE.
- Markson, E. W. (1973). Readjustment to time in old age: A life cycle approach. *Psychiatry, 36*(1), 37-48. https://doi.org/10.1080/00332747.1973.11023744.
- Markus H, & Nurius P. (1986). Possible selves. *Am Psychol*, 41:954–969.
- Markus H, & Wurf E. (1987). The dynamic self-concept: a social psychological perspective. *Annu Rev Psychol*, 38:299–337.

- McCrae RR, & Costa PT. (1982). Self-concept and the stability of personality:cross-sectional comparisons of self-reports and ratings. *J Pers Soc Psychol*, 43(6):1282–1292.
- Neugarten, B. L. (1976). Adaptation and the life cycle. *The counseling psychologist*, *6*(1), 16-20.
- Ng, E. S. & Law, A. (2014). Keeping up! Older workers' adaptation in the workplace after age 55. *Canadian Journal on Aging/La revue canadienne du vieillissement*, *33*(1), 1-14. http://doi:10.1017/S0714980813000639.
- Nilsson, M., Sarvimäki, A., & Ekman, S. L. (2000). Feeling old: Being in a phase of transition in later life. *Nursing Inquiry*, *7*(1), 41-49.
- Raj, U., & Galhotra, A. (2019). The Maintenance and Welfare of Parents and Senior Citizens Act, 2007-Helping the conditions of the elderly in India. *Indian Journal of Community and Family Medicine*, *5*(2), 157.
- Robinson, S. A., Rickenbach, E. H., & Lachman, M. E. (2016). Self-regulatory strategies in daily life: Selection, optimization, and compensation and everyday memory problems. *International journal of behavioral development*, *40*(2), 126-136. http://doi:10.1177/0165025415592187.
- Roy, S. (2019). On development and sustainability: The issue of ageing in India. *Journal of the Anthropological Survey of India*, *68*(1), 27-40. https://doi.org/10.1177%2F2277436X19845734.
- Whitbourne SK. The Me I Know: A Study of Adult Identity. New York,NY: Springer-Verlag; 1986.
- Wortmann, F. C. (2020). The influence of collectivism and individualism on attitudes towards older people: a systematic literature review (Master's thesis, University of Twente).

* * *

AGEING AND ITS MANIFESTATION THROUGH SOCIO-CULTURAL REALM

Aparajita Chakraborty

ABSTRACT

Despite rigorous research on various issues encountered during old age, the biopsychosocial perspectives often fall short to decipher the cultural aspects associated with ageing. Usually, old age is perceived in negative light, owing to the deterioration in health, physical as well as mental, financial dependency and even perceiving as social burden. However, these intersectionality of the aforesaid factors often get unnoticed and proper psychological intervention fails to be strategized. One possible explanation might be giving less importance to the significance of the bigger socio-cultural premise on which these factors are embedded. It is widely known that sociocultural aspects play an important role in determining the societal norms and beliefs, and whether such socio-cultural domains have role to play in old age would be interesting to unearth. This article aims to focus on different socio-cultural factors associated with ageing. Among them, socio-demographic variables, changes in body and mind, engagement in lifestyle activities, marital adjustment, retirement, belief and stigma, death and bereavement are explored extensively. This article would help us to know how these factors are intermingled and often contribute in developing mental health related difficulties, thereby curving path for suitable intervention strategy.

Keywords: Old age, Socio-cultural, Engagement, Transition, Stigma.

Introduction

The gradual debacle in mental health condition, due to augmented stress, is affecting mankind in a ghastly way. Drastic increase in prevalence of mental health illnesses is highly daunting, and it is not even sparing the elderly people. Olson and De Frain (2003) defines old age in terms of three different stages: young old (65 to 74 years), middle old (75 to 84 years) and old-old (85 and older). In order to discuss the process which brings upon the old age manifestation is known as ageing, which can be either functional or chronological in nature. The former one is the measure of the capability and also focuses on social, psychological and physiological age. But Chronological age focuses on the chronology, that is, birth to death (American Psychological Association, 2007). Often, the elderly population suffer through multifaceted issues, like, physical, psychological and social. As per World Health Organization (2017), 15% of adults aged 60 and over suffer from a mental disorder, with mental and neurological disorders accounting for 6.6% of the total disability for this elderly age group. And India is no exception. Census 2011 stated that there are nearly 104 million elderly persons (60 years or above) in India; 53 million females and 51 million males. It is alarming to know that in India, the population of 60 years and above is estimated to increase to 19% (2050) from 8% (2015). The increase in the population of the elderly (80 and above) is also high in India (Fund, U.N.P, 2019). As per report by The 10/66 Dementia Research Group (2000), prevalence rate of dementia in old age (above 65 years of age) ranges from 1.8% to 4.5%. Additionally, the depression rate in 50% in rural part of West Bengal (Nandi et al., 1997). These evidences are distressing, which requires to be addressed by fast, effective, economical as well as parsimonious intervention plans. Theoretical foundations, especially by Erikson (1994) had proposed the advent of integrity among elderly population, in terms of acceptance, wholeness and wisdom. On the contrary, despair would be the consequence for regret, rumination, depression etc. But the major socio cultural contributors in this regard is still misty.

The interface between society and culture form the rudimentary base for any developmental process, including ageing. The overlapping constellation which forms a society and it's cultural attributes that include the cardinal values, norms, customs are language contribute in architecting the socio-cultural realm. Thus the dynamic transaction between society and culture for creating the identity, also includes the geographical contours, demographics, domicile etc. Thus, the ageing need to be scrutinized through the socio-cultural lens, for getting a comprehensive process of ageing.

According to Dua and Erikson (2017), biological, psychological as well as social factors play pivotal role in ageing need to be studied extensively. Thus, the meshwork of different factors related to old age need to be explored extensively. Despite having innumerable research evidences on old age and the issues encountered by them on daily basis, dearth in exploration of socio-cultural factors in regard to old age is evident. Unless the essential socio-cultural factors, and often the regional ones as well, are taken under consideration, designing and delivering of health care services, and other social welfare facilities would not be adequately implemented.

The factors which are going to be discussed here as potential socio-cultural contributors in ageing are: sociodemographic variables, engagement in lifestyle activities, changes in body and mind, belief and stigma, marital adjustment, retirement and death and bereavement. Moreover, how the Indian scenario in terms of ageing differs with that of other Asian countries as well as other continents will also be discussed. It is to be kept in mind that these aforesaid factors do not function in water tight compartment. They interact with each other and create the backdrop of socio-cultural realm associated with ageing.

1. Socio-demographic Variables

Be it gender, marital and economic status, ageing process has been found to vary extensively. The social construction of ageing, in terms of gender, has been seen to vary enormously. A detailed study by Sengupta et al. (2014) had found that increasing age, unmarried/widowed status, illiteracy, unemployment and poverty are significantly associated with cognitive impairment among elderly population of Northern India. As per Devasahayam (2014), women have an advantage that they live longer than men. However, this 'advantage' often plays the opposite tune, as women are more vulnerable to shorter health life expectancy and higher survival rates compared to men, thereby increasing the need to be looked after them (Henrard, 1996). As a result, often women feel that they are 'burden' and a vicious cycle of self hatred and guilt become instrumental, eventually developing depression. According to Sontag (2018), elderly women are judged more harshly than men, which is linked with attractiveness, as the parameter for women's sexuality and physicality are more stringent than men. Numerous studies substantiate the fact that prevalence of depression is more among older women than men (Altun & Yazici, 2015; Eugenia Alvarado et al., 2007). The study by Bhatia et al. (2007) resonates where they found that illness rates are more common among elderly females as well as the fact that elderly females perceived themselves to be lonelier than elderly males.

Additionally, marital status plays an important role too. According to the study done by (Jang et al., 2009), divorced and widowed older men reported higher rate of depressive features than older married men. However, the difference between married and widowed/divorced older women converged with increasing age. Thus, it may be deduced that marriage is a protective factor, which shields from the distresses in old age.

Another important factor which is worth mentioning, in regard to ageing, is socio-economic status (SES). Recent research evidence shows that among older people belonging to lower SES in New Jersy, presence of physical capability, sensory function, physiological function, cognitive performance, emotional well-being, and social function were evident (Steptoe & Zaninotto, 2020). Another interesting finding in this line by Wu and Rudkin (2000) revealed that low SES was associated with poorer health for older Malay, Chinese as well as Indian population. In terms of mental health related issues, the study by Brinda et al. (2016), SES and significant inequalities in lower and middle income countries often predispose as well as maintain depressive symptoms among older population. An interesting finding by John (1996) stated that elderly American Indian population often suffer from economic as well as social challenges, along with health related issues. He had also shown a contrasting difference in personal income among American Indian and non-Hispanic white elders. Source of most of the income of the American Indian elders are derived from social security, public assistance, including Supplemental Security Income, along with engagement in the production of crafts. However, the interest, dividends, and net rental income are the major sources of the non-Hispanic whites. Furthermore, it is evident that the potential determinants for the differences in cognitive performance between and within ethnic and cultural groups in Europe on neuropsychological tests confirmed the role of cultural, linguistic, and educational differences (Nielsen et al., 2012). Thus, dire necessity of health care facilities is required for older people in lower SES.

2. Engagement in Lifestyle Activities

A common notion is that as people get older, their engagements in different sphere diminish. As demands get reduced significantly, their disengagement in endeavours also get evident. It is supported by Disengagement Theory by Cumming and Henry (1961), who proposed that as people get older, their social engagements reduce due to decline in senses or retirement. However, other researcher, like Maddox (1970) had stated that it is the personality factor which determines whether the elderly person would lead a life of 'recluse'. But it has been extensively studied by researchers like Bots et al. (2008) that physical activity, alcohol consumption, smoking behavior, and body weight, are associated with health and functioning among older adults. So, when it comes to lifestyle activities among elderly population, it demands a special attention. For instance, in Iran, ignorance in regard to health in elderly people might take toll in economic, social and health aspects (Mohammadbeigi et al., 2013). The lifestyle also affects the longevity and health in old age. As per Tiwari and Pandey (2013), lifestyles have role in developing cognitive disorders like Alzheimer's disease.

Thus, healthy lifestyle is important in promoting both physical as well as mental health. Healthy lifestyle in elderly individuals include healthy nutrition, sleep hygiene, regular physical activity, nonsmoking, regular periodic examination, participation in social activities as well as being with family (King et al., 2009; Newman et al., 2003). Thus, overall health can be promoted if the old people keep themselves engaged in these activities. Furthermore, Glass et al. (1999) also proposed the engagement in social activities (e.g., church attendance, recreation, and group activities), productive activities (e.g., gardening, preparing meals, and shopping), and fitness activities (e.g., sports, walking, and exercise) are associated with survival of elderly persons. A recent study by Mohta and Halder (2020) found that social networking sites are also used by elderly people, on an average 1 hour 20 minutes. And such technological use was found to be more on males than females. So, it is interesting to know how technological advancement are also getting incorporated in the lifestyle of elderly people. That is, the primitive notion of technology being associated with youth only, is getting revised through this finding. Thus, productive and leisure activities help to improve both physical as well as mental health.

3. Change: Body and Mind

Change in physicality as well as psyche is not an easy matter to deal with in old age, as they go through havoc conundrum. Continuous thought of 'unattractiveness', 'illness', 'loneliness' aggravates the agony faced by the elderly people. But, it is fascinating to know that, the aging process is not similar in nature. For instance, Asian Indian population ages earlier than the reported ages in Caucasian population, which is strikingly contrasting in nature. Furthermore, the earlier signs of aging (in 30–40 years) were more visible in North and East Indian ethnic groups followed by West and South Indians in decreasing order. Also, least signs of ageing was shown by people from South Indian people, considering both early and overall signs together (Shome et al., 2020). Physical changes, ranging from rapid greying hair to extreme case, like arthritis, often take a toll on self-concept among elderly population (Ward, 1985). Concomitantly, rapid changes in metabolism, leading to impaired self-regulation, and structural changes and functional tissues and organs are evident during old age. Other physiological changes include decrease in cardiac output and creatinine clearance, along with lung functionality, increase in blood pressure etc. Furthermore, decline in vision, audition, taste, touch and smell is evident in ageing (Lloyd, 2007). However, research done by Kumar (1997) showed that coronary heart disease, hypertension, mental and many other disorders in the elderly have been reported as isolated observations highlighting differences from those made in the Western countries. As per Thakur, Banerjee & Nikumb (2013), multiple unaddressed health needs, like unoperated cataract, uncontrolled hypertension, uncorrected hearing impairment and tobacco use are prevalent in elderly people, which calls for an immediate health intervention plan for this marginalized group.

It is also to be noted that during old age, the processing of incoming sensory information gets compromised, thereby depreciating the quality of integration and execution of perceptual processes, which might be due to the depreciating schema, which is a pattern of the thought or behavior which helps in organizing the relationship of variables (Paul, 1997). And these changes affect mood, attitude to the environment, physical condition and social activity of older people (Dziechciaz & Filip, 2014). These rapid physical changes often affect the psyche of the elderly people. An interesting finding by Alexopoulos (2005) stated that age as well as disease related issues, along with cognitive impairment and suffering aggravate depression among elderly population.

Thus, it is clear that, psychological changes would also be evident. One of the most significant faculties of psyche is the cognition, and more specifically, information processing. A study by Thapliyal, Halder & Mahato (2016) suggested that deterioration in memory, verbal fluency and response inhibition among people aged 60–70 years, thus, reflecting the underlying neuropsychological phenomena of the difficulty in communication, including compromised responding to external stimuli, thereby getting more prone to isolation and confinement. The change in the information processing is evident from the study by Ebner et al. (2006), which stated that elderly people focus more on the parameters of losses, and less on gains. They get more inclined towards maintenance and preservation of losses, rather than gaining new ones. Similar findings by Depping and Freund (2013) explored that older people remember more loss relevant information. However, literature finding suggests that in processing speed as well as visuospatial working memory tasks, no cultural difference among elderly participants from American and Beijing were noticed (Hedden et al., 2002). It has been supported by the fact that cognitive decline is a universal phenomena and limited to the strategies used during late adulthood, across culture (Park, Nisbett & Hedden, 1999). Another study by Halder and Mahato (2019) had shown identification of deficits in few memory performance tasks in elderly people and they who were categorized as high risk for developing Alzheimer's Disease. Another interesting finding, in contrast, revealed that despite impairment in verbal fluency among elderly people in South India, difficulty in executive functioning and cognitive functioning was not found (D'cruz, Rajaratnam & Kumar, 2013). So, if intervention program incorporates these findings, it would be easier to engage the elderly people, despite few cognitive difficulties, thereby enhancing social functioning.

4. Belief and Stigma

Negative attitude and belief towards elderly population is often disgraceful. By dint of their greying hair and other physical as well as psychological decline in functioning, relatively reduced contribution, old age is associated with stigma, prejudice and stereotype, which caters to coining the term 'ageism' (Butler, 1969). It is interesting to note that elderly people only believe that old age corresponds sickness and disability (Saxena, 2016). Due to stigma, there is discrimination in provision services in older people with mental health related issues (Graham et al., 2003). As stigma often germinates the seed of being 'deviant', 'undesirable', it leads to less care seeking behavior, as in case of older people, who despite being given the opportunity for municipal resources, fail to seek it (De Mendonça Lima, 2004). However, the question remains, whether negative attitude towards elderly people is comprehensive to the range of old aged people, that is 55 years onwards, or it is a particular age range of elderly people who are more stigmatized. As per Neugarten (1974) negative stereotypes are more towards 'old-old' category of aged population, because of their physical ailment, reduced sexuality, poverty etc. However, such observations get generalized to 'young-old' (55 to 75 years). In same line, research by Hummert (1994) suggested that college students perceived early stage of older people with positive stereotype, compared to the 'old old' ones. Thus, it is evident that, the loneliness due to the 'labelling' and the negative attitude, often result in geriatric depression. According to Alexopoulos (2005), socio-economic impoverishment, isolation and bereavement make the elderly people more vulnerable to depression, or triggering depression in already vulnerable elderly individuals. Another important matter of concern is misdiagnosis of depression among elderly population, as it mimics dementia (Lamberty & Bieliauskas, 2003). Thus, the regular screening procedure needs to be advanced and updated in order to reduce such tendency to neglect the series of behavioral manifestation of the elderly people.

Another important determining factor in this regard is the socio-demographics. For instance, urban or rural, eastern or western country are major contributors. A study by Hayslip et al. (2010) found that reported that rural older adults from New York hold a negative attitude toward mental illness. A study done by Loch et al. (2014) stated that in Brazil, the elderly were more discriminators. Another study by Hartini et al. (2018) reported that elderly people from Indonesia had negative attitude towards mental illness. However, the study by Mehra et al. (2020), which was done on elderly people in rural region of Haryana in India showed that older adults had a positive attitude toward mental illness. The reason could be due to contact with a patient of mental illness or experience from the community.

Thus, psychotherapeutic module need to be prepared, along with rigorous propaganda and awareness program in order to alleviate stigma towards elderly population as well as mental illness

5. Marital Relationship and Adjustment

Family dynamics and communication, autonomy in family, domestic violence and other house hold hardships, compatibility with partner, care giving tendency have major influence on quality of life and wellbeing (Hussain, 2021). There are opposing opinion regarding marital health among elderly couple. Few theorists postulate that older married couples are found to be more content than younger married adults (Cunningham & Brookbank, 1988), which may be due to reduced work pressure and less demand. On the other hand, a question remains whether the elderly couple were always happy, or their conflicts have gradually reduced over time (Levenson, Carstensen, & Gottman, 1993). Rowe (2003) divided long term marriages (marriages spanning for 50 years or more) into three groups: couples who are happy together, couples who are unhappy, but continue remaining together and, couples who accept the situation, irrespective of presence or absence of happiness. That means, it is not always true that elderly couple would be happy and contented together. More interestingly, couples who had discord during initial years might get along well in (Brubaker, 1990). Among higher education groups, the marital adjustment was reported to be better among elderly couples in the post parental stages of life. A study by Kumar (2015) showed that as age increases psychological wellbeing decreases among elderly couples in the post parental stages of life. Another important matter of concern in this regard is sexuality among elderly couple. Gibson (1992) proposed that between 10 and 20% of older men and 35% (or more) of older women have no sex life. Physiological problem might be a contributing factor here, which often get unnoticed by health professionals. As per Godschalk, Sison & Mulligan (1997), numerous sexual dysfunction cases among older adults remain untreated. Thus, the general idea regarding sexuality among elderly couple that their sexual drive would be certainly decreasing with age needs to be confronted with rigour. Because, sexual drive differ significantly among individuals (Mastersz & Johnson, 1966). As marital support acts as a protective factors against various stressors, and also known to enhance self-regulation and resilience (DiMatteo, 2004), family and marital therapists as well as gerontologists, in collaboration with other health professionals, need to bring about an extensive intervention program for improving the marital relationship during old age.

6. Retirement

Till the time of retirement, the elderly people have enjoyed significant endeavors, which require deftness and dexterity, along with other work as well as family responsibilities. However, once the person reaches a certain age, there is an abrupt social transition, as if, the pedestal of productivity has drifted once the person retires. The time of progress into retirement offers a remarkable time window that permits researchers to study the adaptation process of the elderly people, that eventually may influence mental and physical health. As per Lindwall et al. (2017), retirement transition is associated with psychological aging, which is defined by biological as well as changes in external environment, which cumulatively influence the psychological health. It is evident that retirement brings about few vacillating changes. For instance, Henning, Lindwall & Johansson (2016) stated that retirement is associated with losses as well as gains. That is, both positive and negative effects of the transition need to be explored. Furthermore, the extensive research done by Lindwall et al. (2017) explored various other factors which also play role in different transition phases. People who are in the beginning of the retirement transition have higher life satisfaction, autonomy, wellbeing and decreased depression. Also, during the middle of the retirement transition, i.e, receiving pension, but still engaged in workforce partly, report improved psychological health. That is, they often feel that, still their 'importance' in the sector has not 'finished'. Research evidences show that voluntariness, sense of control as well as household income moderate the interaction among working in retirement, psychological health and life satisfaction (Nikolova & Graham, 2014; Lux & Schergerhad, 2017). However, it is to be noted that, work-family conflict is a major source of prior role stress for retirees, as work and family are significantly correlated and essential in reciprocal family interaction pattern (Elder, 1994). In this vein, a research by Coursolle et al. (2010) had revealed that those who had more work-based stress which affected family environment, perceive retirement as a relief. However, for women, it is not the case. For retired women, depressive symptoms are more common than employed women because, caring for grandchildren and other household demand may aggravate their stress (Szinovacz & Davey 2006). Thus, gender difference in this regard is also an important matter of interest.

It is evident that, retirement phase meanders through series of events, which are blend of positive as well as negative. From the work of Chanda & Mishra (2019), it is known that cognitive decline resulting from retirement can be addressed if social participation increases. Thus, designing suitable intervention program for preparing the elderly people for retirement need to focus on making them aware of the upcoming changes due to the transition and also to take care of the physiological as well as psychological health effects.

7. Death and Bereavement

Old age is the time when the most 'anticipated', 'fearful', 'avoidant' event, that is death, is generally 'experienced' closely. It is important for the mental health professionals to understand the impact of bereavement among elderly people, as it takes a tremendous toll on physical and mental health. Studies have focused on loss of spouse as the most stressful event experienced by elderly women (Hershberger & Walsh, 1990) or death of parent, siblings and children (d'Epinay et al., 2010). Thus, old age mostly comprises of loss of contemporaries, with whom significant phases of life have been spent. This also indicates that, advent of the most 'dreaded' event, death, is approaching in an accelerated pace.

Research evidence on widowhood is inconclusive. For instance, the study by Lalive d'Epinay et al. (2000) revealed that spousal demise does not necessarily lead to physical ailment among elderly people. On the other hand, the study by Delbès & Gaymu (2000) stated that after mourning period, the widowed become susceptible to depressive symptoms. Another study by Ott et al. (2007) had found that most of the bereaved spouses had depressive mourning period, few showed resilience and relatively lesser percentage of them had chronic depression. Death of a sibling also negatively influences the elderly people. For instance, the study by Hays et al. (1997) had found that death of sibling had impacted physical and cognitive state, just like that of death of spouses. Another significant life event is the death of offspring during old age. Another important aspect which needs to be pondered upon refers to the role of gender of the elderly people in the matter of death and bereavement. That is, whether widow and widower are equally grieved or there lies a difference. An interesting finding by Williams et al. (2006) had found that elderly women are more affected than elderly men when faced with spousal bereavement, however, such finding is also true for death of any other relative or friend. In the same line, the study by Gallagher et al. (1983) had also shown that mental health related issues are more common among elderly women than elderly women. But, another study by Lee, Willetts & Seccombe (1998) showed the opposite.

Thus, death and bereavement among elderly people is an alarm to take initiative on the intervention program. Enhancing social support is another major tread in this regard. According to Hashim et al. (2013), primary care physicians (PCP) play significant role in identifying risk factor for complicated grief among elderly people. Another interesting finding by Brown et al. (2008) also revealed that helping behavior leads to decline in depressive symptoms among people with spousal loss. Thus, these steps can be incorporated to design suitable intervention program for managing grief due death and bereavement among elderly people.

Healthy Ageing: Psychosocial Wellbeing among Elderly Population

All the aforesaid factors aim to depict the intermingling role of society and culture among elderly population. This has to be kept in mind that, the preparation of each stage is preceded by other developmental stages. So, the readiness regarding different issues of quality of life associated during old age need to be instilled since childhood by imparting relevant education in this regard (Jang & Choe, 2006). As per Tyas et al. (2007) healthy ageing comprehends health broadly, taking into consideration the maintenance or enhancement of into older age. In other words, healthy ageing incorporates not only absence of disease, but also enhancing as well as emphasizing the socio-cultural protective factors, which would eventually promote positive mental health.

Few socio-cultural contributors are perceived health status, reduced depression and perceived loneliness, promoting self-esteem, self-achievement and ego-integrity. Mossey and Shapiro (1982) had explored the relationship between well-being and mortality among old people and found that perceived positive health are positively related with wellbeing and less mortality. Additionally, the relationship between self-esteem and work, along with health, inter personal relationship and healthy ageing (Kim, 2013). In the same line, Cha, Sio & Sok (2012) found that sense of self achievement is a major re requisite for self-worth and self-efficacy, thereby enhancing healthy ageing. So, the role of perceived positive health, self-esteem and sense of self achievement are potential protective factors in old age. Cacippo et al. (2006) had found that loneliness and isolation, arising due to decreased personal relationship, among elderly population have significant role to play in geriatric depression. It is widely known how depression can have devastating effect on elderly people, often leading to suicide attempt, due to lack in proper problem solving techniques (Gibbs et al., 2009). It is theorized by Erikson (1993) that psychosocial developmental stages are crucial in integrating one's life experiences, which, as per Erikson, is a major virtue during old age. James and Zarrett (2005) had explored how generativity, which is the major facet during middle adulthood, influences the egointegrity during old age. Torges et al. (2008) also explained that generativity during midlife strongly predicts integrity in later life. Hannah, Domino & Figueredo (1996) explained that resolution of virtues in prior psychosocial stages, lead to an integration of ego during old age, thereby achieving the final virtue, that is, wisdom or 'detached' concern. Thus, exploring these psychosocial factors and their interaction would lead to the final goal, which is, facilitating social and clinical intervention for healthy aging.

Implication

Ageing is a process that meanders through varieties of changes. Since, the time is characterized by series of significant life events, adaptation to those become a dire necessity. However, limited attention given to them is a matter of concern. With abrupt changes in socio-cultural-political-economic changes, little focus is given on how the elderly people are coping with it. The present article, thus, aims to unearth the socio-cultural determinants which are instrumental in ageing.

An important aspect is preparation and the onus is on the society, coupled with cultural factors to promote concern and awareness towards the elderly population. Due to lack of extensive research evidence in Indian population, it is observed that there is significant dearth of comprehensive therapeutic module for old age, essentially based on Indian socio-cultural backdrop. Most of the intervention programme on promoting health and other requisites of elderly people are borrowed from western conceptualizations, which fall short in the Indian realm. Thus, rigorous outcome research in this regard based on Indian population is required direly. This calls for understanding as well as analyzing these factors which are discussed in this article, would help us to plan for intervention diligently.

Conclusion

Ageing is a critical process which calls for special attention. A common idea regarding ageing is the compromised biological functioning. However, there are multiple other factors, namely socio-cultural ones, which influence ageing too. In this article, those socio-cultural factors like socio-demographic variables, changes in body and mind, engagement in lifestyle activities, marital relationship, retirement belief and stigma, death and bereavement are extensively discussed. It needs to be understood that, compartmentalization of socio-cultural variables would neither help in research nor in designing proper awareness and intervention plan. Thus, comprehensive module for intervention, where all the factors, like, biological, along with incorporating socio-cultural variables, must be designed. Emphasis on socio-cultural factors delve to the planning of therapeutic program suitable for Indian elderly population.

References

- Alexopoulos, G. S. (2005). Depression in the elderly. *The lancet, 365*(9475), 1961-1970.
- Altun, F., & Yazici, H. (2015). The relationships between life satisfaction, gender, social security, and depressive symptoms among elderly in Turkey. *Educational Gerontology, 41*(4), 305-314.
- American Psychological Association. (2007). *APA dictionary of psychology*. Washington, DC: American Psychological Association.
- Bhatia, S. P. S., Swami, H. M., Thakur, J. S., & Bhatia, V. (2007). A study of health problems and loneliness among the elderly in Chandigarh. *Indian Journal of Community Medicine*, 32(4), 255.
- Bots, S., Tijhuis, M., Giampaoli, S., Kromhout, D., & Nissinen, A. (2008). Lifestyle-and diet-related factors in late-life depression—a 5-year follow-up of elderly European men: the FINE study. *International Journal of Geriatric Psychiatry, 23*(5), 478-484.
- Brinda, E. M., Rajkumar, A. P., Attermann, J., Gerdtham, U. G., Enemark, U., & Jacob, K. S. (2016). Health, social, and economic variables associated with depression among older people in low and middle income countries: world health organization study on global AGEing and adult health. *The American Journal of Geriatric Psychiatry, 24*(12), 1196-1208.
- Brown, S. L., Brown, R. M., House, J. S., & Smith, D. M. (2008). Coping with spousal loss: Potential buffering effects of self-reported helping behavior. *Personality and Social Psychology Bulletin, 34*(6), 849-861.
- Brubaker, T. H. (1990). Families in later life: A burgeoning research area. *Journal of Marriage and the Family*, 959-981.
- Butler, R. N. (1969). Age-ism: Another form of bigotry. *The gerontologist, 9*(4_Part_1), 243-246.
- Cacioppo, J. T., Hughes, M. E., Waite, L. J., Hawkley, L. C., & Thisted, R. A. (2006). Loneliness as a specific risk factor for depressive symptoms: cross-sectional and longitudinal analyses. *Psychology and aging*, 21(1), 140.
- Census of India (2011). Provisional population totals. *New Delhi: Office of the Registrar General and Census Commissioner.*
- Cha, N. H., Seo, E. J. & Sok, SR. (2012). Factors influencing the successful aging of older Korean adults. *Contemporary Nurse*, 78-87.

- Chanda, S., & Mishra, R. (2019). Impact of transition in work status and social participation on cognitive performance among elderly in India. *BMC geriatrics, 19*(1), 1-10.
- Coursolle, K. M., Sweeney, M. M., Raymo, J. M., & Ho, J. H. (2010). The association between retirement and emotional well-being: Does prior work–family conflict matter? *Journals of Gerontology Series B: Psychological Sciences and Social Sciences, 65*(5), 609-620.
- Cumming, E., & Henry, W. E. (1961). *Growing old, the process of disengagement*. Basic books.
- Cunningham, W. R., & Brookbank, J. W. (1988). Gerontology: The Psychology, Biology, and Sociology of Aging. *Harper & Row, New York.*
- D'cruz, S. M., Rajaratnam, N., & Kumar, M. P. (2013). The effect of aging on verbal fluency in South Indians. *J Dent Med Sci, 6*, 40-2.
- De Mendonça Lima, C. A. (2004). The reduction of stigma and discrimination against older people with mental disorders: a challenge for the future. *Archives of gerontology and geriatrics. Supplement*, (9), 109-120.
- Delbes, A., & GAYMU, J. (2000). Du veuvage à l'isolement. *Gérontologie et société*, (95), 11-26.
- d'Epinay, C. J. L., Cavalli, S., & Guillet, L. A. (2010). Bereavement in very old age: impact on health and relationships of the loss of a spouse, a child, a sibling, or a close friend. *OMEGA-Journal of Death and Dying, 60*(4), 301-325.
- Depping, M., & Freund, A. M. (2013). When choice matters: Task-dependent memory effects in older adulthood. *Psychology and Aging*, 28, 923–936. doi:10.1037/a9934520.
- Devasahayam, T. W. (Ed.). (2014). Gender and ageing: Southeast Asian perspectives (Vol. 229). Institute of Southeast Asian Studies.
- DiMatteo, M. R. (2004). Social support and patient adherence to medical treatment: a meta-analysis. *Health psychology, 23*(2), 207.
- Dua, P., Aging, A., & Erikson, E. (2017). An aging world. A Biopsychosocial Approach to an Aging World.
- Dziechciaz, M., & Filip, R. (2014). Biological psychological and social determinants of old age: Bio-psycho-social aspects of human aging. *Annals of Agricultural and Environmental Medicine, 21*(4).
- Ebner, N. C., Freund, A. M., & Baltes, P. B. (2006). Developmental changes in personal goal orientation from young to late adulthood:

From striving for gains to maintenance and prevention of losses. *Psychology and Aging*, 21, 664–678. doi:10.1037/0882-7974.21.4.664

- Elder Jr, G. H. (1994). Time, human agency, and social change: Perspectives on the life course. *Social psychology quarterly*, 4-15.
- Erikson, E. H. (1993). Childhood and society. WW Norton & Company.
- Erikson, E. H. (1994). Identity and the life cycle. WW Norton & Company.
- Eugenia Alvarado, B., Victoria Zunzunegui, M., Béland, F., Sicotte, M., & Tellechea, L. (2007). Social and gender inequalities in depressive symptoms among urban older adults of Latin America and the Caribbean. *The Journals of Gerontology Series B: Psychological Sciences and Social Sciences*, *62*(4), S226-S236.
- Fund, U. N. P. (2017). Caring for Our Elders: Early Responses. *India Ageing Report–2017.*
- Gallagher, D. E., Breckenridge, J. N., Thompson, L. W., & Peterson, J. A. (1983). Effects of bereavement on indicators of mental health in elderly widows and widowers. *Journal of Gerontology*, *38*(5), 565-571.
- Gibbs, L. M., Dombrovski, A. Y., Morse, J., Siegle, G. J., Houck, P. R., & Szanto, K. (2009). When the solution is part of the problem: problem solving in elderly suicide attempters. *International Journal of Geriatric Psychiatry*, 24(12), 1396-1404.
- Gibson, H. B. (1992). Health and the quality of life in the later years. In *The Emotional and Sexual Lives of Older People* (pp. 183-210). Springer, Boston, MA.
- Glass, T. A., De Leon, C. M., Marottoli, R. A., & Berkman, L. F. (1999). Population based study of social and productive activities as predictors of survival among elderly Americans. *Bmj*, *319*(7208), 478-483.
- Godschalk, M. F., Sison, A., & Mulligan, T. (1997). Management of erectile dysfunction by the geriatrician. *Journal of the American Geriatrics Society*, *45*(10), 1240-1246.
- Graham, N., Lindesay, J., Katona, C., Bertolote, J. M., Camus, V., Copeland, J. R., ... & Wancata, J. (2003). Reducing stigma and discrimination against older people with mental disorders: a technical consensus statement. *International journal of geriatric psychiatry*, *18*(8), 670-678.

- Halder, S., & Mahato, A. (2019). Identifying multiple domain memory impairment in high-risk group for Alzheimer's disorder. *Journal of Geriatric Mental Health*, *6*(1), 14.
- Hannah, M. T., Domino, G., Figueredo, A. J., & Hendrickson, R. (1996). The prediction of ego integrity in older persons. *Educational and Psychological Measurement*, 56(6), 930-950.
- Hartini, N., Fardana, N. A., Ariana, A. D., & Wardana, N. D. (2018). Stigma toward people with mental health problems in Indonesia. *Psychology research and behavior management*, *11*, 535.
- Hashim, S. M., Eng, T. C., Tohit, N., & Wahab, S. (2013). Bereavement in the elderly: the role of primary care. *Mental health in family medicine*, *10*(3), 159.
- Hays, J. C., Gold, D. T., & Pieper, C. F. (1997). Sibling bereavement in late life. *OMEGA-Journal of Death and Dying*, *35*(1), 25-42.
- Hayslip Jr, B., Maiden, R. J., Thomison, N. L., & Temple, J. R. (2010). Mental health attitudes among rural and urban older adults. *Clinical Gerontologist*, *33*(4), 316-331.
- Hedden, T., Park, D. C., Nisbett, R., Ji, L. J., Jing, Q., & Jiao, S. (2002). Cultural variation in verbal versus spatial neuropsychological function across the life span. *Neuropsychology*, *16*(1), 65.
- Henning, G., Lindwall, M., & Johansson, B. (2016). Continuity in well-being in the transition to retirement. *GeroPsych.*
- Henrard, J. C. (1996). Cultural problems of ageing especially regarding gender and intergenerational equity. *Social Science & Medicine*, *43*(5), 667-680.
- Hershberger, P. J., & Walsh, W. B. (1990). Multiple role involvements and the adjustment to conjugal bereavement: An exploratory study. *OMEGA-Journal of Death and Dying*, *21*(2), 91-102.
- Hummert, M. L. (1994). Physiognomic cues to age and the activation of stereotypes of the elderly in interaction. *The International Journal of Aging and Human Development*, *39*(1), 5-19.
- Hussain, S. (2021). The Transcending Age: A Study of Psycho-social Wellbeing of Elderly Women in India. *Journal of Sociological Research*, 12(1):26.
- James, J. B., & Zarrett, N. (2005). Ego integrity in the lives of older women: A follow-up of mothers from the Sears, Maccoby, and Levin (1951) patterns of child rearing study. *Journal of Adult Development*, 12(4), 155-167.

- Jang, I. H., & Choe, S. J. (2006). Social welfare for older persons in aging society. *Seoul: Seoul national University*
- Jang, S. N., Kawachi, I., Chang, J., Boo, K., Shin, H. G., Lee, H., & Cho, S. I. (2009). Marital status, gender, and depression: analysis of the baseline survey of the Korean Longitudinal Study of Ageing (KLoSA). *Social science & medicine, 69*(11), 1608-1615.
- John, R. (1996). Demography of American Indian elders: social, economic, and health status. *Changing numbers, changing needs: American Indian demography and public health*, 218-231.
- Kim, H. K. (2013). Factors affecting successful aging among male elders in Korea. *Journal of Convergence Information Technology*, 8(14), 341.
- King, D. E., Mainous III, A. G., Carnemolla, M., & Everett, C. J. (2009). Adherence to healthy lifestyle habits in US adults, 1988-2006. *The American journal of medicine, 122*(6), 528-534.
- Kumar, P. S. (2015). Psychological well being and marital adjustment: a study on elderly couples in post parental stage of life. *Indian Journal of Gerontology, 29*(1), 77-90.
- Kumar, V. (1997). Ageing in India--an overview. *The Indian journal of medical research, 106*, 257-264.
- Lalive d'Epinay, C. J., Bickel, J.-F., Maystre, C., & Vollenwyder, N. (2000). Vieillesses au fil du temps. 1979-1994: Une révolution tranquille [Old age across the years. 1979-1994: A quiet revolution]. Lausanne: Réalités Sociales.
- Lamberty, G. J., & Bieliauskas, L. A. (1993). Distinguishing between depression and dementia in the elderly: A review of neuropsychological findings. *Archives of Clinical Neuropsychology, 8*(2), 149-170.
- Lee, G. R., Willetts, M. C., & Seccombe, K. (1998). Widowhood and depression: Gender differences. *Research on Aging, 20*(5), 611-630.
- Levenson, R. W., Carstensen, L. L., & Gottman, J. M. (1993). Longterm marriage: age, gender, and satisfaction. *Psychology and aging, 8*(2), 301.
- Lindwall, M., Berg, A. I., Bjälkebring, P., Buratti, S., Hansson, I., Hassing, L., ... & Johansson, B. (2017). Psychological health in the retirement transition: Rationale and first findings in the Health, Ageing and Retirement Transitions in Sweden (HEARTS) study. *Frontiers in psychology, 8*, 1634.

- Lloyd, P. (2007). The Psychology of Ageing: An Introduction, Ian Stuart-Hamilton, *London, Jessica Kingsley Publishers*, 4th edn, 2006, pp. 352, ISBN 1843104261,£ 19.99.
- Loch, A. A., Wang, Y. P., Guarniero, F. B., Lawson, F. L., Hengartner, M. P., Rössler, W., & Gattaz, W. F. (2014). Patterns of stigma toward schizophrenia among the general population: a latent profile analysis. *International Journal of Social Psychiatry, 60*(6), 595-605.
- Lux, T., & Scherger, S. (2017). By the sweat of their brow? The effects of starting work again after pension age on life satisfaction in Germany and the United Kingdom. *Ageing & Society, 37*(2), 295-324.
- Maddox, G. L. (1970). Persistance of Life Style among the Elderly. *Normal Aging I. Durham, NC, Duke University Press, 329*, 331.
- Masters, W. H., & Johnson, V. E. (1966). Human sexual response, Boston (Little, Brown and Company) 1966.
- Mehra, A., Singla, H., Grover, S., & Avasthi, A. (2020). Stigma for mental disorders among the elderly population in a rural setting. *Indian Journal of Social Psychiatry, 36*(3), 184.
- Mohammadbeigi, A., Hassanzadeh, J., Mohammadsalehi, N., Nasimi, B., & Ranjbar-Omrani, G. (2013). Impacts of osteoporosis on quality of life in elderly women. *Chronic Diseases Journal, 1*(1), 13-17.
- Mohta, R., & Halder, S. (2020). Elderly Population and New Age Technology. *Journal of Psychosocial Research, 15*(1).
- Mossey, J. M., & Shapiro, E. (1982). Self-rated health: a predictor of mortality among the elderly. *American journal of public health*, 72(8), 800-808.
- Nandi, P. S., Banerjee, G., Mukherjee, S. P., Nandi, S., & Nandi, D. N. (1997). A study of psychiatric morbidity of the elderly population of a rural community in West Bengal. *Indian journal of psychiatry, 39*(2), 122.
- Neugarten, B. L. (1974). Age groups in American society and the rise of the young-old. *The annals of the American academy of political and social science, 415*(1), 187-198.
- Newman, A. B., Arnold, A. M., Naydeck, B. L., Fried, L. P., Burke, G. L., Enright, P., ... & Cardiovascular Health Study Research Group. (2003). Successful aging: effect of subclinical cardiovascular disease. *Archives of internal medicine, 163*(19), 2315-2322.
- Nielsen, T. R., Vogel, A., Gade, A., & Waldemar, G. (2012). Cognitive testing in non-demented Turkish immigrants-comparison of the

RUDAS and the MMSE. *Scandinavian journal of psychology*, 53(6), 455-460.

- Nikolova, M., & Graham, C. (2014). Employment, late-life work, retirement, and well-being in Europe and the United States. *IZA Journal of European Labor Studies*, *3*(1), 1-30.
- Olson, D. H., & DeFrain, J. (2013). *Marriages and families*. McGraw-Hill US Higher Ed USE.
- Ott, C. H., Lueger, R. J., Kelber, S. T., & Prigerson, H. G. (2007). Spousal bereavement in older adults: Common, resilient, and chronic grief with defining characteristics. *The Journal of nervous and mental disease*, *195*(4), 332-341.
- Park, D. C., Nisbett, R., & Hedden, T. (1999). Aging, culture, and cognition. *The Journals of Gerontology Series B: Psychological Sciences and Social Sciences*, *54*(2), P75-P84.
- Paul, D. M. (1997). Culture and cognition. *American Review of Sociology*, (23), 263-287.
- Retrieved from https://www.who.int/news-room/fact-sheets/detail/mental-health-of-older-adults
- Rowe, C. L. (2003). Family-based interventions for substance abuse: A profile of two models. *The Family Psychologist*, 19(4), 4–9.
- Saxena, R. (2016). Ageism: perception and beliefs towards elderly people in India. *International Journal of Social Sciences and Management Research*. Vol. 2 No.1. Retrieved from https://iiardpub.org/get/IJSSMR/VOL.%202%20NO.%201%202016/Ageism%202.pdf
- Sengupta, P., Benjamin, A. I., Singh, Y., & Grover, A. (2014). Prevalence and correlates of cognitive impairment in a north Indian elderly population. *WHO South-East Asia journal of public health*, 3(2), 135-143.
- Shome, D., Vadera, S., Khare, S., Ram, M. S., Ayyar, A., Kapoor, R., & Desai, N. (2020). Aging and the Indian face: an analytical study of aging in the Asian Indian face. *Plastic and Reconstructive Surgery Global Open*, 8(3).
- Sontag, S. (2018). *The double standard of aging* (pp. 19-24). Routledge.
- Steptoe, A., & Zaninotto, P. (2020). Lower socioeconomic status and the acceleration of aging: An outcome-wide analysis. *Proceedings of the National Academy of Sciences*, *117*(26), 14911-14917.

- Szinovacz, M. E., & Davey, A. (2006). Effects of retirement and grand-child care on depressive symptoms. *The International Journal of Aging and Human Development*, 62(1), 1-20.
- Thakur, R. P., Banerjee, A., & Nikumb, V. B. (2013). Health Problems Among the Elderly: A Cross. Sectional Study. *Annals of medical and health sciences research*, 3(1), 19-25.
- Thapliyal, G., Halder, S., & Mahato, A. (2016). Memory, verbal fluency, and response inhibition in normal aging. *Journal of Geriatric Mental Health*, 3(2), 145.
- The 10/66 Dementia Research Group (2000). Methodological issues in population-based research into dementia in developing countries. A position paper from the 10/66 Dementia Research Group. *International Journal of Geriatric Psychiatry* 15, 21–30
- Tiwari, S. C., & Pandey, N. M. (2013). The Indian concepts of lifestyle and mental health in old age. *Indian Journal of Psychiatry, 55*(Suppl 2), S288.
- Torges, C. M., Stewart, A. J., & Duncan, L. E. (2008). Achieving ego integrity: Personality development in late midlife. *Journal of Research in Personality*, 42(4), 1004-1019.
- Tyas, S. L., Snowdon, D. A., Desrosiers, M. F., Riley, K. P., & Markesbery, W. R. (2007). Healthy ageing in the Nun Study: definition and neuropathologic correlates. *Age and ageing*, 36(6), 650-655.
- Ward, R. A. (1985). Informal networks and well-being in later life: A research agenda. *The Gerontologist, 25*(1), 55-61.
- Williams, B. R., Baker, P. S., Allman, R. M., & Roseman, J. M. (2006). The feminization of bereavement among community-dwelling older adults. *Journal of Women & Aging, 18*(3), 3-18.
- Wu, Z. H., & Rudkin, L. (2000). Social contact, socioeconomic status, and the health status of older Malaysians. *The Gerontologist, 40*(2), 228-234.

* * *

SEXUALITY IN ELDERLY PERSONS

Prerna Sharma, Deepika Srivastav and Dweepchand Singh

ABSTRACT

Ageing is detrimental condition for every individual although it is a significant stage in life span development. Across all genders they have different perspective with related to ageing and their consequences. In 21st century mental health issues are prominent and were seen across the ages and genders. All the international agencies like World Health Organization (WHO), United Nations and American Psychological Association (APA) talks about the epistemology regarding mental health problems and their possible treatment through specific interventions. In the era technological advancement still members of LGBTQAI+ community are not accepted in societies which stigmatize and trigger psychopathology disorder. This chapter is focuses on the prevalence, variance of psychological problems and implication among elderly.

Keywords: Sexuality, Elderly, Gender, Ageing, LGBTQAI+.

Introduction

In nature we see things and being. Being has the capacity to propagate with systematic process. It ensures the continuity of species through reproduction through 'sexual' or 'asexual' modalities. Here, the existence of an individual is not only important, but it is valuable as well. In sexual reproduction there are two opposite individuals known male and female. There are volumes on sex and sexuality across cultures. In modern era, human sexuality has become complicated due to 'population bomb.' At the biological level of anatomy and physiology, children are sexually mature when they become capable of reproduction, which marks the transition to adolescence. The mature stage emerges after a succession of earlier stages of sexual development. Developmental changes are age-related and endogenous due to strong direction by the human genome. Such changes are construed as a universal series of anatomical structures and physiological competencies leading to a universal state of biological maturity - with due consideration of sex differences, need for nutritional and other environmental support, and individual variations. This is the standard stage model.

At the psychological level of behaviour and cognition, standard stage models fit child development to a substantial degree, especially in the early years. In domains ranging from language to reasoning to social cognition, we can identify universal sequences leading to universally achieved states of maturity and can readily supply typical ages of achievement. Development beyond childhood, however, is quite different. There are no biological or psychological milestones universally achieved over the course of the teen years, nor is there biological or psychological evidence for a state of maturity universal among individuals in their twenties but rarely seen among those in their early teens (Moshman, 2015). People continue to change beyond childhood, but they do not change in ways that fit the standard stage model. If that model defines what we mean by development, then development is a phenomenon of childhood.

Psychological changes beyond childhood, however, often seem developmental in some broad sense, even if not in the stringent sense of stage progression to maturity. Changes in cognition, morality, and identity over the course of adolescence and early adulthood often have a developmental flavor even if they are far from universal, occur at widely varying ages, and are more associated with experience than with genes. In sexuality, as in other matters, the changes that strike us as developmental are those that are extended (even if not tied to age), self-regulated (even if not directed by genes), qualitative (even if not broadly structural), and progressive (even if not culminating in a universal state of maturity). A broader definition of development seems to be required to recognize the developmental potential of adolescence and adulthood. National Elderly Policy (1999) defines persons who are above the age of 60 years as the *Elderly Persons.*

With that in mind, development may be defined as change that is extended, self-regulated, qualitative, and progressive (Moshman, 2011). To say development is *extended* is to say that it takes place over time. This is less stringent than the standard expectation that developmental milestones are achieved at specifiable ages or at least within relatively narrow age ranges. To say development is *self-regulated* is to say that it is not simply caused by the environment. This is less stringent than a maturational conception of development as largely directed by genes (at least within any normal human environment) in a universal and predictable direction. To say development is *qualitative* is to require some sort of novelty, rather than more of the same. This is less stringent than to insist on broad-ranging structural transformation. Finally, to say development is *progressive* is to reserve the term for changes that represent progress. This is less stringent than a requirement that change leads inexorably to a universal state of maturity in order to qualify as developmental. Sexuality development in adolescence does not fit the standard stage model but is, nonetheless, developmental in the broader sense of meeting all four of these criteria.

Sexuality

According to the World Health Organization (WHO), sexual health is defined as "a state of complete physical, mental, emotional and social wellbeing related with sexuality" (Srithanaviboonchai, et al., 2019). The importance of the sexual health for the experiencing of the life at the fullest for all people, especially in older age, who represent a population group comprised of those who are aged 50 or over. The concept of sexuality is a multifaceted construct that encompasses sexual activity, function and behavior. In the Older age, Sexual activity is vital marker of quality of life, which is associated with mental and physical well-being, satisfactory relationships, and reduced risk of chronic diseases. Many recent studies have analysed overall sexual attitudes (such as sexual desire and sexual satisfaction) during aging in different age groups (Ricoy-Cano, et al., 2020).

Disorders Related to Sexual Attitude

Sexual desire disorders are characterized by the lack or diminished desires, interests, thoughts, motivation, or fantasies related to sexual activities, including hypoactive sexual desire disorder. Sexual aversion disorder is aversion or avoidance of genital contact of a sexual partner in activity. Sexual desires are affected by the various disease. There is a clear-cut connection between low desire and depression, which selective serotonin reuptake inhibitors can further compound. Coronary heart diseases and myocardial infractions are also found to be led to a reduction in sexual desires. Renal failure, urinary tract symptoms in women, diabetes, hyperprolactinaemia, primary and secondary hypogonadism in men, bilateral oophorectomy in women, adrenal disease, neurological damage to brain regions related to processing sexual stimuli due to neurological or cardiovascular disease are also found to be a cause of reduced sexual desire and subjective arousal (Basson & Schultz, 2007).

Sexual arousal disorders are different for both men and women. Male erectile dysfunction is characterized by difficulty or failure to maintain an appropriate erection until the completion of the last phase of the sexual activity or by lack of sexual excitement (subjective sense) and pleasure during sexual activity. In female sexual arousal disorders, attaining and maintaining the appropriate level of lubrication swelling response till the last phase of the sexual activity cycle or lack of sexual excitement and pleasure (subjective sense) during sexual activity is generally seen. Coronary artery disease, renal failure, lower urinary tract symptoms, cardiac failure, hypertension, diabetes, hypogonadism, depression, sleep apnoea, and neurological disorders involving the autonomic nervous system are the primary cause of erectile dysfunction in men. Sexual dysfunction due to cardiovascular disease, diabetes, and renal failure are much less common in women than men. Atheroma of hypogastric and pudendal arteries is found to be associated with reduced lubrication in women. Oestrogen deficiency is also more frequently associated with reduced response to sexual stimuli (Basson & Schultz, 2007).

Orgasm disorders are characterized by absent or delayed orgasm followed by an expected level of arousal and excitement phase of the sexual activity cycle of adequate intensity and duration in both males and females. Another male orgasm disorder, called premature ejaculation characterized by ejaculation either before, upon, or shortly after penetration, with minimal sexual stimulation or before a man wants it. Prostatitis, epididymitis, spinal cord injury, low testosterone in men, damage to pelvis nerves, urethritis, pelvic floor dysfunction, post-menopause in women are the most common causes of sexual dysfunctions of orgasm and ejaculation in men (Basson & Schultz, 2007).

Sexual pain disorders include dyspareunia and vaginismus. In dyspareunia, genital pain is experienced by either sex, before, during, or after sexual intercourse, given the pain must not be caused by lack of lubrication or vaginismus. Vaginismus is characterized by involuntary spasms in one-third of vaginal musculature that interfere with coitus (Halvorsen & Metz, 1992). Peyronie's disease, phimosis, priapism, sickle cell disease, thalassemia, leukaemia, dermatological diseases, sexually transmitted diseases, and penile cancer are the most common causes dyspareunia in men. Vulvovaginal atrophy, hypothalamic or pituitary disease, bilateral oophorectomy, pelvic radiation, lower urinary tract symptoms, chronic vulvovaginal candidosis, fibromyalgia, genital mutilation, dermatological disease, and anatomical variations are seen in women as a cause of dyspareunia (Basson & Schultz, 2007).

Misconceptions and Myths about Sexuality and Ageing

The concept of Sexuality in older adults can represent as "a dark continent", which most of the people, including physicians, prefer not to think about. Unfortunately, this stereotypical thinking, prejudice and ignorance still dominate current views on sexuality in old age. Mentioned below are some of the misconceptions and myths about it (Domingues & Barbagallo, 2016).

2.1. *"Sexuality does not exist in old age"*

The belief that sexuality vanishes during old age is frequent among the general population, but among health care providers. For example, a study showed that most nurses interviewed did not believe that people in their 70's had sexual needs.

2.2. *"Sexuality among older persons is comical"*

Sexuality in old age is frequently seen as laughable, which is illustrated by the jokes about it and humorous birthday cards that refer to the potency decline over the years. This may be partly explained by the general attitudes linking sexuality to physical attractiveness and beauty, incorrectly regarding both as necessary components for relationships, while the media creates an amusing picture of seniors' sexuality.

2.3. *"Sexuality among older persons is disgusting"*

This stereotype makes older people feel shame or guilty about feelings of sexual desire and precludes to openly express these concerns and needs to the medical staff for fear of being branded as inappropriate, bizarre, obscene, or as "dirty old people".

2.4. *"Sexual activity in long-term care (LTC) facilities is against the rules"*

A study conducted in residential retirement facilities, which involved white men and women aged 80–102 years using an anonymous 117-item questionnaire found that 62% of men and 30% of women over 80 years had recent intercourse, and 87% of men and 68% of women had physical intimacy of some sort (Bretschneider & McCoy, 1988). Another study in 15 LTC facilities, interviewing seniors with a mean age of 82 years showed that 81% of men and 75% of women reported sexual desire, but were currently sexually inactive because of lack of opportunity (Hajjar & Kamel, 2003).

2.5. *"Assumed to be heterosexual"*

The presence of lesbian, gay, bisexual and transgender (LGBT) older adults is often not considered (Frediksen-Goldsen & Kim, 2015; Griebling, 2016). A study reported that staff members tend to have more negative views of same-sex intimacy (Hinrichs & Vacha-Haase, 2010).

Sexual Identities

Largely it is seen that the significant growth in sixty five plus population those include gay, lesbian, bisexual and transgender as a part of LGBT population. This population experience almost similar challenges, barriers and inequalities that disrupt their quality of life.

Challenges faced by LGBT Elders: The aging is not a very smooth process. Moreover, it is more difficult for a member of disfavoured legally and social minority as the real life challenges are comparatively more than their heterosexual community.

Challenges Associated with Social Stigma: The stigma associated with LGBT community stand in a way of participating fully in society. The historical prejudice have an impact on their overall well-being.

Existence in Society and Families of Choice: Presently, the society is quite modern yet somewhere people are failing to accept the concept of homosexuality. At home LGBT elders are more likely to be childless, single and unaccepted by family members whereas the heterosexual elder have a family and receive proper care from family members. Having same sex partner is still perceived as a crime by society therefore, the acceptance towards this community is less.

Legal Biasness: Law is failing to provide the financial security and social acceptance for LGBT elders. There is a need to address the security issues with these elders which our system is failing to do. The barriers in society make the successful aging harder of this community.

Financial Insecurities: The lifetime of discrimination faced by LGBT elders– combined with the resulting effects on financial security–is compounded by major laws and safety net programs that fail to protect and support LGBT elders equally with their heterosexual peers.

Difficulties associated with Health related facilities: Health care is an important problematic issue for elderly people of LGBT community as they lack social support and financial security. There are related needs of health care are as follows:

1. The LGBT elders' are overlooked in terms of their health. Service providers should provide some extra care of this population and this population has higher rates of chronic illness.
2. The government and social support for families are limited. LGBT elders rely on family-of-choice caregivers, who often do not receive the same legal or social recognition as biological family caregivers.
3. The trained professionals are required in health sector for the treatment of LGBT elderly as many professionals may be discriminate or unaware about the existence of LGBT elderly.
4. There is high demand of providing friendly environment in Nursing homes, clinics and hospitals.
5. Insurance policies in health care system should give family of choice to such individuals.

Psychological Intervention

The prognosis of psychological interventions is much less with the Elderly as there is higher prevalence of medical disorders makes attention to physical causes of symptoms and to iatrogenic effects of medications as causes of symptoms highly important as well. There are many benefits of providing psychotherapeutic intervention for this population.

1. **Rebuilding Self-concept and Self-esteem:** The main task of psychotherapy is to understand the self-perception and helping individual of this community. As loss in biopsychosocial functions are associated with various physical and psychological limitations therefore, impact self-esteem. Psychotherapeutic sessions help individual in restoring a more positive view of themselves as an important and competent person hence, restore of feelings of mastery and self-esteem.

2. **Helping through Grief Process:** The loss of loving one is unbearable and difficult to process. Elderly go through multiple losses of friends, spouse, relatives and their own roles as an authority figure. It is important to resolve these feelings. Therapeutic intervention helps elderly to deal with these painful emotions smoothly.

3. **Dealing with Problems of Aging, Illness, and Possible Dependence:** For elderly patients facing the many changes and narcissistic losses of aging, including increased dependency and anticipation and fear of dependency and physical illnesses, the process of psychotherapy can offer a safe and trusting relationship in which to examine those most frightening feelings. These fears may be of being hated by or disgusting to the caretaker, or perhaps it is intolerable to be "in someone else's hands." The experience of therapy offers the elderly person a chance to respond to these frightening feelings in a manner that is life enhancing rather than stagnating. Aging well depends on the ability to mourn for the self, which opens possibilities and freedom in the years that are to come. For those with sufficient internal resources, aging, despite all its losses, may be a spur to positive development of the personality.

4. **Dealing with concept of Death and Dying:** In old age, impending death becomes a reality that can no longer be denied and facing this can be a challenge. For an old person

with a poor ego function, this task can be quite overwhelming. However, death-related anxiety is more a part of early adult life than of old age because, for elderly individuals, pain and suffering related to death are more of a concern than the fear of death itself. The concern about death itself does not end here, because for some people the thought of not existing or not being is not a possibility they can imagine. Even if they are not religious, the thought of life after death is a pressing question that should be explored, as it is clinically significant.

5. Transference and Countertransference: Transference occurs when a patient experiences the therapist as a significant figure from the past with whom he or she had a highly significant and developmentally important relationship. The therapist, empathically understanding the transference relationship, aims to respond differently from the figures of the past, which creates a more positive experience for the patient. In this way, the patient develops a more positive view of the self. Transference phenomenon unique to psychotherapy with the elderly in which the therapist is viewed as the child of the patient, and he termed it reverse transference. Countertransference is defined here as the therapist's experience of the elderly patient. The therapist needs to pay special attention to any positive or negative feelings he or she has toward the patient. For the therapist, a relationship with an elderly person can be anxiety provoking because of the possible physical problems, dementing illness, apparent helplessness, and dependency that the elderly person may have. This therapist anxiety in turn can promote fear of engulfment by the patient and can lead to withdrawal from or rejection of the patient. Overidentification with the patient's problems can also invoke feelings of sadness and pity, which can block accurate empathy and realistic exploration of the possibilities of change.

Conclusion

There are various issues in the sexuality when related with different gender orientations, these issues may vary due to numerous reasons, it is important to wider and perspective for the sexuality among older men and women. The myths need to be clarified and interventions are needed in the prospective area to manage these psychosocial issues.

References

- Atiq, R. (2006). Common Themes and Issues in Geriatric Psychotherapy. *Psychiatry (Engmont), 3*(6), *53-56.*
- Basson, R., & Schultz W. (2007). Sexual sequelae of general medical disorders. *The Lancet, 369*, 409–24.
- Braun, M., Wassmer, G., Klotz, T. et al. (2000). Epidemiology of erectile dysfunction: Results of the 'Cologne Male Survey'. *Int J Impot Res, 12*, 305-311.
- Camacho, M. E., & Reyes-Ortiz, C. A. (2005). Sexual dysfunction in the elderly: Age or disease? In *International Journal of Impotence Research* (Vol. 17, Issue SUPPL. S1). https://doi.org/10.1038/sj.ijir.3901429.
- Chew, K.K., Bremner, A., Stuckey, B., et al. (2009). Sex life after 65: How does erectile dysfunction affect ageing and elderly men? *Aging Male, 12*, 41-46.
- DeBusk, R., Drory, Y., Goldstein, I., et al. (2000). Management of sexual dysfunction in patients with cardiovascular disease: recommendations of the Princeton Consensus Panel. *American Journal of Cardiology, 86*,175–81.
- Fedele D, Bortolotti A, & Coscelli C, et al. (2000). Erectile dysfunction in type 1 and type 2 diabetics in Italy. *International Journal of Epidemiology*, 29, 524– 31.
- Halvorsen, J. G., & Metz, M. E. (1992). Sexual dysfunction, Part I: Classification, etiology, and pathogenesis. *The Journal of the American Board of Family Practice*, 5(1), 51-61.
- Hatzimouratidis, K., & Hatzichristou, D. (2007). Sexual dysfunctions: classifications and definitions. *The journal of sexual medicine*, 4(1), 241-250.

- Kennedy, S. & Rizvi, S. (2009). Sexual dysfunction, depression, and the impact of antidepressants. *Journal Clinical Psychopharmacology, 29*, 157–64.
- Kostis, J., Jackson, G., Rosen, R., et al. (2005). Sexual dysfunction and cardiac risk (the Second Princeton Consensus Conference). *The American Journal of Cardiology, 96*, 313–21.
- Lindau, S.T., Schumm, L.P., Laumann, E.O., et al. (2007). A study of sexuality and health among older adults in the United States. *N Engl J Med*, 357, 762- 774.
- Moshman, D. (2009). *Liberty and learning: Academic freedom for teachers and students.* Portsmouth, NH: Heinemann.
- Meador, K. & Davis, C. (1996). Psychotherapy. In: Busse E, Blazer D (eds): The American Psychiatric Press Textbook of Geriatric Psychiatry. Washington, DC: American Psychiatric Press, Inc., 395–412.
- Sathyanarayana Rao TS, Ismail S, Darshan MS, Tandon A. (2015). Sexual disorders among elderly: An epidemiological study in south Indian rural population. *Indian J Psychiatry*, 57, 236-41.
- Sarkadi, A., & Rosenqvist, U. (2001). Contradictions in the medical encounter: Female sexual dysfunction in primary care contacts. *Fam Pract, 18*, 161-166.
- Selvin, E., Burnett, A.L., & Platz, E. A. (2007). Prevalence and risk factors for erectile dysfunction in the US. *Am J Med*, 120, 151-157.
- Rees, P., Fowler, C., & Maas C. (2007). Sexual function in men and women with neurological disorders. *The Lancet*, 369, 512–25.
- Valadares, A.L., Pinto-Neto, A.M., Osis, M.J., et al. (2008). Prevalence of sexual dysfunction and its associated factors in women aged 40-65 years with 11 years or more of formal education: A population-based household survey. *Clinics (Sao Paulo)*, 63, 775-782.
- Wagner, G., & Mulhall, J. (2001). Pathophysiology and diagnosis of male erectile dysfunction. *BJU Int, 88*, 3-10.
- Wylie, K., & Kenney, G. (2010). Sexual dysfunction and the ageing male. *Maturitas*, 65(1), 23–27. https://doi.org/10.1016/j.maturitas.2009.10.018.
- Zheng, H., Bidasee, K., Mayhan, W., et al. (2007). Lack of central nitric oxide triggers erectile dysfunction in diabetes. American Journal of Physiology, 292, 1158-64.

* * *

A PROBE INTO THE ENVIRONMENTAL IMPACT ON HEALTH AND WELLBEING IN OLD AGE

Mohua Chatterjee

Introduction

The origin of Environmental Psychology may be traced back to the person-in-context approach of Kurt Lewin. Behaviour is the resultant of the person, his environment, and the interaction between the person with his environment. Environmental Psychology does not study person and environment as separate entities; rather focuses on the reciprocal interplay or transaction between people and environment, the way people shape their environment, and the impacts those transactions create upon people's attitudes, values, behaviours and experiences. Environmental Psychology considers both natural and man-made environments, with due importance to the socio-cultural domains; and purports to shape and modify the physical environment so as to make it congenial and user friendly based on research-based intervention strategies. The discipline follows an interdisciplinary perspective; and works in collaboration with the experts from various fields like architecture, geography, environmental science, gerontology and so on.

Environmental gerontology, being a sub-discipline under environmental psychology deals with human-environment interaction in association with ageing; and aims to ascertain, analyze, assess, modify and optimize the impacts of natural, built and social environments on health and general wellbeing of elderly people. A person's functioning depends on his resources, such as, interests, abilities, skills, training, experience etc., the physical and/or social context or environment in which the person is embedded, and the compatibility between the person and his environment. With ageing, the person-environment compatibility declines with the gradual decrement in the individual's physical and psychological health; and he may find it increasingly difficult to keep pace with the changing demands of his environment, owing to poor health and reduced competencies. The subject matters of environmental gerontology include differential effects of natural and built environments on older adults, space perception of elderlies, variation in the need for privacy, personal space and perceived control over space, impacts of physical barriers on restricted mobility, consequences of voluntary or involuntary relocation on health and quality of life, psychophysical problems associated with detachment from familiar places, objects and people, changes in place attachment and personal identity owing to relocation, difficulties in adjustment to new places and so on.

The following section has focused on the behavioural and health consequences of elderly people of natural and built environment components.

Impact of Natural Environment

The roots of mankind are based in nature. Looking at the nature containing mountains and glaciers, water bodies, farmland, clumps of trees and bushes makes us feel refreshed, energetic and relaxed. Regular and sustained exposure to nature has been found to reduce mental health problems among the elderlies, such as, slower cognitive decline

(Mullenbach et al., 2018), subjective wellbeing (Ola & Mathur, 2018), and ensure healthy ageing. Natural environmental conditions may sometimes pose threats to human health; and may be perceived as stressors when the human adaptive resources fall short or fail to cope with them. Environmental stressors comprise both cataclysmic events and ambient stressors.

Cataclysmic events including natural disasters, such as, flood, drought, earthquake, tsunami, cyclone, volcanic eruption, and technological catastrophe are sudden, powerful events attributed to human actions and errors. These events affect a large section of community within a small span of time, and require major adaptive resources and intervention.

There has been debate among the researchers over the years concerning the vulnerability of the older people to cataclysmic events in comparison to the younger ones. Several researchers have found that physical well-being (Alipour et al., 2015; and Jia et al., 2010) and psychological health (O'donnell and Forbes, 2016; Alipour et al., 2015; and Srinivasan et al., 2014) of older adults are more affected by natural disasters compared to their younger counterparts. The researchers have subjected elderly people's growing vulnerability to natural disasters to their deteriorating physical and psychological health and functional capacity. They suffer from decreased sensory and motor skills, elevated reaction time, increased information processing time, poor cognitive abilities, physical impairment, restricted mobility, chronic illnesses requiring continuous medical supervision, physical and emotional dependence on others, socioeconomic limitations, diminished resilience and coping skills, and several other problems. Consequently, when faced with a disaster, older people become slower than younger ones in seeking assistance from others, procuring aids, resolving problems encountered during the catastrophe, and even evacuating the space. Another group of researchers stresses that elderly people are less vulnerable to psychological impacts of disasters compared to the younger survivors (Banks, 2013 & Cherniack, 2008). Elderlies do not easily fall prey to such events because of their maturity, experience, and greater exposure to life's stressors which enhance their resilience and coping skills, inoculate them against the negative effects of similar stressors, and help them to resist and combat the stressors.

Ambient stressors, including climate change, pollution, noise, overpopulation, etc., are chronic and continuous in nature; and take their toll on human health slowly. Individuals are differentially susceptible to the impacts of ambient stressors, based on their age, condition of health, exposure and adaptive resources.

The vast climate change throughout the globe over the years has severe consequences on human health. The excessive rise in temperature followed by heat waves, increased rainfall causing flood, river bank erosion, snowstorm and blizzards, hurricanes, typhoons, tornados, lack of rain causing drought, loss of forest, forest fire, disappearance of water bodies and desertification, etc., impact the physical and psychosocial health of the community, especially the vulnerable population of older adults. The venerable section may suffer from psychophysical pathologies, mental and physical weakness, hypertension, headache, hyperalgesia and pains, and autonomic symptoms, such as, mood disturbances, irritability and anxiety (Mazza et al., 2012).

The adverse impacts created by the environmental pollutants on the aged people are matters of grave concern and challenge. Due to a weak immune system, decreased vigour, and chronic physical pathologies, they become easily susceptible to the environmental toxicants; and the damage becomes irreparable. Aging causes alterations in neuroendocrine and neurotransmitter levels and the thyroid-pituitary axis; decrement in the secretion of significant hormones like growth hormone, insulin, and sex steroids; and enhancement in levels of glucocorticoids and cytokines. All these alterations make the elderlies more vulnerable to the environmental adversities than the younger section of the society.

Older individuals have been found to suffer from environmentally associated adverse health effects, such as, neurotoxicity (Kodavanti, 1999), cancer (Akman, 2003), cardiovascular and pulmonary morbidity (Bateson & Schwartz, 2004; Lippman et al., 2003; Reaven, 2003), inflammatory responses (McCord, 2003), and gastrointestinal effects caused by several waterborne pathogens (Naumova et al., 2003). The increased levels of air pollutants including nitrogen dioxide, sulphur dioxide, ground level ozone, carbon monoxide, benzene and particle pollution caused by dust, dirt, smoke, etc., in the major cities of the world, nowadays, are related to the enhanced rate of chronic obstructive pulmonary disease (COPD), chronic bronchitis (CB), asthma, cancer, and cardiac problems among the dwellers. Numerous researchers have recorded evidences of ambient particulate matter causing respiratory and cardiovascular diseases (Zeng et al., 2010; Cakmak et al., 2007; Fischer et al., 2003), hospitalization for respiratory illness (Schwartz, 1995), pneumonia (Zanobetti & Schwartz, 2006; Medina-Ramon et al., 2006), COPD (Medina-Ramon et al., 2006; Yang et al., 2005; Chen et al., 2004), emergency department visit for asthma (Villeneuve et al., 2007), and cough and phlegm (Bentayeb et al., 2010) among the aged population. Outdoor pollution exposure has been linked to increased mortality rate among the older people relating to respiratory issues (Dong et al., 2012; Romieu et al., 2012; Brunekreef et al., 2009; Jerrett et al., 2009; Franklin et al., 2007; Filleul et al., 2004; & Aga et al., 2003), COPD (Romieu et al., 2012; Naess et al., 2007; Aga et al., 2003; & Fischer et al., 2003), cardiopulmonary causes (Romieu et al., 2012; Aga et al., 2003), and pneumonia (Aga et al., 2003; & Fischer et al., 2003).

Noise affects the human health and wellbeing in a number of ways including, annoyance, irritability, mood swing, aggression, depletion of attentional capacity, reduced energy, sleep disturbances, interference with communication, impaired task performance, temporary or permanent hearing loss, decreased prosocial behaviour, and so on. Elderly people due to their ailing health and decreasing cognitive capacities fall under the vulnerable group, being affected by the adverse effects of noise more than the younger ones. Uncontrolled and unpredictable noise may take a toll on them by creating an attentional overload, which, in turn, disturbs their performance and interpersonal relations. Noise pollution has been found to be significantly related to depressed or negative mental condition of the older adults in India (Firdaus, 2016).

Extreme temperature can be detrimental for the elderlies, due to the age specific deteriorations in the ability to sustain the adverse effects of heat and cold stress. The internal system regulating the body temperature becomes weak with increasing age, owing to certain diseases, chronic dehydration, and medications. Older people suffer more than the younger ones from reduction in heat loss responses of sweating, skin vasodilation, and impaired body heat dissipation. Consequently, they take longer to perceive the changes in ambient air temperature and respond to it, and fall prey to heat related morbidity and mortality (Kenney & Hodgson, 1987). Though the capacity of acclimatization is person-specific, those with pre-existing health conditions are particularly vulnerable to heat stress and heat stroke.

Impact of Built Environment

Built environment, as per Grant et al. (2000) comprises "all buildings, spaces, and products that are created and modified by humans". Van Cauwenberg et al. (2011) conceived of built environment as the objective and perceived characteristics of the physical context in which people spend their time. Built environment includes the broad features of urban layout such as, cityscapes (building heights, shapes, design and architecture, and overall density), streetscapes (street width, tree cover, housing density, zoning etc.) and the basic services or infrastructure that are required to keep the society running and healthy (transportation, water supply, sewerage system, utilities such as, electricity and gas, services related to education, recreation, bureaucracy, and emergency services such as, police and fire). The mutual dependence and interactions among these core components of the built environment greatly impact the health and well-being of individuals and their communities. The elements of built environment have profound effects on the psychological health of people. Low rise housing, better housing condition and healthy physical and social environment have a significant impact on positive mental health of the elderlies (Firdaus, 2016). The health, wellbeing and quality of life of older adults are more influenced by the aspects of built environment, since this age group spends more time at home in comparison to younger adults (Garin et al., 2014).

Place Identity and Relocation

People's identities are based on the interplay among genetic, environmental and socio-cultural factors. Place identity being a sub-domain of an individual's personal identity, consists of his or her knowledge and feelings about the physical spaces based on regular interactions with them (Proshansky et al., 1983). People develop place identities in multiple ways, in which place functions to provide a sense of belonging, construct meaning, foster attachment and mediate change. Place identity being a dynamic concept undergoes continuous modifications throughout a person's life. The concepts related to place identity include place attachment, that is, a positive emotional bond grown between individuals and their environment (Altman & Low, 1992), and sense of place, that is, a sense of belonging to a physical environment, personal and collective identity being the by-products of this sense of belonging.

Abandonment of a familiar place and subsequent movement to a new setting is not only stressful but also requires skills of adaptation and reconstruction. When cherished places, spaces, and settings are destroyed or irrevocably changed beyond control, people feel a sense of loss and grief, and feel that their personal identities are at stake. Forced removal from place and land has been catastrophic for many indigenous people. Voluntary evacuation and subsequent relocation to other settings may also be impactful for people, especially the vulnerable section. Stresses relating to relocation are magnified for aged people, as their physiological capacities and psychological resources gradually decline with age, and fall short of demand. The aged people's abilities to cope with relocation may be limited, and may result in a syndrome, that is, "a state in which an individual experiences physiological and/or psychological disturbances as a result of a transfer from one environment to another" (Brugler et al., 1993).

Borup (1982) mentioned about four types of relocation, namely, interinstitutional (moving from one place to another such as, hospital), intrainstitutional (moving from one room to the other in the same institution such as, care home), residential (moving from one residence to another), and residential or institutional (moving from the residence to an institution such as, old age home, or vice versa), which may be experienced by the elderlies. Residential relocation may be taxing for the aged people, as they have to bear with the psychological pain associated with moving away from the place with which they have formed strong emotional attachments over the years. Adaptation with the new setting requires them exploring the space and forming new contacts, which may not be possible always due to ailing health and restricted mobility. Shamian et al. (1984) finds the movement from the residence to the institution as the most stressful of all the four types of relocation for the aged persons. Mikhail (1992) has attributed this perceived stress to loss of friendship, possessions and personal autonomy.

The negative impacts of relocation on the elderly people include deterioration in general health (Lawton & Yaffe, 1970; Percy, 1974), and increased mortality rate (Percy, 1974). Residential relocation has been found to be associated with damaged health status (Ferraro, 1982), decrease in functional health and psychological wellbeing (Ben-Sira, 1991), and depression resulting from lack of control over the new setting. Gass et al., (1992) reported that when people perceive the move as threatening, a decrease in their psychological health and morale results.

Age, gender, physical status, economic condition, experience of relocation, quality of the new environment, and population density of the environment determine a person's adjustment to relocation to a new setting. People who live alone, belong to low socioeconomic strata, are undergoing some kind of rehabilitation, possess lower levels of life satisfaction and aggressive coping style are more susceptible to the adverse impacts of relocation. Movement away from a familiar area (Mikhail, 1992), and to the setting with high population density (Carsrud et al., 1979) create stress for the relocates. On the other hand, the aged people may be able to adapt to a relocation that is planned (Mikhail, 1992), does not last long (Chenitz, 1983), or is voluntary. They can better adapt to the relocation and view themselves in control of the situation, when they are prepared beforehand. Such persons can perceive the relocation experience positively; and exhibit evidences of higher morale and physical health. Moreover, when the new setting offers more benefits, or is perceived as an improved one than the previous environment, people can adjust easily (Kowalski, 1981).

Sense of Community and Neighbourhood Attachment

Sense of community involves the feeling of belongingness shared by the members of a group, mutual trust and faith among them that they matter to one another, and a shared conviction that their needs will be met through their commitment to be together (McMillan & Chavis, 1986). Built environment through enhanced social interaction and participation can nurture and enhance the sense of community and community cohesion, which are significant for community mental wellbeing. However, graffiti, litter, broken benches, poor maintenance of parks, poorly designed and ill-maintained footpaths with obstacles, uneven surface and potholes, and an overall lack of safety can create difficulties for older adults to navigate, thereby limiting their physical activities (Adlakha et al., 2020). Stathi et al., (2012) also assert that the factors such as, attractiveness, availability of public transport, access to seating and green space improve the neighbourhood quality; and facilitate the use of local neighbourhood by older adults. Too much traffic on the street disrupts the social cohesion of a neighbourhood (Halpern, 1995), as it makes difficult for people to sit outdoors or to converse on the street. Moreover, excess traffic increases the number of strangers in the neighbourhood, which in turn, increases the fear of crime among the people (Fowler, 1987); and enhances noise and pollution in the environment. All these take a toll on the physical and mental health of people, especially of the vulnerable section of aged people; and reduce social support and sense of community. Neighbourhood amenities such as libraries and community centres and community-based cultural programmes have been found to provide the aged people with indispensable opportunities for social participation and community engagement (Adlakha et al., 2020).

Neighbourhood attachment has been observed to promote social networks, norm of reciprocity and mutual trust among people (Putman, 2000); and to correlate positively with health (Andrew & Keefe, 2014), wellbeing (Cramm et al., 2013), quality of life (Lucumi et al., 2015; Buffel et al., 2012), lower prevalence of mental health disorder (Friedman et al., 2012), and reduced mortality rate (Lochner et al., 2003) among old people. Oswald et al., (2011) has found neighbourhood quality to explain life satisfaction of the elderly dwellers aged above 65 years. Neighbourhood walkability (that is, availability of pedestrian-friendly spaces and restricted motor traffic) can decrease depressive symptoms (Berke et al., 2007); and neighbourhood context has been found to determine the cognitive function (Sheffield & Peek, 2009) among old adults. Aversive neighbourhood environments, on the contrary, may bring about functional deterioration (Balfour & Kaplan, 2002) among the aged inhabitants.

Perception of Neighbourhood Safety

Perception of neighbourhood safety may reduce the prevalence of mental health disorders (Friedman et al., 2012). It strengthens neighbourhood attachment and community mental health by facilitating neighbourhood walkability and regular interactions among the residents. One of the most important predictors of perceived neighbourhood safety is the satisfaction with the features of the local built environment. The relationship between environmental design and crime has two dimensions. First, levels of crime can be reduced through environmental design (Newman, 1972); and second, environmental design contributes to fear of crime, which becomes even more problematic than the actual levels of crime (Halpern, 1995; Heinzelmann, 1981). Oscar Newman (1973) in his Defensible Space Theory suggested about certain design features which may enhance the residents' sense of security and decrease crime in the territory. He proposed to use real or symbolic barriers to separate public and private territories, and to provide opportunities for surveillance over the territory to the owners. However, the erection of barriers, either symbolic or real, has not been proved to be effective enough for preventing crime. The size and homogeneity of the neighbourhood, physical appearance of the neighbourhood in terms of vacant properties, graffiti, broken windows, etc., reflecting physical incivilities and lack of order, the presence of gangs of youths, homeless people and poverty, and low levels of social cohesion, social integration, and lack of community feeling contribute to the fear of crime or perceived lack of safety in the environment.

Among older people, feelings of lack of safety can have negative consequences on health (Jackson & Stafford, 2009), and psychological wellbeing (Firdaus, 2016; Van Dyck et al., 2015). Elderly people are one of the strongly affected groups by the safety implications of isolation.

Privacy and Crowding

Privacy is the selective control over another's access to one's self, one's group, or one's environment. People depend on two mechanisms to gratify their need for privacy: personal space and territorial behaviour. Personal space is an invisible bubble that people maintain around themselves, wherever they go. It determines how closely one will approach others, or will allow others to approach his or her self during an interaction. The size of the personal space bubble may shrink depending on age, sex, socioeconomic status, personality variables, quality of relationship, nature of task, perceived safety of the environment etc. Territories, on the other hand, are visible and static boundaries that people maintain to find solitude and identify with the place. Crowding is the psychological counterpart of density; and results from the violation of personal space and territory. It is the subjective perception of people feeling physically constrained and overburdened with too many interactions beyond cognitive capacity. Crowding, invasion of privacy, decreased personal space and disturbed territorial behaviour harm physical and psychological health of people; and cause damaged social relationships, increased aggression, abusive behaviour, substance abuse, decreased prosocial behaviour, and limited ability to function in an environment. Firdaus (2016) found the depressed mental condition of the Indian older adults to be significantly related with overcrowding. At old age, people's need for personal space increases (Hayduk, 1983), which may contribute to higher density stress among the aged than the young ones. However, aged people's desires for communication should be met, for helping them not to experience feelings of isolation, loneliness and depression.

Concluding Remark

Environmental gerontology with an applied and multidisciplinary approach addresses the problems of old people, emerging as a consequence of person-environment interaction. The discipline focuses on ascertaining the factors underlying the problems, and finding solutions to them. It is practically difficult, if not impossible, to discuss the impacts of environment on the aged people, taking all the aspects of natural and built environments into account. However, an attempt has been made here, to throw light on some of the important areas of environmental influence on the vulnerable section of aged population.

Along with alpha matching or congruence among different components of the built environment from the objective point of view, the environmental psychologists and designers should aim at beta batching or making the environment habitable, with due consideration to various elements like spatial allocations, aesthetic of space, lighting, temperature, access to nature, colour, indoor air quality, noise, user control of space, imageability, surveillance and perceived safety, maintenance of personal space and privacy etc. The amount, distribution, and form of interior spaces should be given importance so as to make the environment coherent and meaningful, and satisfy the territorial behaviours of the users. Comfortable, soothing and sustainable indoor air quality, thermal comfort, natural ventilation, access to sufficient amount of daylight, lack of glare, and proper insulation of walls ensuring privacy of the owners should be made available; and planning must be done accordingly. Efforts should be made not only toward improving the fit between users and their environments but also toward reducing differences between designers' and occupants' definitions of good design. In old age, multiple morbidity, cognitive and motor disability, and frailty create special needs. The design process, therefore, should consider such needs, so as to minimize the adverse impacts as well as enhance the liveability of the space.

Sense of community among the residents may be enhanced by a thoughtful urban planning that ensures visual coherence, legibility and orientation, diversity and attractiveness of the buildings, privacy and territorial behaviour, recreation and entertainment facilities, opportunities for creative involvement in the transformation of the place, safety, social interaction and participation in cultural activities, availability and easy access to amenities, connectivity to community resources, and availability of regular public transport.

Finally, satisfaction with the environment may be achieved when the design allows social support, and perceived control over privacy at the same time. The design which allows the opportunities for interaction without hindering one's autonomy of determining where, when, how much and with whom to interact provides utmost satisfaction and ensures better mental health.

The social awareness and policies regarding community care, health promotion and related concerns for the elderlies can be guided by the researches on ageing and environment. More researches in the areas such as, impacts of environmental determinants on quality of life of old people, associations between aspects of built environment and physical and mental health of the users, relation between neighbourhood quality and residents' satisfaction, and impacts of relocation and readjustment in the new setting on the psychosocial health; with an action research methodology characterized by the collaboration among all the stakeholders including the representatives from different age groups, especially the elderlies, urban planners and architects, health care professionals, municipal authorities are needed, so as to facilitate the construction of an age-friendly society and bring about positive changes in the mindsets of people in general, towards the aged people. From the user's perspective, it will be a setting favouring preservation and restoration of the natural environment and construction of a built environment equipped with all basic amenities simultaneously; which will enable the occupants not only to maintain their health, wellbeing and quality of life, but also to fulfil their basic needs of autonomy and identity.

References

- Adlakha, D., Krishna, M., Woolrych, R., & Ellis, G. (2020). Neighbourhood Supports for Active Ageing in Urban India. *Psychology and Develop Societies,* 32 (2), 254-277.
- Aga, E., Samoli, E., & Touloumi, G. (2003). Short-term effects of ambient particles on mortality in the elderly: results from 28 cities in the APHEA2 project. *Eur Respir J Suppl, 40,* 28s-33s.
- Akman, S. (2003). Overview of oxidative stress and cancer. In Cutler, R. & Rodriguez, H. (Eds). *Critical Reviews of Oxidative Stress and Aging.* Hackensack, NJ: World Scientific, 925–954.

- Alipour, F., Khankeh, H., Fekrazad, H., Kamali, M., Rafiey, H., & Ahmadi, S. (2015). Social issues and post-disaster recovery: a qualitative study in an Iranian context. *Int Soc Work, 58*(5), 689–703.
- Altman, I., & Low, S. (Eds.). (1992). *Place attachment.* New York: Plenum.
- Andrew, M. K., & Keefe, J. M. (2014). Social vulnerability from a social ecology perspective: A cohort study of older adults from the National Population Health Survey of Canada. *BMC Geriatrics, 14,* 90.
- Balfour, J. L., & Kaplan, G. A. (2002). Neighborhood environment and loss of physical function in older adults: Evidence from the Alameda County Study. *American Journal of Epidemiology, 155,* 507–515.
- Banks, L. (2013). Caring for elderly adults during disasters: improving health outcomes and recovery. *South Med J., 106* (1), 94–98.
- Bateson, T.F., & Schwartz, J. (2004). Who is sensitive to the effects of particulate air pollution on mortality? A case-crossover analysis of effect modifiers. *Epidemiology, 15,*143–149.
- Ben-Sira, Z. (1991). Regression, stress, and readjustment in aging. New York: Praeger.
- Bentayeb, M., Helmer, C., & Raherison, C. (2010). Bronchitis-like symptoms and proximity air pollution in French elderly. *Respir Med, 104,* 880-888.
- Berke, E. M., Gottlieb, L. M., Moudon, A. V., & Larson, E. B. (2007). Protective association between neighborhood walkability and depression in older men. *Journal of the American Geriatrics Society, 55,* 526–533.
- Borup, J. (1982). The effects of varying degrees of inter-institutional environmental change on long-term care patients. *The Gerontologist, 22,* 409-17.
- Brunekreef, B., Beelen, R., & Hoek, G. (2009). Effects of long-term exposure to traffic-related air pollution on respiratory and cardiovascular mortality in the Netherlands: the NLCS-AIR study. *Res Rep Health Eff Inst, 139,* 5-71.
- Buffel, T., Verte, D., De Donder, L., De Witte, N., Dury, S., Vanwing, T., & Bolsenbroek, A. (2012). Theorizing the relationship between older people and their immediate social living environment. *International Journal of Lifelong Education, 31,* 13–32.

- Cakmak, S., Dales, R.E., & Vidal. C.B. (2007). Air pollution and mortality in Chile: Susceptibility among the elderly. *Environ Health Perspect, 115*, 524–527.
- Carsrud, A. L., Carsrud, K. B., Henderson, D. P., Alisch, C. J., & Fowler, A. V. (1979). Effects of social and environmental change on institutionalized mentally retarded persons: The relocation syndrome considered. *American Journal of Mental Deficiency, 84*, 266-72.
- Chen, Y., Yang, Q., & Krewski, D. (2004). Influence of relatively low level of particulate ar pollution on hospitalization for COPD in elderly people. *Inhal Toxicol, 16*, 21-25.
- Chenitz, W. C. (1983). Entry into a nursing home as status passage: A theory to guide nursing practice. *Geriatric Nursing* (March/April), 92-97.
- Cherniack, E.P. (2008). The impact of natural disasters on the elderly. *Am J Disaster Med., 3*(3), 133–139.
- Cramm, J. M., van Dijk, H. M., & Nieboer, A. P. (2013). The importance of neighborhood social cohesion and social capital for the wellbeing of older adults in the community. *The Gerontologist, 53*, 142–152.
- Dong, G.H., Zhang, P., & Sun, B. (2012). Long-term exposure to ambient air pollution and respiratory disease mortality in Shenyang, China: a 12-year population-based retrospective cohort study. *Respiration, 84*, 360-368.
- Ferraro, K.F. (1982). The health consequences of relocation among the aged in the community. *Gerontol, 38*,90-96.
- Filleul, L., Le Tertre, A., & Baldi, I. (2004). Difference in the relation between daily mortality and air pollution among elderly and all-ages populations in southwestern France. *Environ Res, 94*, 249-253.
- Firdaus, G. (2016). Built Environment and Health Outcomes: Identification of Contextual Risk Factors for Mental Well-being of Older Adults. *Ageing International,* 42, 62-77.
- Fischer, P., Hoek, G., & Brunekreef, B. (2003). Air pollution and mortality in The Netherlands: are the elderly more at risk? *Eur Respir J Suppl, 40*, 34s-38s.
- Fowler, E.P. (1987). Street management and city design. *Social Forces, 66* (2), 365-389.
- Franklin, M., Zeka, A., & Schwartz, J. (2007). Association between PM2.5 and all-cause and specific-cause mortality in 27 US communities. *J Expo Sci Environ Epidemiol, 17*, 279-87.

- Friedman, D., Parikh, N. S., Giunta, N., Fahs, M. C., & Gallo, W. T. (2012). The influence of neighborhood factors on the quality of life of older adults attending New York City senior centers: Results from the Health Indicators Project. *Quality of Life Research, 21,* 123–131.
- Garin, N., Olaya, B., Miret, M., Ayuso-Mateos, J. L., Power, M., Bucciarelli, P., & Haro, J. M. (2014). Built environment and elderly population health: A comprehensive literature review. *Clinical Practice and Epidemiology in Mental Health: CP and EMH, 10,* 103–115.
- Gass, K., Gaustad, G., Oberst, M., & Hughes, S. (1992). Relocation appraisal, functional independence, morale, and health of nursing home residents. *Issues in Mental Health Nursing, 13,* 239-253.
- Grant, J., O'Neill, M., & Petersen, B. (2000). Our Built and Natural Environments: A Technical Review of the Interactions between Land Use, Transportation, and Environmental Quality, U.S. Environmental Protection Agency, Washington, DC, USA.
- Halpern, D. (1995). Mental Health and the Built Environment: More Than Bricks and Mortar? Taylor & Francis, Abingdon.
- Hayduk, L. A. (1983). Personal space: Where we now stand. *Psychological Bulletin, 94*(2), 293–335.
- Heinzelmann, F. (1981). Reactions to crime: Impacts of crime: Crime prevention and the physical environment. *Sage Criminal Justice System Annuals, 16,* 87–101.
- Jackson, J., & Stafford, M. (2009). Public health and fear of crime. A prospective cohort study. *British Journal of Criminology, 49,* 832–847.
- Jerrett, M., Burnett, R.T., & Pope, C.A. (2009). Longterm ozone exposure and mortality. *N Engl J Med, 360,* 1085-1095.
- Jia, Z., Tian, W., Liu, W., Cao, Y., Yan, J., & Shun, Z. (2010). Are the elderly more vulnerable to psychological impact of natural disaster? A population-based survey of adult survivors of the 2008 Sichuan earthquake. *BMC Public Health, 10*(1), 1–11.
- Kenney, W.L., & Hodgson, J.L. (1987). Heat tolerance, thermoregulation and ageing. *Sports Med, 4,* 446-456.
- Kodavanti, P.R.S. (1999). Reactive oxygen species and antioxidant homeostasis in neurotoxicology. In: *Neurotoxicology* (Tilson HA, Harry G, eds). Target Organ Toxicology Series. Philadelphia: Taylor and Francis, 157 -178.

- Lawton, M. P., & Yaffe, S. (1970). Mortality, morbidity, and voluntary change in residence by older people. *Journal of the American Geriatric Society, 18*, 823-831.
- Lippman, M., Frampton, M., Schwartz, J., Dockery, D., Schlesinger, R., & Koutradis, P. (2003). The U.S. Environmental Protection Agency particulate matter health effects research centers program: a midcourse report of status, progress, and plans. *Environ Health Perspect*, 11, 1074–1092.
- Lochner, K.A., Kawachi, R.T., & Buka, S.L. (2003). Social capital and neighborhood mortality rates in Chicago. *Social Science and Medicine (1982), 56*, 1797-1805.
- Lucumi, D.I., Gomez, L.F., Brownson, R. C., & Parra, D. C. (2015). Social capital, socioeconomic status, and health-related quality of life among older adults in Bogota (Colombia). *Journal of Aging and Health, 27*, 730-750.
- Mazza, M., Di Nicola, M., Catalano, V., Callea, A., Martinotti, G., & Harnic, D. (2012). Description and validation of a questionnaire for the detection of meteoropathy and meteorosensitivity: the METEO-Q. *Compr Psychiatry, 53*, 103-106.
- McCord, J. (2003). Oxidative stress related disease—overview. In: *Critical Reviews of Oxidative Stress and Aging* (Cutler R, Rodriguez H, Eds.). Hackensack, NJ: World Scientific, 883-895.
- McMillan, D.W., & Chavis, D.M. (1986). Sense of community: A definition and theory. *Journal of Community Psychology, 14*(1), 6-23.
- Medina-Ramón, M., Zanobetti, A., & Schwartz, J. (2006). The effect of ozone and PM10 on hospital admissions for pneumonia and chronic obstructive pulmonary disease: a national multicity study. *Am J Epidemiol, 163*, 579-588.
- Mikhail, M. (1992). Psychological response to relocation to a nursing home. *Journal of Gerontological Nursing, 18*, 35-39.
- Mullenbach, L.E., Mowen, A.J., & Baker, B.L. (2018). Assessing the Relationship between a Composite Score of Urban Park Quality and Health. *Prev Chronic Dis, 15*: 180033.
- Naess, O., Nafstad, P., & Aamodt, G. (2007). Relation between concentration of air pollution and cause-specific mortality: four-year exposures to nitrogen dioxide and particulate matter pollutants in 470 neighborhoods in Oslo, Norway. *Am J Epidemiol, 165*, 435-443.

- Naumova, E., Egorov, A., Morris, R., & Griffiths, J. (2003). The elderly and waterborne Cryptosporidium infection: gastroenteritis hospitalizations before and during the 1993 Milwaukee outbreak. *Emerg Infect Dis, 9*, 418-425.
- Newman, O. (1972). Defensible space: crime prevention through urban design. New York: Macmillan.
- Newman, O. (1973). Defensible space: crime prevention through urban design. New York: Collier Books.
- O'donnell, M.L., & Forbes, D. (2016). Natural disaster, older adults, and mental health–a dangerous combination. *Int Psychogeriatr, 28* (1), 9-10.
- Ola, M., & Mathur, R. (2018). Various Environmental Factors and their impact on subjective well-being on the older adults. *Indian Journal of Health & Wellbeing*, 9 (1), 89-92.
- Oswald, F., Jopp, D., Rott, C., & Wahl, H. W. (2011). Is aging in place a resource for or risk to life satisfaction? *The Gerontologist, 51*, 238-250.
- Percy, C.H. (1974). The need for redefinition of long-term care facilities. *The Congressional Record*, 30: 25693-25705.
- Putman, R. D. (2000). Bowling alone. The collapse and revival of American community. New York: Simon and Shuster.
- Reaven, P. (2003). Roles of oxidative stress and other novel risk factors in cardiovascular disease, in Cutler, R. and Rodriguez, H. (Eds.) *Critical Reviews of Oxidative Stress and Aging*. Hackensack, NJ: World Scientific, 896-924.
- Romieu, I., Gouveia, N., & Cifuentes, L.A. (2012). Multicity study of air pollution and mortality in Latin America (the ESCALA study). *Res Rep Health Eff Inst*, 171, 5-86.
- Schwartz, J. (1995). Short term fluctuations in air pollution and hospital admissions of the elderly for respiratory disease. *Thorax, 50*, 531-538.
- Shamian, J., Clarfield, A. M., & Maclean, J. (1984). Arandomized trial of intra-hospital relocation of geriatric patients in a tertiary-care teaching hospital. *Journal of the American Geriatrics Society, 32*, 794-800.
- Sheffield, K. M., & Peek, M. K. (2009). Neighborhood context and cognitive decline in older Mexican Americans: Results from the Hispanic established populations for epidemiologic studies of the elderly. *American Journal of Epidemiology, 169*, 1092-1101.

- Srinivasan, S., Llorente, M.D., & Magley, M. (2014). Mental Health Consequences of Disaster Exposure in Older Adults. Disaster Preparedness for Seniors. New York, NY: Springer, 311-327.
- Stathi, A., Gilbert, H., & Fox, K.R. (2012). Determinants of neighborhood activity of adults age 70 and over: a mixed-methods study. *J. Aging Phys. Act., 20* (2), 148-170.
- Van Cauwenberg, J., De Bourdeaudhuij, I., De Meester, F., Van Dyck, D., Salmon, J., Clarys, P., & Deforche, B. (2011). Relationship between the physical environment and physical activity in older adults: A systematic review. *Health and Place, 17*, 458-469.
- Van Dyck, D., Teychenne, M., McNaughton, S. A., De Bourdeaudhuij, I., & Salmon, J. (2015). Relationship of the perceived social and physical environment with mental health-related quality of life in middle-aged and older adults: Mediating effects of physical activity. *PLoS One, 10.*
- Villeneuve, P.J., Chen, L., & Rowe, B.H. (2007). Outdoor air pollution and emergency department visits for asthma among children and adults: a case-crossover study in northern Alberta, Canada. *Environ Health, 6*, 40.
- Yang, Q., Chen, Y., & Krewski, D. (2005). Effect of short-term exposure to low levels of gaseous pollutants on chronic obstructive pulmonary disease hospitalizations. *Environ Res, 99*, 99-105.
- Zanobetti, A., & Schwartz, J. (2006). Air pollution and emergency admissions in Boston, MA. *J Epidemiol Community Health, 60*, 890-895.
- Zeng, Y., Gu, D., & Purser, J. (2010). Associations of environmental factors with elderly health and mortality in China. *Am J Public Health, 100*, 298-305.

* * *

COVID-19 PANDEMIC: IMPACT ON GERIATRIC POPULATION

Susmita Halder and Shinjini Samajdar

Introduction

The Corona Virus Disease 2019 (COVID-19) has impacted numerous lives and is gradually increasing its peak worldwide (McKibbin & Fernando, 2020). While Indian Government has taken rigorous actions to control the extend of COVID-19, including nation-wide lockdown, it is also significant for each one of us to pursue the protocols and take essential measures and precautions to discontinue the chain of contamination of the disease (Kumar et al., 2020). People in old age are at a higher risk of COVID-19 infection and also due to their decreased resistance, immunity, and health reserves, as well as multiple related comorbidities like hypertension, diabetes, chronic kidney disease and COPD. Also, course of infection tends to be more affective in case of elderlies resulting in higher death (Li & Mutchler, 2020). The COVID-19 epidemic is impacting the overall population in extreme ways. In several countries, older people are in front of the most intimidation and challenges at this instance (Richardson et al., 2020). Even though all age groups are at hazard of constricting COVID-19, older people face noteworthy menace of developing severe disease if they catch the disease due to physiological impact that move toward ageing and potential underlying health conditions (Pelicioni & Lord, 2020).

The COVID-19 situation inflated the health condition of 26% of the elderly population in India, who ranked it as their leading reason of apprehension, while 25% said the pandemic has caused emotional issues to them. A study conducted by NGO Agewell Foundation interacted with 10,000 senior citizens across 27 States and Union territories, result suggested that ascertaining changing needs of the elderly people is due to the impact of the pandemic on them. It has been revealed that the pandemic has not just deteriorated the health condition of the elderly population, but has also disfigured their pattern of social interaction and affected their psychosocial wellbeing and economic security. People expressed that, COVID-19 and the consequential lockdowns affected their health condition, societal lives and their primary concern was related to the impact of the pandemic (Kämpfen et al., 2020).

India has the second-largest population in the world with more than 1.34 billion people, making it hard to manage the spread of COVID-19 (Ghosh et al., 2020; Siddiqui et al., 2020). The Ministry of Health and Family Welfare of India has taken a variety of awareness schemes to sensitize the people to provide the knowledge regarding the Do's and Don'ts and the safety measures that require to be taken in opposition to Coronavirus (Roy et al., 2021). The pattern of community interaction defines the outbreak of COVID-19 and in the nonappearance of vaccine and heals; the only way to evade the increase is to persuade social distancing.

The pandemic has an unparalleled consequence on the lives of citizens, regardless of their demographic profile. The older people are at a higher threat of getting infected. It is consequently advised, to keep social distance and pursue the essential guiding principle to keep own and loved one's protected (Nagarkar, 2020). The casualty rate for elderly is more than contrasted to other age groups. The pandemic is putting elders at a higher risk of inequity, solitude, and scarcity besides the threat to life. COVID-19 has disturbed the lives and living of people, especially in rural India. The lockdown has reduced earnings, increased job insecurity and intimidate the food supply of the rural population. One-quarter of India's population is under the poverty level and roughly half a billion individuals are doing jobs in the unstable sectors, and surviving on daily wages. The lockdown has affected millions of lives, and they are being hungry and destitute, and with no wealth and means to earn, these people are depend on others for food and help, while there are many more who are in starving.

COVID-19 pandemic has restricted lives of almost everyone of all age groups, including aging population. Older adults are identified as vulnerable group in terms of physical and psychosocial stability. In terms of morbidity and mortality, elderly people faced more fatality of disease conditions. Negative impact in terms of psychological distress, decision making, planning capabilities and perception of helplessness are observed; those are needed to be identified and modified at early stage in elderly population. In this chapter, the focus would be on the overview of impact of pandemic situation on cognitive and psychological functioning of elderly population along with challenges in treatment process. Preventing and modifying symptoms manifestations are necessary to provide cognitive and mental health services to ageing population, by reaching them personally or via online telepsychotherapy services.

Impact of Pandemic Across Age Groups

Corona Virus Disease 2019 (COVID-19) was first identified in December 2019 and the World Health Organization declared the outbreak as pandemic in March 2029. This is a contagious disease caused by acute respiratory syndrome. Outbreak of corona virus has negatively impacted the physical as well as the psychological health of the individuals globally. Galloping spread of infection and increased mortality due to COVID-19 were causes of great concern among the health policy makers. It became a priority to implement guidelines and control the devastating situation. Total death due to COVID-19 was 393,338 and pre-COVID complications were also followed by. In pandemic the precautionary measures were focused on physical distancing, being at home, sanitization and compulsory using of masks. Declaration of pandemic had changed the functionality and routine of every individual. Global lockdown was proclaimed, and the individuals were vulnerable in terms of psychological and social health. Changes in daily routine and restricted measures were adversely deteriorated wellbeing of everyone. Dependency on digital and virtual platform impacted daily living (Haleem et al., 2020). From online classes, financial transactions, virtual meetings, social interactions, medical and professional practices are becoming essential to individuals across different age groups (Belot et al., 2020). Various factors such as, separation from loved ones, financial uncertainty, major changes in daily routines, concerns regarding health and medical emergencies are causing enormous stress to the individuals. Frequent exposure of media or load of information or news also accelerate stress and exacerbate the psychological outcomes. During the pandemic, when staying at home is the norm, exploring the ways to live, practicing or coping with situations in a particular way might decrease psychosocial vulnerabilities (Kar et al., 2020). Traumatic stress is a predictor to deterioration of physical and mental health consequences. The concerns regarding the pandemic are varied among different phases of life or age groups. In children, the change denotes restrictions to socialization, physical activities, i.e., playing, going to school etc. Reduced social interactions among them imply limited chances to improve social skills and maintenance of peer relationships. In adolescents, the methods of study have changed and focusing on future accomplishments through performance has deteriorated. Uncertainty, helplessness, and lack of focus are leading them to emotional turmoil. (De Figueiredo et al., 2021). Young and middle adults were adversely impacted due to preoccupations to financial conditions, future plans, disrupted familial relationship along with decreased social interaction and self accomplishments. The most vulnerable group during this pandemic is older adults. Infection severity and rate of mortality are higher among the older adults. The worsening of physical, psychological and social functioning is evident with age. As old age and comorbidity are important risk factors of COVID-19, it is required to give special attention to elderly population. Restricted social interactions and worries regarding others' health conditions are the triggering events to focus. Precipitating factors related to ageing and complications related to ageing are needed to be focused during the pandemic (Monahan et al., 2020).

COVID-19 and Vulnerability in Elderly

According to epidemiologist, ageing is one of the most vulnerable factors which indicates the reduced chances of survival during COVID-19 pandemic. After the age of 65, physical co-morbidities diminish and restrict the physical functioning. Along with physical functioning, pandemic and stay-home protocols are affecting the mental and emotional wellbeing of older adults. However, government strategies and policies regarding the pandemic has been specifically focused on health of elderly in many countries (Benksim et al., 2020). Objectives of government policies focused on elderly people are to convince them to comply with the policies and to maintain the role of responsible citizens in order to control the spread of corona virus. As older adults are most vulnerable group to infection, it was aimed to take and maintain the preventive measures more than young fellow citizens. In studies it has been found that the compliance regarding self isolation is less among the older adults and they would prefer dying from the disease rather than staying at home (Daoust, 2020). COVID-19 is not the only disease which suggests intensive care for elderly people. In case of pneumococcal diseases, cardiovascular disorder or stroke, risks of mortality are also high among the elderly people. As older adults are more vulnerable to the disease condition, the consequences are related to increased risk of hospitalization, delayed recovery time, decrease in pulmonary functions and faster disease progression among them (Liu et al., 2020). In COVID-19 infection the severity and seriousness of the disease condition is much more, and elderly people are perceived to be more dutiful regarding maintenance of government preventive policies. Identification of factors which are worsening the condition of geriatric population due to COVID-19 emergence is needed as soon as possible. The most identified factors are pre-existing disabilities, cognitive and affective disorders, polypharmacotherapy, nutritional deficits and absence of feasibility of long-term treatment for elderly population. Alterations of immune system related to age increases the chances of nutritional deficits which reinforces the progress of immediate systematic inflammation among older adults (Aiello et al., 2019). Older population is more susceptible to poor physiological functioning and physical fitness, restricted social functioning and decline in cognitive abilities than other age groups and it impacts their psychological health negatively. Older adults might be in a risk zone due to age, but they're not perceived as weak if proper and adequate care is taken. Senior-friendly and pandemic related policies should be present to prevent the expectable outcomes due to their age-related vulnerabilities.

In case of institutionalized elderly individual, the risks are less than others as they're living in an environment where the accessibility to go out to outer world is less. The speed of spread of the disease and contagion nature of the virus are affecting individuals and the policies recommended to stay at home thus, institutionalized individuals are safer than others. Hence, infected individuals, staying in elderly institute might have less opportunity to get proper medical support and it increases the risks to deteriorated health conditions. In elderly patients, urgent medical attention and supervision is more required which can be provided immediately after symptoms developed. Early identification and assessment of severity of symptoms are necessary in elderly but in case institutionalized elderly the limited resources might delay the treatment procedure. Staying away from family and dependent environment has prior decrement in mental health and induced emotional vulnerabilities can be observable after COVID-19 pandemic (Sacco et al., 2020). More restricted social interaction and limited resources causing more distress during this pandemic condition.

Cognitive-Affective-Social Functioning in Elderly during Pandemic

Seniors are considered to be more effete group of decreased physiological immune conditions and often interrelated with chronic disease conditions. Chronic disease itself has psychosocial impact on functioning of elderly population. Decreased physical fitness and limited performance inclined to dependency and helplessness in older adults. Feelings of loneliness, depressed mood and apprehending situations negatively can be seen among older adults more than others. In the COVID-19 pandemic, in healthy elderly the distress and hopelessness regarding own health and situations are deteriorating the mental health conditions. The desire to meet loved ones, being engaged in social interactions, living life in own ways could not be fulfilled due to the pandemic which encourages the distress and leading to irritability, anger outburst or emotional turmoil in older adults. Changes in psychological and emotional functioning in elderly caused due to COVID-19 pandemic should be focused thoroughly and comprehensively as they're in high risk group. Emotional response in relation to pandemic declaration is more prevalent among the older adults compared to other groups (Sardella et al., 2021). Avoidance of social activities, social isolation and being cautious most of the time increased the mental health concerns and they're experiencing social isolation most of the time. Intolerance and irritability among the older adults are more prevalent which is maintained by fear and anger outbursts. Uncertainty and unpredictable nature of pandemic induced their symptom manifestations and maintaining anxiety and stress responses to most vulnerable group. Fear related to loss of near ones, own health condition, financial concerns, and reduced social interaction affected adversely on mental health. In last 1 year, getting negative news and information in adding more distress and making them defensive in terms of emotional catharses and behavioural control. Lack of connection with surrounding and reduced physical presence along with exaggeration of negative news is impacting over coping strategies of health elderly individual. Psychological squeal of COVID-19 pandemic produced more fear and anxiety than the pandemic itself (Bidzan-Bluma et al., 2020). The unforeseeable and doubtful nature of prolong pandemic inducing disharmony between thoughts and actions. In a study conducted by Halder et al., (2021), it has been showed that psychological impact is more among the older adults in terms of maintaining daily routines, trouble in sleeping, worries regarding health concerns of themselves and their family members, being irritable, feelings of lack of control over situations, and worries regarding financial constraints. Deteriorated coping due to pandemic implicated as preoccupations over uncontrolled situations and difficulties in alternating negative thoughts and behaviors in adaptive ways. In elderly population, another distressing and devastating trauma have been death of near ones. Sudden death of young family members or friends or companions leads to complicated grief and bereavement. Difficulties in accepting the unfortunate event and finding out alternative reactions are increasing the emotional turmoil and distress among older adults. Prolonged concerns since the primary period of pandemic are making them helpless and the death of loved ones precipitating mental health disorders. In case of repetitive incidents of death inclining maladaptive behaviors and which might have influencing physical health conditions negatively.

Ageing brain is associated with decline of cognitive functioning and can be manifested as mild cognitive impairment (MCI) or dementia. The progression of cognitive decline in elderly could be influenced by physical health conditions, nurturance, proper nutrition, prolonged psychological distress and neurological deficits. In pandemic situation, the increased psychological stress and emotional agitation influenced brain functioning and the rate of progression of cognitive functioning has been reportedly declined. Decline has been seen to be started prior to old age and deteriorated with time (Thyrian et al., 2020). Identification of deficits can be reflected in intermittent daily functioning

(Rosenblum et al., 2021), difficulties in reaction time, cognitive control and flexibility. In last 2 years, the focus is mostly given on immediate physiological affect due to COVID-19 virus, immediate assessments and treatment process were conducted but the impact on cognitive functioning should also be elaborated and illustrated. Early identification by changed cognitive abilities and functioning is necessary along with management plans.

Altered emotional and cognitive performance leads to impulsiveness, rigidity, irritability, negative apprehensions, lack of resilience and adjustment in older adults which can influence the social functionality. Government protocols are encouraging the social isolation and are influencing everyone to reduce social gatherings and prolonged social isolation affecting the societal behaviors. Poor or lack of support and supervision has been limited due to social isolation. Contagious nature of disease is reducing the chances to help others for the sake of own health concerns. People could not able to be there when they're needed. Usefulness of technology and digital connection are helping elderly people to keep in touch with loved ones and maintaining social relationship. Virtual social meet platforms have become convenient and constant connection increases resilience and reduce worries due to pandemic (Jnr, 2020). In regard to lack of social interaction and emotional catharses elderly people has become more irritable and inflexible which leads to quarrelsome behaviors. Habit of being closer through physical connections of elderly people has been changed and the adaption to the new normal has become a bit difficult to them. It is affecting their mental health and they are being apprehensive regarding their pre-existing relationships and connections with others. COVID-19 protocols should exchange the word "social distancing" to "physical distancing" in regard to maintain healthy positive relationship along with growth.

Psychological and Cognitive Functioning of Elderly COVID-19 Survivors

COVID-19 infection might need intensive care, hospitalization and help of ventilator for prolonged period in older adults. Systematic inflammation and pulmonary deterioration lead to oxygen deprivation in brain cells which implicated as confusion, difficulties in memory functioning, working memory deficits and exaggerated progression of cognitive impairment (Alonso-Lana et al., 2020). Research findings on older adults indicated that severity of infection associated with cognitive decline in domains of concentration, memory and cognitive control which lead to decrement in functioning of daily living activities. COVID-19 infected older adults with co-morbid conditions like Alzheimer's disease and delirium could deteriorate cognitive functioning more than without infected older individuals (Alonso-Lana et al., 2020). Prolonged loneliness and isolation during illness and hospitalization also may have significant impact upon reduced brain volume and which is related to left medial temporal lobe associated with memory functioning and in long term lead to Alzheimer's disease. Social isolation and labeling on the infected patients lead to psychological distress, self criticalness, and feelings of helpless and intolerant implies to reduce energy, sleep disturbances, subjective feelings of loneliness and depressed mood. Sudden and impoverished social environment resulting from the current situation is detrimental to older people and increase the chances of neuro-degenerative disorders and psychological complications.

Stress, Grief, Loss and Resilience during COVID-19 Pandemic

It has been obvious that the pandemic situation symbolized major change of scenery. In this sense, revolutionize was pragmatic in the social and family environments (Ando, 2020). In addition to the ordinary sources of stress noted, which leads to decreased physical activity and changes in sleeping hours and deteriorated lifestyle. Elderly people are having high levels of stress, other psychological symptoms, and a deep concern about after effects of the pandemic such as post-traumatic stress disorder (Essadek & Rabeyron, 2020). Coping approaches are often allied with the need to conflict a perceived intimidating situation (Martínez et al., 2020). Furthermore, cultural factors mediated the use of these strategies; In a study it has been seen that, coping strategy during COVID-19, were followed by acceptance, self-destruction, and other active coping techniques (Salman et al., 2020). In pre-COVID periods, considerable positive relationships had also been found between the commitment in avoidant behaviors and perceived stress (Oliva et al., 2018), as well as downbeat interaction between higher community support and lower stress levels.

Resilience can be definite as a person's capability to face the confrontations and difficulties of existence in a positive and adaptive approach, as well as the competence to get well from an unfavorable occurrence (Cénat et al., 2020; Glass et al., 2020). During confinement, the association between resilience and stress was also evaluated, and it became clear that it was multifaceted (Ando, 2020; Marchini et al., 2020). According to Liu C. H. et al. (2020) found that resilience was associated with low levels of hopelessness and nervousness, but not with post-traumatic stress disorder. In pre-COVID periods, it was observed that the execution of problem-solving focused behaviors had a reducing effect on stress levels (Keech et al., 2018).

Theoretical viewpoint on coping imply that ageing may be beneficial for coping appropriate to an addition of life understanding that promote the modification of coping proficiency (Aldwin & Igarashi, 2016; Neupert et al., 2019). Moreover, according to the strength and vulnerability integration (SAVI) model, older adults have better emotional regulation while evaluated with younger persons (Charles, 2010), which can be advantageous to coping healthy (Skinner & Zimmer-Gembeck, 2007). Current research suggests older adults are additionally skilled at coping than younger individuals (Neubauer et al., 2019). Aldwin and Igarashi (2016) disagree that the progression of coping with stress can form resilience, in addition to older adults are likely to have increased coping resources and approaches to illustrate upon from their precedent occurrences. The COVID-19 pandemic is a noteworthy life stressor. It is indefinite how elongated the pandemic will continue, or how longer older adults will require to socially segregate to keep away from contracting the infection. In cooperation with gerontologists and behavioral health specialists have expressed apprehension that increased tension and loneliness due to the virulent disease could negatively influence older adults' comfort. For example, solitude resulting as of social isolation has been connected to negative health outcomes for older adults and increased transience (Shankar et al., 2011). It is essential that the impacts of such proceedings on older adults to enhance appreciate how they deal with and whether lessons well-read from their understandings can assist arrange individuals of every ages for similar prospect measures.

Perception of Elderly Population during Pandemic

During the pandemic situation, it has been seen that, like other ages, older adults are also had an huge impact in following the restricted and unpredictable lifestyles. Spending whole time in a planned and constructive way can create intense anxiety and apprehensions while living a life in unplanned way. Other than the predictability, there is other points to discuss on the basis of loss of near ones, loss of persons who are younger than them, emotional turbulence, shook up financial equilibrium inclined to the poor coping and resilience in older people. In a qualitative research, individuals were asked to express their point of view regarding the pandemic situation,

64 years old, male conveyed in this regard as *"I have had a cardiac arrest. I either way do not venture out or stay at home. Now I need to be more cautious and won't go out unless very necessary."* While he was asked if he is fearful of the situation due to pandemic or not; he said *"No, I don't fear, but I need to be careful of the situation"*. 82 years old, male expressed as *"I am already 82 years old, and at this stage, why COVID, anything can happen to me. I used to walk a little and go out, even that has stopped now; I am not fearful of me, rather worried about my family members"*. In both the narrations, it has been seen that, they are accepted that, as they're in the stage of life where death is inevitable and the physical co-morbidities are already present. So, somehow they have accepted the fact COVID infection might not have any extra effect on their lives whereas they're more concerned regarding the changed lifestyle and worried about family members.

70 years old, female has expressed her impressions as *"Both my son and daughter stay abroad. I am too much worried, if something happens to me or even to them; I won't be able to see them again; I only worry that no one should get infected with it (COVID)"*. From this unfolding, the worries and apprehensions not specified to fear of losing near ones and this is creating emotional disturbances among her.

In point of view from the coping and resilience, there are individuals who are characteristically see the life in different way or in more positive way but the situations have trembled up their thought pattern and they might have tried to stay vigilant during the situation but somehow they've also fell under the condition of pandemic emotional misbalance. 66 years old, male has said *"I've always been positive during the lifetime, I've faced difficulties tremendously financially or emotionally, but somehow I've managed all those things and walked forward in life. In this situation I've not faced that much difficulties but somehow I became more vulnerable with the fact that, I am being restricted in house and could not able to fight physically as I've done before. But I do believe this will end and again everything will fall into places"*. Another individual who is 63 years old male, has been said that *"As my age is increasing I might not get all I want in my life, but I do belief COVID-19 pandemic has given me the strength to live my life as it would end soon. I've done so many new things that were not possible in other times. Yes, I do have fear regarding the situation, but I have seen so much of life, has no fear to die."* In both the narrations, the acceptance of the situation has become prominent and they're comparing their life time experiences and using it as coping with this novel and unpredictable situation.

Psychotherapeutic Intervention Facilities during Pandemic for Elderly Population

Along with health care facilities, psychotherapeutic interventions are needed to give due importance in government plans; and already psychological interventions were included in service following protocols and regulations. In-person psychotherapy has become constraint in pandemic situations but in the era of virtual reality, it was easy to conduct and providing psychotherapy is necessary to control mental and cognitive health of every individuals. Contributing psychotherapeutic intervention to older adults is itself challenging due to their rigid cognitive flexibility and reduced capacity to understand. Telecommunication via computer, smart phone or any other electronic devices has become tougher due to their unconventionality towards technology usage, but it helps in reducing emotional distress and cognitive impairment and improve functioning in pandemic situation (Bodner et al., 2020). For children, adolescents and young adults, telepsychotherapy is very convenient, and they've comfort in the process. In case of older adults, the boundary of telepsychotherapy will be restricted. In management of physiological symptoms of anxiety, deep diaphragmatic breathing relaxation therapy has been proved to be efficient and it helps to engage older adults in activities in pandemic isolation situation. Involvement in well-organized schedule and increasing skills could increase the self efficacy and distract from the distressing thoughts and triggers (Halder et al., 2020). Older adults look forward to interacting to catharses emotional turmoil and reduce subjective feelings of loneliness. Cognitive behavioural therapy (CBT) helps in modulating emotional dysregulation, faulty beliefs, and alteration of maladaptive behaviors through reducing irritability, anger outbursts and restlessness (Razai et al., 2020; Girdhar et al., 2020). Neuro-degenerative symptoms are evident among older adults in pandemic situation, which requires assessment and identification domains related to cognitive decline and functional disability. Pre-existing cognitive impairment in older adults could be deteriorated in pandemic situation because of limited supervision of impairment condition and gaps between cognitive training and rehabilitation (Rebok et al., 2014). In older adults, intermission between training could deteriorate functioning and improvement becomes delayed. Early identification and training could restrain the progression of cognitive impairment. Home-based intervention programmes for each older adult can be customized about their mental health conditions and new additions to activities could also be manualized. Requirement of each individual may not be same but in home-based intervention programmes the focuses would be given on present functional status and impairment.

Conclusion

Constant monitoring and supervision would help to identify the problems; and maintain the positive outcomes of psychotherapeutic intervention. Motivating older adults to take vaccination and educating regarding after effect of the process is presently in concern. The process of accelerating positive mental health through virtual and telepsychotherapy would be the primary goal of mental health professionals. In this difficult times, mental health in elderly can be facilitated by desensitizing anxiety, reducing distressing thoughts, and preventing cognitive impairment along with positive family and social support.

References

- Aiello, A., Farzaneh, F., Candore, G., Caruso, C., Davinelli, S., Gambino, C. M., ... & Accardi, G. (2019). Immunosenescence and its hallmarks: how to oppose aging strategically? A review of potential options for therapeutic intervention. *Frontiers in immunology, 10,* 2247.
- Aldwin, C. M., Igarashi, H., Bengston, V., & Settersten, R. A. (2016). Coping, optimal aging, and resilience in a sociocultural context. *Handbook of theories of aging, 3,* 551-576.
- Alonso-Lana, S., Marquié, M., Ruiz, A., & Boada, M. (2020). Cognitive and neuropsychiatric manifestations of COVID-19 and effects on elderly individuals with dementia. *Frontiers in aging neuroscience, 12.*
- Ando S. (2020). University teaching and learning in a time of social distancing: a sociocultural perspective. *J. Hum. Behav. Soc. Environ.* 31 435–448. 10.1080/10911359.2020.1814928

- Belot, M., Choi, S., Jamison, J. C., Papageorge, N. W., Tripodi, E., & Van den Broek-Altenburg, E. (2020). Unequal consequences of COVID 19 across age and income: representative evidence from six countries.
- Benksim, A., Rachid, A. I. T., & Cherkaoui, M. (2020). Vulnerability and fragility expose older adults to the potential dangers of COVID-19 pandemic. *Iranian Journal of Public Health.*
- Bidzan-Bluma, I., Bidzan, M., Jurek, P., Bidzan, L., Knietzsch, J., Stueck, M., & Bidzan, M. (2020). A Polish and German Population Study of Quality of Life, Well-Being, and Life Satisfaction in Older Adults During the COVID-19 Pandemic. *Frontiers in psychiatry, 11.*
- Bodner, K. A., Goldberg, T. E., Devanand, D. P., & Doraiswamy, P. M. (2020). Advancing Computerized Cognitive Training for MCI and Alzheimer's Disease in a Pandemic and Post-pandemic World. *Frontiers in Psychiatry, 11,* 1286.
- Cénat, J. M., Mukunzi, J. N., Noorishad, P. G., Rousseau, C., Derivois, D., & Bukaka, J. (2020). A systematic review of mental health programs among populations affected by the Ebola virus disease. *Journal of Psychosomatic Research, 131,* 109966.
- Charles, S. T. (2010). Strength and vulnerability integration: a model of emotional well-being across adulthood. *Psychological bulletin, 136*(6), 1068.
- Daoust, J. F. (2020). Elderly people and responses to COVID-19 in 27 Countries. *PloS one, 15*(7), e0235590.
- De Figueiredo, C. S., Sandre, P. C., Portugal, L. C. L., Mázala-de-Oliveira, T., da Silva Chagas, L., Raony, Í., & Bomfim, P. O. S. (2021). COVID-19 pandemic impact on children and adolescents' mental health: Biological, environmental, and social factors. *Progress in Neuro-Psychopharmacology and Biological Psychiatry, 106,* 110171.
- Essadek, A., & Rabeyron, T. (2020). Mental health of French students during the COVID-19 pandemic. *Journal of affective disorders, 277,* 392-393.
- Ghosh, A., Nundy, S., & Mallick, T. K. (2020). How India is dealing with COVID-19 pandemic. *Sensors International, 1,* 100021.
- Girdhar, R., Srivastava, V., & Sethi, S. (2020). Managing mental health issues among elderly during COVID-19 pandemic. *J. Geriatr. Care Res, 7,* 32-35.

- Glass M., Rana S., Coghlan R., Lerner L. I., Harrison J. D., Stoltenberg M., et al., (2020). Global palliative care education in the time of COVID-19. *J. Pain Symptom Manag,* 60, 14–19. 10.1016/j.jpainsymman.2020.07.018
- Halder S, Mahato A, Samajdar S, Manot S & Ghosh S. (2021) Psychological impact and its coping in COVID-19 pandemic: A study across India. Journal of Psychosocial Research. (Under publication).
- Halder, S., Mahato, A., & Manot, S. (2020). COVID-19: Psychological impact and psychotherapeutic intervention. *EC Psychology and Psychiatry*, *9*(2020), 32-35.
- Haleem, A., Javaid, M., & Vaishya, R. (2020). Effects of COVID-19 pandemic in daily life. *Current medicine research and practice.*
- Jnr, B. A. (2020). Use of telemedicine and virtual care for remote treatment in response to COVID-19 pandemic. *Journal of Medical Systems*, *44*(7), 1-9.
- Kämpfen, F., Kohler, I. V., Ciancio, A., Bruine de Bruin, W., Maurer, J., & Kohler, H. P. (2020). Predictors of mental health during the COVID-19 pandemic in the US: Role of economic concerns, health worries and social distancing. *PloS one*, *15*(11), e0241895.
- Kar, S. K., Arafat, S. Y., Kabir, R., Sharma, P., & Saxena, S. K. (2020). Coping with mental health challenges during COVID-19. In *Coronavirus disease 2019 (COVID-19)* (pp. 199-213). Springer, Singapore.
- Keech J. J., Hagger M., O'Callaghan F. V., Hamilton K. (2018). The influence of university students' stress mindsets on health and performance outcomes. *Ann. Behav. Med.* 52 1046–1059. 10.1093/abm/kay008
- Kumar, S. U., Kumar, D. T., Christopher, B. P., & Doss, C. (2020). The rise and impact of COVID-19 in India. *Frontiers in medicine*, *7*, 250.
- Li, Y., & Mutchler, J. E. (2020). Older adults and the economic impact of the COVID-19 pandemic. *Journal of Aging & Social Policy*, *32*(4-5), 477-487.
- Liu C. H., Zhang E., Wong G., Hyun S., Hahm H. C. (2020). Factors associated with depression, anxiety, and PTSD symptomatology during the COVID-19 pandemic: clinical implications for U.S. young adult mental health. *Psychiatry Res.* 290:113172. 10.1016/j.psychres.2020.113172

- Liu, K., Chen, Y., Lin, R., & Han, K. (2020). Clinical features of COVID-19 in elderly patients: A comparison with young and middle-aged patients. *Journal of Infection, 80*(6), e14-e18.
- Marchini S., Zaurino E., Bouziotis J., Brondino N., Delvenne V., Delhaye M. (2020). Study of resilience and loneliness in youth (18-25 years old) during the COVID-19 pandemic lockdown measures. *J. Community Psychol.* 49 468–480. 10.1002/jcop.22473
- McKibbin, W., & Fernando, R. (2020). The economic impact of COVID-19. *Economics in the Time of COVID-19, 45*(10.1162).
- Monahan, C., Macdonald, J., Lytle, A., Apriceno, M., & Levy, S. R. (2020). COVID-19 and ageism: How positive and negative responses impact older adults and society. *American Psychologist.*
- Nagarkar, A. (2020). Challenges and concerns for older adults in India regarding the COVID-19 pandemic. *Journal of gerontological social work, 63*(4), 259-261.
- Neubauer, B. E., Witkop, C. T., & Varpio, L. (2019). How phenomenology can help us learn from the experiences of others. *Perspectives on medical education, 8*(2), 90.
- Neupert, S. D., Neubauer, A. B., Scott, S. B., Hyun, J., & Sliwinski, M. J. (2019). Back to the future: Examining age differences in processes before stressor exposure.
- Oliva, E. I., Gherardi-Donato, E. C., Bermúdez, J. A., and Facundo, F. R. (2018). Uso de Facebook, estrés percibido y consumo de alcohol en jóvenes universitarios. *Ciência Saúde Coletiva* 23, 3675–3681. doi: 10.1590/1413-812320182311.27132016
- Pelicioni, P. H., & Lord, S. R. (2020). COVID-19 will severely impact older people's lives, and in many more ways than you think!. *Brazilian journal of physical therapy, 24*(4), 293.
- Razai, M. S., Oakeshott, P., Kankam, H., Galea, S., & Stokes-Lampard, H. (2020). Mitigating the psychological effects of social isolation during the COVID-19 pandemic. *bmj, 369.*
- Rebok, G. W., Ball, K., Guey, L. T., Jones, R. N., Kim, H. Y., King, J. W., ... & ACTIVE Study Group. (2014). Ten-year effects of the advanced cognitive training for independent and vital elderly cognitive training trial on cognition and everyday functioning in older adults. *Journal of the American Geriatrics Society, 62*(1), 16-24.

- Richardson, S. J., Carroll, C. B., Close, J., Gordon, A. L., O'Brien, J., Quinn, T. J., ... & Witham, M. D. (2020). Research with older people in a world with COVID-19: identification of current and future priorities, challenges and opportunities. *Age and ageing, 49*(6), 901-906.
- Rodriguez-Morales, A. J., Cardona-Ospina, J. A., Gutiérrez-Ocampo, E., Villamizar-Peña, R., Holguin-Rivera, Y., Escalera-Antezana, J. P., Alvarado-Arnez, L. E., Bonilla-Aldana, D. K., Franco-Paredes, C., Henao-Martinez, A. F., Paniz-Mondolfi, A., Lagos-Grisales, G. J., Ramírez-Vallejo, E., Suárez, J. A., Zambrano, L. I., Villamil-Gómez, W. E., Balbin-Ramon, G. J., Rabaan, A. A., Harapan, H., Dhama, K., ... Latin American Network of Coronavirus Disease 2019-COVID-19 Research (LANCOVID-19). Electronic address: https://www.lanCOVID.org (2020). Clinical, laboratory and imaging features of COVID-19: A systematic review and meta-analysis. *Travel medicine and infectious disease, 34,* 101623. https://doi.org/10.1016/j.tmaid.2020.101623
- Rosenblum, S., & Elimelech, O. C. (2021). Gender Differences in State Anxiety Related to Daily Function Among Older Adults During the COVID-19 Pandemic: Questionnaire Study. *JMIR aging, 4*(2), e25876.
- Roy, A., Singh, A. K., Mishra, S., Chinnadurai, A., Mitra, A., & Bakshi, O. (2021). Mental health implications of COVID-19 pandemic and its response in India. *The International journal of social psychiatry, 67*(5), 587.
- Sacco, G., Lléonart, S., Simon, R., Noublanche, F., Annweiler, C., & TOVID Study Group. (2020). Communication technology preferences of hospitalized and institutionalized frail older adults during COVID-19 confinement: cross-sectional survey study. *JMIR mHealth and uHealth, 8*(9), e21845.
- Salman, M., Asif, N., Mustafa, Z. U., Khan, T. M., Shehzadi, N., Hussain, K., ... & Khan, M. T. (2020). Psychological impact of COVID-19 on Pakistani university students and how they are coping. *Medrxiv.*
- Sardella, A., Lenzo, V., Bonanno, G. A., Basile, G., & Quattropani, M. C. (2021). Expressive Flexibility and Dispositional Optimism Contribute to the Elderly's Resilience and Health-Related Quality of Life during the COVID-19 Pandemic. *International journal of environmental research and public health, 18*(4), 1698.

- Shankar, A., McMunn, A., Demakakos, P., Hamer, M., & Steptoe, A. (2017). Social isolation and loneliness: Prospective associations with functional status in older adults. *Health psychology, 36*(2), 179.
- Siddiqui, A. F., Wiederkehr, M., Rozanova, L., & Flahault, A. (2020). Situation of India in the COVID-19 pandemic: India's initial pandemic experience. *International Journal of Environmental Research and Public Health, 17*(23), 8994.
- Skinner, E. A., & Zimmer-Gembeck, M. J. (2007). The development of coping. *Annu. Rev. Psychol., 58,* 119-144.
- Thyrian, J. R., Kracht, F., Nikelski, A., Boekholt, M., Schumacher-Schönert, F., Rädke, A., & Kreisel, S. H. (2020). The situation of elderly with cognitive impairment living at home during lockdown in the Corona-pandemic in Germany. *BMC geriatrics, 20*(1), 1-15.

* * *

PSYCHOTHERAPEUTIC INTERVENTION ON AGEING POPULATION IN RECENT PERSPECTIVES

Sneha Das, Sneha Patel and Sampurna Chakraborty

Introduction

Aging is a result of accumulated molecular and cellular changes over time, marked by a gradual decline in physical and mental capacity, increased vulnerability for diseases, and finally death. Globally, the elderly population is increasing rapidly, and it is estimated that older people aged 60 years and over will constitute 22% of the total world population by 2025 (WHO, 2018). Older people are more vulnerable to age-related diseases and disabilities caused by biological and physical changes, accompanied by social facets like retirement, moving to new living arrangements, death of spouse, friends, and relatives, and financial constraints which acts as a burden to the person and society as a whole. Furthermore, mental health issues are critical issues that also come with aging as the well-being of the individual and the individual's harmonious integration into society, are at stake. Despite recent advances in mental health treatments for older adults (age 65 and older), less than one-third of older individuals with a mental health or substance use disorder receive treatment. (Regier et al., 1993; Karlin et al., 2008)

Older adults may suffer relapses of psychological disorders when they are young, or newer problem arises during developmental stresses of late-life or neuropathology. Medical problems are more common in older adults, and psychological symptoms and syndromes often coexist with them. Manifestations of mental disorders may be different in the elderly, compared with younger age groups, and there may be difficulties in separating symptoms of mental disorders from those occurring in normal aging. For example, there is an overlap in symptoms of depression, physical disorders, and in normal aging as a loss of appetite, fatigue, and sleep disturbances are common in all. This may lead not only to over diagnosis but also to underdiagnoses if depressive symptoms are thought to be due to physical disorders or normal aging (Ernst & Angst, 1995; Skoog et al., 1993; Blanchard et al., 1994; Lehtinen et al., 1990; Rorsman et al., 1990; Wallace et al., 1995). Thus understanding the comorbidity of mental and medical disorders is a central task in assessing and treating psychological problems in older adults. Additionally, psychiatric conditions are also related to greater subjective impairment and disability, and more limitations in activities of daily living (Karlsson et al., 2009; Cairney et al., 2008) thus, management of these issues apart from the symptomatology of psychiatric condition is also a primary goal in psychological intervention planning to improve treatment outcomes.

Choice of Psychotherapy

There has been always a dilemma as to which psychological intervention is ideal for older adults. The treatment of choice is guided by the nature of the problem, therapeutic goals, preferences of the older adult, and practical considerations from the client's point of view. It also largely depends upon the availability of experts. Although older people share similar generational experiences, there are differences among them in terms of race, culture, gender, sexual orientation, and social class that need to be taken into account in understanding the problems of older adults before planning their intervention. However, if a range of therapies is made available to the clientele they might be the best scenario for the patient and the therapist.

Clinical and research evidence has shown that in the case of uncomplicated depressive illness, cognitive behavioral therapy (CBT) or interpersonal psychotherapy (IPT) may be provided as a first preference with or without pharmacological treatment. Psychotherapeutic intervention is useful in preventing relapse in recurrent depression. IPT is noted to work best when there is evidence of conflict in relationships; while CBT is suited more for cognitively sophisticated individuals and those with trait level anxiety. Patients with depressive illness secondary to borderline or narcissistic personality traits often have a history of traumatic experiences in childhood or earlier in their adult lives and dysfunctional family background. Cognitive analytic therapy (CAT) or psychodynamic therapy may be the treatment of choice. Depressive illness in later life may worsen due to the expressed emotion or changes in the family structure where systemic therapy can be the therapy of choice. Even with the wide array of intervention strategies available, CBT is the most preferred mode of treatment for its wide acceptance in terms of effectiveness and feasibility, (Kiosses et al., 2011).

Evidence-based Practices in Geriatric Mental Health Care

The application of intervention is shifting from adapting current interventions for different populations and settings to investing in novel, potentially more effective, personalized, and tailored interventions (Chambers et al., 2010). The NIMH report of *From Discovery to Cure* on future directions for interventions, recommends that interventions researchers focus on understanding moderators of treatment response to better match patients to existing evidence-based practices and to develop new interventions for those who do not respond to any existing treatments (NAMHC, 2010). A wide range of psychological treatments has now been validated for use with older adults. Evidence-based therapies for elderly patients include IPT, CBT and problem-solving therapy (PST), and, to a lesser extent, reminiscence therapy (RT) and short-term psychodynamic therapy. Newer approaches are also emerging, including mindfulness-based approaches, and therapies delivered with the use of technology (Bryant, 2016).

The common psychological interventions for the elderly for various psychiatric conditions:

1. Cognitive rehabilitation: It is a behavior change intervention, based on an understanding of the cognitive changes seen in mild to moderate dementia, which builds on relatively better-preserved cognitive abilities to address and overcome the impact of cognitive impairment. Evidence-based techniques used in cognitive rehabilitation interventions include both enhanced learning methods and the introduction of compensatory strategies. One study investigated the effect of cognitive rehabilitation including tasks of cognitive training on the performance of everyday activities in early-stage of Alzheimer's disease. Forty-three elderly people were divided into two groups: the cognitive rehabilitation group (experimental) and the control group. Cognitive rehabilitation comprises of 8 sessions, each lasting 60 minutes (individual 30 min, group 30 min). Individual sessions focus on personal meaningful goals, time-and-place orientation, matching faces and names, and learning memory and sustaining attention.

Significant improvements were observed in occupation performance and satisfaction, Quality of Life in Alzheimer's Disease (QOL-AD), and the orientation subscale of the MMSE in the experimental group (Kim, 2015). Another review study analyzed the effect of cognitive interventions for improving or maintaining the general cognitive status of older adults who were of different cognitive levels. It reviewed studies published between 2010 and 2019 and included 13 systematic reviews and/or meta-analyses, it showed that the cognitive intervention programs improved general cognitive functioning and specific cognitive functions with a gradual decline in cognitive functions in older persons with dementia; and there was an improvement in activities of daily living. It was also seen that it preserved the cognitive improvement for periods of 2 months to 5 years. Cognitive interventions have proven effective for maintaining and/or improving cognitive functioning in older adults regardless of their initial cognitive status (Sanjuán et al., 2020).

2. **Psychodynamic therapy:** Psychodynamic therapy has been widely used in all age groups including later life (Garner, 2002; Arden, 2002). Psychodynamic approaches focus on the development of insight into repressed unconscious material from earlier life experience and working on it in the therapeutic relationship. However, the client's age can be an important factor in the line of transference, countertransference, and resistance towards therapy. While treating elderly patients, the therapist might experience unconscious fear of dependence and helplessness which create a barrier to acknowledge the need of the elderly clients. The client's situation may elicit in the therapist idealized care fantasies resulting from the therapist's unconscious fears and concerns about their own older family members. However, irrespective of this the psychodynamic model is suited well

with older adults as therapy derived from the client's 'feelings of abandonment and despair, intimacy and isolation, arrogance and disdain, stagnation, and creativity are the struggles each of us face as a developmental task of "the third age". Studies have reported that brief psychodynamic therapy was better than waitlist control at post-treatment and equally effective compared with CBT in older adults recruited from the community (Thompson et al., 1987; Gallagher et al., 1994). A systematic review (Pinquart & Sorensen, 2001) noted that there are very few published studies on the effects of psychodynamic interventions. The limited evidence available suggests that psychodynamic therapy is as effective as cognitive or behavioral approaches in the treatment of depression (Thompson et al., 1987; Gallagher-Thompson et al., 1990). Yet another study compared short-term psychodynamic psychotherapy and CBT. Patients with GAD received either CBT (n = 29) or short-term psychotherapy (n = 28). Results showed both CBT and short-term psychodynamic psychotherapy yielded significant, large, and stable improvements using the primary outcome measures symptoms of anxiety and depression. CBT was superior in secondary measures of trait anxiety, worry, and depression with findings remained stable at the 12-month follow-up (Salzer et al., 2010).

3. **Cognitive analytic therapy:** It is an integration of analytic (object relations theory) and cognitive psychotherapy. It is a brief, structured and collaborative therapeutic journey from past trauma into reconnection with dialogue and meaning. It focuses on shared meaning in the context of the client's life story and emphasizes the cathartic approach with the help of dialogue used by the client (Hepple, 2002). In the elderly population, coping mechanisms are challenged by losses, disability, and changes in the social role where

preexisting trauma and low self-esteem can resurface to produce anxiety, depression, and self-destructive behaviors, which can be understood in terms of the person's whole life story. CAT connects the past with the present with a focus on shared meaning across generational and cultural boundaries.

4. **Behavior therapy (BT):** Behaviour therapy has been widely recognized as very successful for treating a wide variety of mental/behavioral problems, ranging from anxiety disorders to developmental disabilities. Studies indicate that behavioral activation (BA) may help in reducing depressive symptoms by activity restriction. Behavioral activation is efficacious as a treatment for geriatric depression (Yon & Scogin, 2008). A recent systematic review on psychotherapy for PTSD with older adults indicate that all the case studies and treatment outcome studies utilizing exposure therapy (e.g., imaginal exposure only; in vivo exposure only; full, manualized prolonged exposure) reported at least some effectiveness in ameliorating symptoms related to trauma (Dinnen et al., 2015). A review of muscle tension in GAD evaluated 13 controlled studies and suggested that muscle relaxation therapy and CBT are the most effective treatments for GAD even in the geriatric age group. The investigators indicated that the efficacy of muscle relaxation therapy for GAD lies primarily in its function of stress reduction and in helping to distract from excessive worry by focusing on the muscles. (Pluess et al., 2009).

5. **Cognitive behavioral therapy :** Cognitive behavioral therapy is a form of psychotherapy that is most widely used in all age groups including older people. In controlled clinical studies, it is found efficacious in the treatment of depression, anxiety, and behavioral problems in the context of dementia. A more recent trial (Barrowclough et al., 2001) indicates the effectiveness of CBT in anxiety symptoms of older adults and

subjective reporting of anxiety and depression over 12 months. Research suggests that while working with older people, adaptations to CBT techniques such as an increased emphasis on maintenance in areas of work, validate feelings of guilt and helplessness following the onset of the disability and other life events need to be incorporated. Brief group CBT was also found effective for older people suffering from chronic obstructive pulmonary disease in a study (Kunik et al., 2001). Several meta-analyses have reported large effect sizes for CBT in the treatment of late-life depression (Pinquart et al., 2007; Gould et al., 2012; Wilson et al., 2008) and late-life anxiety and 71% shows improvement even at 12-month follow-up in anxiety symptoms (Stanley et al., 2003).

6. **Interpersonal psychotherapy:** Interpersonal therapy addresses communication, emotional reciprocity, and support through renegotiated role relationships with the result of symptom reduction and improvement in functionality. It is directly applicable to the relationship and developmental issues relevant to people in later life (Miller & Reynolds, 2002). Reasonable evidence exists to support its efficacy in the treatment of depression in older people, both in the acute phase and in relapse prevention (Reynolds et al., 1999). Van Schaik and colleagues (2006) recruited patients from general medicine clinics with a diagnosis of Major Depressive Disorder. In another study Mossey and colleagues (1996) used a modified version of IPT, called interpersonal counseling (IPC), to treat medically hospitalized patients with minor depression shortly after their discharge. In both studies, IPT and the treatment-as-usual group (TAU) were equally effective on measures of depression severity at the post-treatment phase. However, at a 6-month follow-up, both studies reported significantly more improvement in the IPT/IPC groups compared with TAU.

7. Systemic (family) therapy: A model that looks at individuals in the context of their wider family and the larger social system seems to have wide applicability among the elderly (Pearce, 2002). Older adults are being taken care of by their family members for their psychological problems. Thus, coordination among family members is a very important factor. It may be particularly helpful in communicating and processing the diagnosis of dementia in a family setting, the role of reinforcement in somatization, and the concept of the sick role and its validation. This approach views presenting symptoms in the patient as may result from a dysfunctional family structure or function and it addresses the issue through techniques such as circular questioning, positive communication, paradoxical intervention, reframing, and exploration of the shared genogram (family tree). This therapy may tip the system into positive changes and gradually help in better integration of the elderly and improving their well-being.

8. Reminiscence therapy: Reminiscence intervention is based on Erikson's last stage of life span development entitled "reflection on life." RT involves recalling the past problem and solution into the focus of discussion to increase self-esteem and social connection. RT typically occurs in a group format where individuals are encouraged to recall and share memories of the past, with personal artifacts, newspapers, and/or music often used to stimulate memories. It is regularly used with the elderly to gain perspective on their lives and thus is popular in senior centers, residential settings, and retirement communities rather than as clinical intervention for those older adults with major mental health or personality disorders (Thorton & Brotchie, 1987). Research suggests that it is a potentially useful intervention for the treatment of late-life depression; however, more research to generalize its efficacy when compared with other therapies is warranted. Group RT was found effective in improving depression in the elderly but efficacy was not maintained at 5-week follow-up (Goldwasser et al., 1987). The study concluded that this therapy should be offered continuously to maintain improvements in the quality of life. RT improves reality orientation, cognition, communication, and behavior of confused elderly (Baines et al., 1987). In a randomized controlled study, a significant reduction in depression in people aged 65-74 was noted using this therapy (Youssef, 1990). Reminiscence, involving peer and family participation has been widely used in dementia (Woods et al., 2006), depression (Pinquart et al., 2007) in both the community and care homes.

9. **Life review therapy (LRT):** It is a more intense type of RT, which involves the reworking of past conflicts to gain a better understanding and acceptance of the past. This therapy is also based on the work of Erik Erikson's (1966) psychosocial development and it emphasizes resolving conflict on ego integrity versus despair and his eight-stage model of psychosocial development. This therapy aims at helping a client to get satisfactorily formulate and accept personalized answers to existential questions such as, 'Who am I?' and 'How did I live my life?' LRT is found to be effective for depression management (Arean et al., 1993).

10. **Problem-solving therapy:** Problem-solving therapy aims to reduce psychological distress through a highly structured process, where the PST therapists develop patients' problem-solving capabilities through psychoeducation, interactive exercises, and motivational homework assignments. Thus, PST can support depressed home-living vulnerable patients in dealing with common stressors in their daily life (e.g., resulting from medical illness and limited resources) and meeting their needs. PST is also suitable for

patients with cognitive impairments. In a comparative study between PST and supportive psychotherapy (SPT), PST was found more effective than SPT in reducing disability in older patients with major depression and executive dysfunction, and its benefits were retained after the end of treatment. PST also has an effect suggesting it may be a treatment alternative in an older patient population likely to be resistant to pharmacotherapy (Areán et al., 2010; Alexopoulos et al., 2011).

11. Grief therapy: Older adults may often experience complicated grief. They think about dying rather than living as they age. Loss of a loved one trigger feeling of loneliness and fear along with increased dependency and illness (Miller, 2012). The grieving process may bring feelings of fear, anxiety, shame, or unhappiness. Over time, positive feelings like: joy, peace, or happiness are linked to memories of the loved one. Complicated patterns of grief occur in approximately 10-20% of bereaved individuals (Shear & Shair, 2005; Miller, 2012). In these cases, accepting the death of a loved one and continuing with one's own life in a meaningful and active way becomes difficult. Invasive and repetitive intense yearning and longing for the deceased may become apparent; impeding or preventing individuals from completing daily activities. Individuals with complicated grief often believe that they can stay connected to their lost love through their ongoing expression of loss and mourning and learn to grow from the grief.

12. Existential psychotherapy: In old age, death is inevitable, pain and suffering related to death are more of a concern than the fear of death itself. Existential therapy is appropriate for the elderly facing boundary situation like retirement transitions, chronic illness, and irreversible decisions. The aim of the therapy is consolidation through the process of mastering the past and adapting to the present like acceptance of aging, reduction of anxiety, and treatment of specific disorders (Knight, 1986). Existential psychotherapy is ideal for those facing an existential crisis where the goal of therapy is in an existential frame of reference, to assist the client for self-investigation by exploring the four ultimate areas: freedom, isolation, meaninglessness, and death. The existential aim is to liberate patients from being passive victims of circumstance and motivate them to become active participants in their lives through heightened awareness and responsibility. Taking meaningful ownership of one's life, feelings, choices, and beliefs promote authentic relatedness with oneself, the world, and others and help the elderly to bear the burden of their suffering and deal with the eventual death with strength and dignity (Heidegger, 1962; May, 1979; May, 1983).

A study investigating the effectiveness of Gestalt therapy found that gestalt group therapy increased the expression of anger, left clients less hostile, clearer-headed, and less confused (O'Leary, 2001). O'Leary and Nieuwstraten (2003) in their qualitative study found that gestalt RT elicited certain types of memory that were posited as being therapeutic.

13. Supportive psychotherapy: Supportive psychotherapy is the integration of various psychotherapeutic approaches such as psychodynamic, cognitive-behavioral, and interpersonal conceptual models and techniques (Winston, 2004). In supportive psychotherapy, the therapist plays an active and directive role to strengthen the patient's social functioning and coping skills. It is a poorly understood but very practical means of helping people with dementia to adjust to the effects of their illness. Based on the patient's needs and deficits, individual sessions can be tailored. Understanding the components of supportive psychotherapy and its benefits helps clinicians to improve the quality of life of people with dementia and their caregivers within the ever-present constraints of limited time and resources (Junaid & Hegde, 2007).

14. Acceptance and commitment therapy: Acceptance and commitment therapy focuses on psychological flexibility and its therapeutic techniques are effective in the treatment of depression in long-term care (Davison et al., 2017). A randomized study evaluated the effectiveness of a blended ACT intervention for older adults with anxiety symptoms (Witlox et al., 2018) and found its efficacy in all outcome variables in post-treatment and follow-up assessment. Recent studies support the efficacy of ACT with people with chronic pain (Alonso-Fernández et al., 2016). The first comparative study examined the effectiveness between brief blended ACT and face-to-face CBT intervention for older adults with anxiety symptoms found large reductions in anxiety symptom severity in both conditions post-treatment, and these changes were maintained at the 12-month follow-up. The long-term impacts on positive mental health and treatment satisfaction are noted to be significantly higher in the blended ACT group than the CBT group. Thus, the blended ACT is a valuable treatment alternative to CBT for anxiety in later life (Witlox et al., 2021).

Psychoeducational approaches developed particularly for family members caring for older adults with cognitive loss are of great utility. Education about the nature of cognitive loss, problem-solving strategies for practical problems, and the provision of emotional support are key components of such psychoeducation. A similar psychoeducational approach may be useful for relatives caring for older adults with depression or anxiety disorders. Research shows psychoeducation training is highly effective in the reduction of psychological distress (depression and anxiety) and elevating self-esteem among elderly residing in old-age homes (Maheshwari et al., 2021). Most of the psychosocial and psycho-educational interventions described are person-centered strategies based on the cognitive-behavioral approach or informational tools to enhance care providers' knowledge of disorders such as dementia. Most studies showed that psychoeducation achieved successful results in handling behavioral and psychological symptoms in dementia (BPSD) and mood-anxiety symptoms of care providers, contributing to an overall improvement in dyad life (Alves et al., 2020).

Technology-based Intervention

Nowadays, tele-health services are an alternative, cost-effective treatment approach. These interventions help overcome barriers to psychotherapeutic care for older physically impaired people. Psychological consultation is provided either online (via the internet) or via telephone. Especially patients, hailing from a rural background or people with limited mobility, maybe benefitted from tele-health services. According to health care professionals, tele-health is a practical and economical way of providing treatment facilities. However, a significant proportion of older adults lack access to the necessary technology which remains a major drawback to the application of technological advancement in therapy (Hunsaker & Hargittai, 2018). Additionally, a systematic literature overview emphasized that certain aspects, such as living arrangements, level of education and functionality, comfort with using the internet, and satisfaction as well as experience with psychotherapy need to be considered when evaluating tele-health as an appropriate treatment approach (Harerimana et al., 2019). Especially in a psychotherapeutic context where the formation of a therapeutic alliance plays a central role, studies suggested that while such an alliance may be successfully formed, especially patients with neuropsychological deficits, those highly susceptible to distractions or frail patients tended to perceive the therapeutic relationship as weaker (Titov et al., 2015) while some patient groups may completely oppose tele-delivered psychotherapy (Frost et al., 2019). Therefore although positive outcomes of tele-health intervention are present, the application and its effectiveness in the elderly population are inconsistent and inconclusive. Furthermore, there is also a dearth of studies regarding the implementation of tele-health, for vulnerable older adults.

One qualitative study aimed at studying the main technology-based intervention in supporting quality of life or psychological well-being in the elderly population. Existing scientific literature was investigated to find how technology can be implemented into the therapeutic management of older adults. Thematic analysis suggested that virtual reality (VR), robots, telemedicine, software, video games, and smartphones, etc., are useful tools for psychological treatment in the current era and its incorporation in the elderly population is warranted as the existing findings from the literature are encouraging, although most of these results are only preliminary (Vailati et al., 2020).

Why adaptations are necessary?

Adaption is necessary for working with older adults this is necessary because older adults' problem-solving, learning, and behavioral changes can be assessed and modified at a much slower pace than working with adolescents and young adults. Interventions like CBT are provided with written material as such it is easily understandable and it should be printed large enough for visually impaired older clients. In the case of cognitively impaired older adults, interpersonal support and environmental/behavioral modification may play a greater role. Many late-life mental disorders are recurrent or chronic, the therapist needs to be flexible about setting therapeutic goals considering the current conditions. Goals may emphasize managing symptoms, preventing relapse, and enhancing functional capacity rather than completely ameliorating the presenting problem.

Psychotherapy of Elderly Population in India

Geriatric mental health has yet not received adequate recognition in India. Geriatric mental health is hindered by several challenges which prevent the development and progress of its services. It includes several challenges like: demographic characteristics of the Indian aging population, sexual issues, poor primary, secondary, and tertiary health care services, poor infrastructure and resources to deal adequately with dementia care, geriatric depression, and various issues related to policy and research. Geriatric mental health needs to be incorporated into primary health care along with the training of primary care workers and preventive work to enhance well-being in the elderly and to prevent severe depression and suicide in the elderly (Lodha & De Sousa, 2018).

In India, progressive muscle relaxation therapy (PMRT) has been a proven effective therapy technique in the management of anxiety and depression among elderly people. A study was conducted at old age homes in Rajasthan where everyone had depressive features and 28.0% were diagnosed with moderate anxiety. PMRT was found to play a major and effective role in the significant reduction of anxiety and depression (Ghodela et al., 2019). Bansal and Gill (2018), examined the efficacy of RT among 150 geriatric populations with cognitive impairment. RT intervention module included 6 sessions (twice weekly for 3-weeks). The post-test result indicates that RT was effective in decreasing the cognitive function impairment among the study participants. RT was also found to play a major role in improving Health-Related Quality of Life (HRQOL). Another study was conducted at an old age home in Bengaluru, India, using Group RT (10 sessions, 6 groups, 5 members in each group) in the management of HRQOL. Childhood memories, education pattern, first job and first salary, marriage, first child, etc., were kept as major themes of group discussion and the study yielded similar trends of efficacy (Shah et al., 2018). The mindfulness-based intervention has also been recorded to be effective in the older Indian population. Mindful meditation exercises were successful in effectively targeting depression among senior members in Vasavi Muthiyor Illam at Coimbatore. The finding promises the efficacy of mindful meditation and requires greater application and research (Unnikrishnan, 2014).

Challenges and Barriers towards Implementation of Psychotherapy

When working with an older population, difficulties that may arise include health issues, mobility problems due to fibromyalgia, arthritis, and other physical diseases, full-time assistance by a caregiver, and financial constraints. These difficulties may activate stereotyped and ageist attitudes on the part of the psychotherapist and may pose obstacles in therapy such as the therapist may not be motivated enough to adopt helpful and empathetic approaches due to a stereotype belief of ageism like older patients are confused and forgetful. This attitude restricts the therapist from using helpful approaches (e.g., audiotaping therapy sessions for review at home, ensuring good lighting in the therapy room, slowing the pace of speech and lowering the tone of voice, etc., (Wyman et al., 2011). Transference and counter-transference are two issues that can also be a barrier in psychotherapy even in the elderly group.

Psychotherapists may often perceive older patients as incompetent, disabled, and rigid to acknowledge the changes that come with age, social roles within the family and work environment, intergenerational gaps, etc. Such stereotypical attitudes toward aging create a barrier in psychotherapist's insight into these issues and eventually impact the effectiveness of therapy. Negative beliefs about old age might block the psychotherapist's ability to effectively work with the patients and maintain a positive regard, non-judgmental and empathetic stance towards the elderly patient.

Therefore in conclusion it can be said that for effective management of psychiatric disorders, distress, and age-related issues in the elderly population it is of utmost importance to understand the lifestyle pattern and changes, the demands, and expectations of that age, and take the emotional, cognitive and physical flexibility and constraint into consideration before planning and tailoring the intervention. The intervention may need a high degree of modification, personalization in terms of time course or techniques to increase treatment outcome and address the needs of the elderly. Therefore, the goals and modality of intervention must be chosen with great care and therapist variables such as empathy, non-judgmental behavior, and positive regard must be ensured. Most importantly, fundamental and clinical research in this area is warranted and may be made part of public health policymaking and implementation.

References

- Alexopoulos, G. S., Raue, P. J., Kiosses, D. N., Mackin, R. S., Kanellopoulos, D., McCulloch, C., & Areán, P. A. (2011). Problem-solving therapy and supportive therapy in older adults with major depression and executive dysfunction: effect on disability. *Archives of general psychiatry, 68*(1), 33-41.
- Alonso-Fernández, M., López-López, A., Losada, A., González, J. L., & Wetherell, J. L. (2016). Acceptance and commitment therapy and selective optimization with compensation for institutionalized older people with chronic pain. *Pain medicine, 17*(2), 264-277.
- Alves, G. S., Casali, M. E., Veras, A. B., Carrilho, C. G., Bruno Costa, E., Rodrigues, V. M., & Dourado, M. C. N. (2020). A systematic review of home-setting psychoeducation interventions for behavioral changes in dementia: some lessons for the COVID-19 pandemic and post-pandemic assistance. *Frontiers in psychiatry, 11*, 1028.
- Areán, P. A., & Cook, B. L. (2002). Psychotherapy and combined psychotherapy/pharmacotherapy for late-life depression. *Biological psychiatry, 52*(3), 293-303.
- Arean, P. A., Perri, M. G., Nezu, A. M., Schein, R. L., Christopher, F., & Joseph, T. X. (1993). Comparative effectiveness of social problem-solving therapy and reminiscence therapy as treatments for depression in older adults. *Journal of consulting and clinical psychology, 61*(6), 1003.
- Areán, P. A., Raue, P., Mackin, R. S., Kanellopoulos, D., McCulloch, C., & Alexopoulos, G. S. (2010). Problem-solving therapy and supportive therapy in older adults with major depression and executive dysfunction. *American journal of psychiatry, 167*(11), 1391-1398.
- Bansal, N., & Gill, K. (2018). Effectiveness of Reminiscence Therapy on cognitive function impairment among Geriatric Population living in old age homes of Punjab. *Indian Journal of Psychiatric Nursing, 15*(1), 48.
- Barrowclough, C., King, P., Colville, J., Russell, E., Burns, A., & Tarrier, N. (2001). A randomized trial of the effectiveness of cognitive-behavioral therapy and supportive counseling for anxiety symptoms in older adults. *Journal of consulting and clinical psychology, 69*(5), 756.
- Blanchard, M. R., Waterreus, A., & Mann, A. H. (1994). The nature of depression among older people in inner London, and the contact with primary care. *The British Journal of Psychiatry, 164*(3), 396-402.

- Bodner, E., Palgi, Y., & Wyman, M. F. (2018). Ageism in mental health assessment and treatment of older adults. *Contemporary perspectives on ageism*, 241-262.
- Bryant, C., Bei, B., Gilson, K. M., Komiti, A., Jackson, H., & Judd, F. (2016). Antecedents of attitudes to aging: A study of the roles of personality and well-being. *The Gerontologist*, *56*(2), 256-265.
- Chambers, D. A., Wang, P. S., & Insel, T. R. (2010). Maximizing efficiency and impact in effectiveness and services research.
- Davison, T. E., Eppingstall, B., Runci, S., & O'Connor, D. W. (2017). A pilot trial of acceptance and commitment therapy for symptoms of depression and anxiety in older adults residing in long-term care facilities. *Aging & mental health*, *21*(7), 766-773.
- Dinnen, S., Simiola, V., & Cook, J. M. (2015). Post-traumatic stress disorder in older adults: A systematic review of the psychotherapy treatment literature. *Aging & mental health*, *19*(2), 144-150.
- Ernst, C., & Angst, J. (1995). Depression in old age. *European Archives of Psychiatry and Clinical Neuroscience*, *245*(6), 272-287.
- Frost, R., Beattie, A., Bhanu, C., Walters, K., & Ben-Shlomo, Y. (2019). Management of depression and referral of older people to psychological therapies: a systematic review of qualitative studies. *British Journal of General Practice*, *69*(680), e171-e181.
- Gallagher-Thompson, D., & Steffen, A. M. (1994). Comparative effects of cognitive-behavioral and brief psychodynamic psychotherapies for depressed family caregivers. *Journal of consulting and clinical psychology*, *62*(3), 543.
- Gallagher-Thompson, D., Hanley-Peterson, P., & Thompson, L. W. (1990). Maintenance of gains versus relapse following brief psychotherapy for depression. *Journal of Consulting and Clinical Psychology*, *58*(3), 371.
- Garner, J. (2002). Psychodynamic work and older adults. *Advances in psychiatric treatment*, *8*(2), 128-135.
- Ghodela, A. K., Singh, V., Kaushik, N., & Maheshwari, S. K. (2019). Effectiveness of progressive muscle relaxation therapy on anxiety and depression: A pre-experimental study on elderly people of old age homes. *Indian Journal of Psychiatric Nursing*, *16*(2), 56.
- Goldwasser, A. N., Auerbach, S. M., & Harkins, S. W. (1987). Cognitive, affective, and behavioral effects of reminiscence group therapy on demented elderly. *The International Journal of Aging and Human Development*, *25*(3), 209-222.

- Gould, R. L., Coulson, M. C., & Howard, R. J. (2012). Cognitive-behavioral therapy for depression in older people: a meta-analysis and meta-regression of randomized controlled trials. *Journal of the American Geriatrics Society, 60*(10), 1817-1830.
- Harerimana, B., Forchuk, C., & O'Regan, T. (2019). The use of technology for mental healthcare delivery among older adults with depressive symptoms: a systematic literature review. *International journal of mental health nursing, 28*(3), 657-670.
- Heidegger, M. (1962). Being and time (J. Macquarrie and E. Robinson, trans.) Harper & Row. *New York.*
- Hepple, J., & Sutton, L. (Eds.). (2004). Cognitive analytic therapy and later life: A new perspective on old age. Psychology Press.
- Hunsaker, A., & Hargittai, E. (2018). A review of Internet use among older adults. *New Media & Society, 20*(10), 3937-3954.
- Junaid, O., & Hegde, S. (2007). Supportive psychotherapy in dementia. *Advances in Psychiatric Treatment, 13*(1), 17-23.
- Karlin, B. E., Duffy, M., & Gleaves, D. H. (2008). Patterns and predictors of mental health service use and mental illness among older and younger adults in the United States. *Psychological Services, 5*(3), 275.
- Karlsson B, Klenfeldt IF, Sigström R, et al. (2009). Prevalence of social phobia in non-demented elderly from a Swedish population study. *Am J Geriatr Psychiatry*, 17:127–135.
- Kim, S. (2015). Cognitive rehabilitation for elderly people with early-stage Alzheimer's disease. *Journal of physical therapy science, 27*(2), 543-546.
- Kiosses, D. N., Leon, A. C., & Areán, P. A. (2011). Psychosocial interventions for the acute treatment of late-life major depression: A systematic review of evidence-based treatments, predictors of treatment outcomes and moderators of treatment effects. *The Psychiatric Clinics of North America, 34*(2), 377.
- Knight, B. G. (2004). *Psychotherapy with older adults*. Sage.
- Lehtinen, V., Joukamaa, M., Lahtela, K., Raitasalo, R., Jyrkinen, E., Maatela, J., & Aromaa, A. (1990). Prevalence of mental disorders among adults in Finland: basic results from the Mini Finland Health Survey. *Acta Psychiatrica Scandinavica, 81*(5), 418-425.
- Leichsenring, F., Salzer, S., Jaeger, U., Kächele, H., Kreische, R., Leweke, F., ... & Leibing, E. (2010). Short-term psychodynamic

psychotherapy and Cognitive-Behavioral Therapy in generalized anxiety disorder: A randomized, controlled trial. *Focus, 8*(1), 66-74.

- Lodha, P., & De Sousa, A. (2018). Geriatric mental health: The challenges for India. *Journal of Geriatric Mental Health, 5*(1), 16.
- Maheshwari, S. K., Chaturvedi, R., & Sharma, P. (2021). Effectiveness of psycho-educational intervention on psychological distress and self-esteem among resident elderly: A study from old age homes of Punjab, India. *Clinical Epidemiology and Global Health, 11*, 100733.
- May, R. (1996). *Psychology and the human dilemma.* WW Norton & Company.
- May, R. (1983). The discovery of being. New York: W. W. *W Norton & Co.*
- Miller, M. D. & Reynolds, C. F. (2002). Interpersonal psychotherapy. In Psychological Therapies with Older People. Developing Treatments for Effective Practice (eds J. N. Hepple, J. Pearce & P. W. Wilkinson). Hove: Brunner-Routledge.
- Mossey, J. M., Knott, K. A., Higgins, M., & Talerico, K. (1996). Effectiveness of a psychosocial intervention, interpersonal counseling, for subdysthymic depression in medically ill elderly. *The Journals of Gerontology Series A: Biological Sciences and Medical Sciences, 51*(4), M172-M178.
- NAMHC, W. (2010). From discovery to cure: Accelerating the development of new and personalized interventions for mental illnesses. *Rockville, MD: National Institute of Mental Health, National Institutes of Health, US Department of Health and Human Services.*
- Pearce, J. (2002). Systemic therapy. In Psychological Therapies with Older People. Developing Treatments for Effective Practice (eds J. N. Hepple, J. Pearce & P. W. Wilkinson). Hove: Brunner-Routledge.
- Pearce, J. (2014). Systemic therapy. In *Psychological Therapies with Older People* (pp. 76-102). Psychology Press.
- Pinquart, M., & Sorensen, S. (2001). Influences on loneliness in older adults: A meta-analysis. *Basic and applied social psychology, 23*(4), 245-266.
- Pinquart, M., Duberstein, P. R., & Lyness, J. M. (2007). Effects of psychotherapy and other behavioral interventions on clinically depressed older adults: A meta-analysis. *Aging & mental health, 11*(6), 645-657.

- Pluess, M., Conrad, A., & Wilhelm, F. H. (2009). Muscle tension in generalized anxiety disorder: a critical review of the literature. *Journal of anxiety disorders, 23*(1), 1-11.
- Regier, D. A., Narrow, W. E., Rae, D. S., Manderscheid, R. W., Locke, B. Z., & Goodwin, F. K. (1993). The de facto US mental and addictive disorders service system: Epidemiologic Catchment Area prospective 1-year prevalence rates of disorders and services. *Archives of general psychiatry, 50*(2), 85-94.
- Reynolds, C. F., Frank, E. & Perel, J. M. (1999) Nortriptyline and interpersonal psychotherapy on maintenance therapies for recurrent major depression: a randomized controlled trial in patients older than 59 years. *JAMA*, 281, 39–44.
- Rorsman, B., Gräsbeck, A., Hagnell, O., Lanke, J., ÖHman, R., Öjesjö, L., & Otterbeck, L. (1990). A prospective study of first-incidence depression. *The British Journal of Psychiatry, 156*(3), 336-342.
- Sanjuán, M., Navarro, E., & Calero, M. D. (2020). Effectiveness of Cognitive Interventions in Older Adults: A Review. *European Journal of Investigation in Health, Psychology, and Education, 10*(3), 876-898.
- Shah, L. K., Rashmi, S., & Nanjundappa, D. (2018). Effectiveness of reminiscence therapy on health-related quality of life among the old age people residing at a selected old age home, Bengaluru, India. *Janaki Medical College Journal of Medical Science, 6*(2), 44-54.
- Shear, K., & Shair, H. (2005). Attachment, loss, and complicated grief. *Developmental Psychobiology: The Journal of the International Society for Developmental Psychobiology, 47*(3), 253-267.
- Shear, M. K., Frank, E., Houck, P. R., & Reynolds, C. F. III (2005). Treatment of complicated grief: A randomized controlled trial. *JAMA, 293*, 26012608.
- Skoog, I., Nilson, L., Landahl, S., & Steen, B. (1993). Mental disorders and the use of psychotropic drugs in an 85-year-old urban population. *International Psychogeriatrics, 5*(1), 33-48.
- Thompson, L. W., Gallagher, D., & Breckenridge, J. S. (1987). Comparative effectiveness of psychotherapies for depressed elders. *Journal of consulting and clinical psychology, 55*(3), 385.
- Thornton, S., & Brotchie, J. (1987). Reminiscence: A critical review of the empirical literature. *British Journal of Clinical Psychology, 26*(2), 93-111.

- Titov, N., Dear, B. F., Ali, S., Zou, J. B., Lorian, C. N., Johnston, L., & Fogliati, V. J. (2015). Clinical and cost-effectiveness of therapist-guided internet-delivered cognitive behavior therapy for older adults with symptoms of depression: a randomized controlled trial. *Behavior therapy*, *46*(2), 193-205.
- Unnikrishnan, N. (2014). *Effectiveness of Mindful Meditation on Depression among Senior Citizens in a Selected Old Age Home at Coimbatore* (Doctoral dissertation, Cherraan's College of Nursing, Coimbatore).
- Vailati Riboni, F., Comazzi, B., Bercovitz, K., Castelnuovo, G., Molinari, E., & Pagnini, F. (2020). Technologically-enhanced psychological interventions for older adults: a scoping review. *BMC geriatrics*, *20*, 1-11.
- Van Schaik, A., Van Marwijk, H., Adèr, H., Van Dyck, R., De Haan, M., Penninx, B., ... & Beekman, A. (2006). Interpersonal psychotherapy for elderly patients in primary care. *The American Journal of Geriatric Psychiatry*, *14*(9), 777-786.
- Wallace, J., & Pfohl, B. (1995). Age-related differences in symptomatic expression of major depression. *Journal of Nervous and Mental Disease*.
- Winston, A., Rosenthal, R. N., & Pinsker, H. (2004). *Introduction to supportive psychotherapy*. American Psychiatric Publishing, Inc.
- Witlox, M., Garnefski, N., Kraaij, V., de Waal, M. W., Smit, F., Bohlmeijer, E., & Spinhoven, P. (2021). Blended Acceptance and Commitment Therapy Versus Face-to-face Cognitive Behavioral Therapy for Older Adults With Anxiety Symptoms in Primary Care: Pragmatic Single-blind Cluster Randomized Trial. *Journal of Medical Internet Research*, *23*(3), e24366.
- Witlox, M., Kraaij, V., Garnefski, N., De Waal, M. W., Smit, F., Hoencamp, E., ... & Spinhoven, P. (2018). An Internet-based Acceptance and Commitment Therapy intervention for older adults with anxiety complaints: study protocol for a cluster-randomized controlled trial. *Trials*, *19*(1), 1-14.
- World Health Organization, "Elderly population. Health situation and trend assessment 2018," 2018.http://www.searo.who.int/entity/health_situation_trends/data/chi/elderlypopulation/en/.
- Yon, A., & Scogin, F. (2008). Behavioral activation as a treatment for geriatric depression. *Clinical Gerontologist*, *32*(1), 91-103.

* * *

ABOUT THE CONTRIBUTORS

1. **Ajaz Ahmad Sofi:** Ajaz Ahmad Sofi is a licensed Clinical Psychologist, registered with the Rehabilitation Council of India (RCI) since 2017. He is a Gold Medalist in M.Phil. Clinical Psychology from Amity Institute of Behavioural and Allied Sciences (AIBAS), Amity University, Jaipur, Rajasthan. Currently, he is working as Mental Health Supervisor in a mental health project in Srinagar. He has good experience of working with patients in different age range, presented with mood disorders, anxiety, substance abuse, behavioral problems, developmental disorders, and personality disorders. He mostly employs Cognitive Behavioural Therapy, Dialectical Behavioural Therapy, Motivational Enhancement Therapy, and Play Therapy with his clients.

2. **Aparajita Chakraborty**: Ms. Aparajita Chakraborty is a Clinical Psychologist and currently teaching at Amity University, Kolkata. She completed her M.Phil. in Clinical Psychology from Institute of Psychiatry (IOP), Center of Excellence in the year 2017. She has actively participated in teaching and clinical work in the field of mental health. Her areas of interest include self-harm Behavior, Borderline Personality Disorder, and Marital Therapy. She has also published many research articles in indexed and peer reviewed journals.

3. **Debolina Roy**: Debolina Roy is an Assistant Professor of Clinical Psychology in the Department of Behavioral and Allied Sciences, Amity University, Mumbai. Her research interests include Clinical Neuropsychology,

Developmental Psychopathology and Cross Culture Psychology. Her recent research interest focused at evolutionary and adaptive approach to geriatric studies.

4. **Deepika Srivastav**: Deepika Srivastav, is a registered clinical psychologist, currently working as an assistant professor grade-I with Department of Clinical Psychology (AIBHAS) at Amity University, Noida. She received her M.Phil. in Clinical Psychology degree from Institute of Human Behaviour and Allied Sciences (IHBAS) Delhi. She has recently submitted her PhD in psychology on "Effect of cognitive behaviour therapy on Parkinson's Disease" at University of Delhi.

5. **Dweepchand Singh**: Dr. Dweepchand Singh did his M.Phil. in Clinical Psychology from NIMHANS in 1987. He completed his PhD from University of Delhi. He had his association with All India Institute of Medical Science (AIIMS) and GB Pant hospital Delhi. He is with Amity University, Noida for more than 16 years. He has his contribution into international and national level psychology publications.

6. **Lakshmi Priya K.**: Lakshmi Priya K. has completed her M.Phil. in Clinical Psychology from Institute of Psychiatry and is a Rehabilitation Council of India registered practitioner. She has been working in a private capacity with clinical as well as non-clinical cases. She has published in The Journal of Child Psychology and Psychiatry and presented various papers in National as well as International Conferences. She is a certified Acceptance and Commitment Based Therapist and uses an eclectic approach to help her clients with an array of problems faced in adult life.

7. **Madhurima Dey Sarkar**: Madhurima Dey Sarkar is a Clinical Psychologist (RCI Registered) and is currently a PhD scholar and Guest Lecturer at the Department of Applied Psychology, University of Calcutta. Her research interests include therapeutic interventions for geriatric population, and she also takes a keen interest in working with the adolescent population and researching various neuropsychological correlates of various childhood disorders.

8. **Mohua Chatterjee**: Dr. Mohua Chatterjee is an Assistant Professor of Psychology at Bethune College, Kolkata. She has done her M.Sc. with specialization in Organizational and Environmental Psychology and received her doctoral degree on Environmental Psychology from the University of Calcutta.

9. **Megha Choudhary**: Megha Choudhary has completed her M.Phil in Clinical Psychology from Institute of Psychiatry, Kolkata and her PhD tenure in Clinical Psychology from Central Institute of Psychiatry, Ranchi. She is a Rehabilitation Council of India registered practitioner and is working as a Clinical Psychologist at NIMHANS, Bengaluru. She has published in the Journal of Psychosocial Research and presented various papers in National and International Conferences. She has won several awards as best paper in most of the conferences as well. She is a certified Acceptance and Commitment Based Therapist and uses dynamic, mentalization and mindfulness-based interventions to help clients with various problems.

10. **Prerna Sharma**: Ms. Prerna Sharma is registered clinical psychologist, currently working as an Assistant Professor at Amity University, Noida in the department

of Clinical Psychology. She has been working in the field for the last 6 years she has completed her M.Phil. from Amity University, Rajasthan. She is pursuing PhD from Amity University, Gurgaon. She has several publications in peer reviewed journals.

11. **Rithvik S. Kashyap**: Rithvik S. Kashyap is a clinical psychologist by profession and a Vedic scholar by passion. He completed his M.Phil. in Clinical Psychology from Osmania University and is currently carrying his doctoral research work in the area of Mindful based parenting interventions for childhood behavioural problems from University of Mysore. He had always been keen in eastern psychological perspectives and had carried out several research studies. Being in a multi-speciality hospital setting, he has been consistently working with geriatric population serving their psychological needs working as a clinical psychologist. He is a part of various interdisciplinary studies and has various publications to his credit. He is currently working as an Assistant Professor in the Department of Clinical Psychology, JSS Medical College and Hospital, JSS Academy of Higher Education and Research, Mysuru.

12. **Sahithya B.R.**: Dr. Sahithya B.R., M.Phil., PhD, is a registered clinical psychologist working as an Assistant Professor of clinical psychology in Manipal Academy of Higher Education, Udupi, Karnataka. She has an experience ranging over 10 plus years, working in mental health sector addressing various mental health issues in both child and adult population. She has previously worked as a clinical psychologist at NIMHANS, Bangalore, and as Assistant Professor at

DIMHANS, Dharwad. She has published several research and review papers in journals and has written several articles for news magazines and blogs.

13. **Sampurna Chakraborty**: Sampurna Chakraborty is the Program Manager of Project Stree Manoraksha, NIMHANS, Bangalore. She is also pursuing her Ph.D. program in Clinical Psychology from the Central Institute of Psychiatry (CIP), Ranchi. Her previous professional engagements include working as a Clinical Psychologist and Researcher for 2.5 years in CIP and as an Assistant Professor in Psychology for 1 year in Mount Carmel College, Bangalore. Her areas of interest include Anxiety Disorders, OCD, Psychological Trauma, Gender-based Violence, and Cognitive Therapy. She aspires to be an academician and contribute to the field of Clinical Psychology and Women's Mental Health.

14. **Shinjini Samajdar**: Ms. Shinjini Samajdar is registered Clinical Psychologist and she is currently working as an Assistant Professor in Clinical Psychology at Sweekar Academy of Rehabilitation Sciences, Secunderabad. She completed her M.Phil. in Clinical Psychology. She also worked as research assistant in Intel CSR funded project at Amity University. She has several publications in peer reviewed and indexed journals.

15. **Shridhar Utagi:** Dr. Shridhar Utagi is currently pursuing Doctor of Medicine in Psychiatry at the National Institute of Mental Health and Neurosciences, Bengaluru. He is a research enthusiast, and his interest lies in Cognitive Neurosciences, Dementia, Brain Stimulation, Child and Adolescent Psychiatry and Neurophysiological tools to understand the

neurobiology of various psychiatric diseases. He aspires to be a cognitive neuroscientist in the future.

16. **Sneha Das**: Sneha Das is a RCI licensed Clinical Psychologist, specialized in dialectical behavior therapy and other cognitive based interventions, neuro-rehabilitation, and mindfulness-based interventions. She has completed her M.Phil. in Clinical Psychology from Institute of Psychiatry, Kolkata and pursuing her PhD in clinical psychology from Central Institute of Psychiatry, Ranchi. She is currently working as an Assistant Professor in Clinical Psychology in Indian Naval Hospital Ship (INHS) Asvini, Centre of Excellence, Mumbai. She has been working in the field of mental health for last 8 years. Her expertise areas are working with children, adolescents, and young adults.

17. **Sneha Patel**: Sneha Patel is a licensed Clinical Psychologist. She has completed her M.Phil. in Clinical Psychology from S.C.B Medical College, Cuttack. She is a PhD Scholar from Central Institute of Psychiatry, Ranchi. She is currently working as an in-house Clinical Psychologist in Tata Digital Health. She has been working in the field of mental health for the last 4 years. She provides psychological services to people suffering from mental health issues across all age groups. Her expert areas are psychosis, neurosis, and child psychology.

* * *